Charles Bettelheim

The Transition to Socialist Economy

**Translated from the French by
Brian Pearce**

Humanities Press

This edition first published
in the U.S.A. in 1975 by
Humanities Press Inc.
Atlantic Highlands, N.J. 07716

© The Harvester Press Limited
First published in France as
La transition vers l'économie socialiste
by Francois Maspero, 1968

Library of Congress Cataloging in Publication Data
Bettelheim, Charles.
    The transition to socialist economy.

    (Marxist theory and contemporary capitalism)
    Translation of La Transition vers l'èconomie socialiste.
        Bibliography: p. 244.
        Includes index.
        1. Marxian economics. 2. Socialism.
    3. Prices—Communist countries. II. Title
    II. Series
    HB97. 5.B413   335.4'11   75-16385
    ISBN 0-391-00396-8

Printed in England by
Latimer Trend & Company Ltd Plymouth

Contents

223859

Preface to the English Edition

I have already mentioned, in the preface to the French edition of this book, that the reader will find in it formulations which reflect stages in the evolution of my ideas about the problems dealt with in the following pages. I referred at the same time to my intention to carry through a critical analysis of some of the concepts employed here.

The reader of this English version of my book should be informed that during the last few years I have tried to fulfil this plan, but that the results have not taken the form I originally intended to give them.

In fact I sought, on the one hand, to define more precisely the nature of economic calculation, so as to bring out more clearly the point that what is usually meant by this term is in reality only a monetary calculation, of limited significance; and, on the other, to elucidate the nature of the social relations which make possible a monetary calculation of this sort.[1] At the same time, in a discussion with Paul Sweezy, I gave greater precision to my thinking about the problems of the transition to socialism and about the existence of a struggle between a socialist tendency and a capitalist tendency within the social formations in transition.[2]

Subsequently, I have undertaken a fresh critical evaluation of the economic, social and political changes that the U.S.S.R. has experienced since the revolution of 1917,[3] with a view to defining the limitations of these changes and the nature of the modifications undergone by the changes themselves in the course of time, as a result of class struggles. Thereby I have sought to identify more exactly the social foundations of present-day Soviet policy and its increasing subordination to the interests of a privileged minority which has *de facto* control of the means of production. Furthermore, the experience of the Chinese Revolution, and especially the lessons of the Cultural Revolution has led me to give greater emphasis to changes in the superstructure of society as a condition for progress towards socialism, and to stress that only a certain type of development of the productive forces can ensure genuinely socialist planning.[4] These different concrete analyses have consequently caused me to define more precisely and correct a number of my theoretical concepts. In view of all this, the following pages need to be read today not without taking account of the critical developments that I have mentioned.

CHARLES BETTELHEIM
Paris, February, 1974.

NOTES TO PREFACE

1 Cf. Charles Bettelheim, *Calcul économique et formes de propriété*, Paris, Maspero, 1970. To be published in U.K. by Routledge and Kegan Paul and in the U.S.A. by Monthly Review Press.

2 Cf. Paul Sweezy and Charles Bettelheim, *On the Transition to Socialism*, New York, Monthly Review Press, 1971 (122 pp.).

3 This investigation has resulted in the publication of a work entitled *Les Luttes de Classes en URSS*. The first volume, covering the period 1917–23, was published jointly, in 1974, by Maspero and Editions du Seuil.

4 Cf. Charles Bettelheim, *Révolution culturelle et organisation industrielle en Chine*, Paris, Maspero, 1973.

TRANSLATOR'S NOTE

Since this book was translated and set in type ready for press, some books which are referred to in the original French editions have appeared in English. These are:

Charles Bettelheim, *Cultural Revolution and Industrial Organisation in China*, London, 1974.

L. Althusser, E. Balibar, R. Establet, *Reading 'Capital'*, London, 1970.

N. I. Bukharin, *The Economy of the Transition Period*, New York, 1971.

K. Marx, *Contribution to the Critique of Political Economy*, London, 1971.

L. Althusser, *For Marx*, London, 1970.

K. Marx, *Grundrisse*, London, 1973.

Foreword

This work is devoted to a group of theoretical and practical questions the importance of which increases from year to year but studies of which are nevertheless extremely rare. What is published here is, in essentials, a synthesis of lectures given at the École Pratique des Hautes Études (Sorbonne), a number of articles, and thoughts formulated in the course of the seminar for which I am responsible at the École Normale Supérieure.

The problems examined are among those which are at the heart of the most topical concerns of the day in economic, social and political matters. The theoretical analyses to which these problems can give rise must therefore necessarily be enriched and diversified as a result of the *real developments* on the basis of which these analyses can be worked out. This explains the *evolution* in certain formulations which the reader will be able to observe in these papers, the writing of which has been spread over a period of about four years.

What gives unity to the chapters that follow is that they form the beginning of a fresh critical consideration of the problems which are currently spoken of as those of "the transition to socialism". It will be seen that this expression is far from adequate as a description of the reality it is supposed to describe. It suggests a "forward march" at the end of which there is in some sense guaranteed to be socialism. However, what in fact is so described is an historical period that can more properly be called that of "transition *between* capitalism and socialism". Such a period does not lead in single-line fashion to socialism; it may lead to that, but it may also lead to renewed forms of capitalism, in particular to state capitalism.

That this possibility is a real one emerges with increasing clarity in the course of the following chapters, though it is not explicitly formulated until Chapter 6 (see especially page 223), so that the terminology I have used still reflects only to a limited extent the conclusion that I eventually reach.

The comment I have just made has a general bearing. It relates also to other expressions which suggest a certain "single-line development of history". To admit this is, of course, as I have already said, to become drawn into a fresh critical consideration (which is barely outlined in these pages) that must focus upon a number of notions in current use such as "socialist economy", "socialist planning", "socialist property", and so on. Some results of such an analysis will be presented in another work, now being prepared, dealing with "the structures of transitional economies" (this title is probably not definitive).[1]

It is worth stressing at the outset that the critical analyses demanded by the realities described below, and the concepts by means of which I have endeavoured to grasp these realities, cannot be restricted merely to the economic plane of the various social formations, but must also deal with the political and ideological planes and with the relations between these two and between them both and the economy. A way of proceeding such as this must, moreover, lead to critical analysis of certain generalisations that have been made at certain moments, on the basis of some aspect or other of Soviet economic reality or Soviet economic policy; for instance, some generalisations of the arguments put forward by Lenin in favour of the New Economic Policy.

What will be found here is thus merely the beginning of such an approach. Except in Chapter 6, the reader will find here no analyses dealing with economic calculation, and more especially with economic calculation on the scale of society. These analyses will not be made public until after critical consideration of the structures of economies in transition between capitalism and socialism. Nor will any analyses dealing with the People's Republic of China be found here; such an analysis has already been offered in another work—a book containing contributions by other economists who also take part in the work of the *Centre d'Études de Planification Socialiste* (Centre for Study of Socialist Planning) and which appeared in the *Economie et Socialisme* series.[2]

These papers thus constitute only a first collection of thoughts aroused by the progress and difficulties of planning, and the political and ideological developments experienced by the socialist countries. These thoughts are put forward for discussion, which is indispensable if research and analysis are to be usefully carried on, so that, by an examination of the current phases of development, theoretical lessons and practical results may be drawn from them.

CHARLES BETTELHEIM
(August 1967)

NOTES TO FOREWORD

1 Now published as *Les Luttes de Classes en URSS*, Vol. 1, 1917–23, Paris, Senil/Maspero, 1974.
2 Ch. Bettelheim, J. Charrière, H. Marchisio, *La Construction du socialisme en Chine* (Building Socialism in China), series *Economie et Socialisme*, Paris, Maspero, 1965. Reissued in the *Petite Collection Maspero*, March 1968.

1: The problematic of the economy of transition

The basic purpose of this chapter is to study the economies of transition, and thereby the problems posed by their structure and evolution.

My aim is to arrive, if possible, at the scientific establishment of a certain number of concepts essential to knowledge of the economies of transition and of the laws of development to which they are subject. It is clearly impossible to say whether this aim can be realised, since, for the moment, we possess, in this field, mainly descriptions and "practical concepts". By "practical concepts" I mean, like Louis Althusser, concepts which still derive, in the way they are formulated, from a previous way of seeing the problems, a way that it is our very task to replace, because it is still uncertain of itself, being uncertain what its scientific object actually consists of.

Such practical concepts point out to us where the problems are that we have to solve, within the old ways of seeing the problems and on the plane of theoretical practice. If we do not take care, these practical concepts can seem to be solutions of problems which in fact they merely describe.

The objects described by the term "economy of transition" are obviously among those a scientific awareness of which is essential to the understanding of our epoch, since this appears to us precisely as an *age of transition*.

Empirically, this transition, or rather these transitions, appear to us in two forms.

One is a form of radical transition: transition from the capitalist mode of production to the socialist mode of production, that is, a country's passage from one period of the history of mankind to another, through an upheaval in production-relations and class relations and the replacement of one state machine by another with a different class nature. There is another, more limited, form of transition, with a much more uncertain content, namely, that of the economies and societies that were formerly under colonial domination and have now entered a post-colonial period. This second type of transition itself throws up the problems described by those other practical concepts, the terms "neo-imperialism", "neo-colonialism" and "specific form of socialism". The last-mentioned expression is commonly used both for certain social realities and for the ideological concepts that describe them, such as, for instance, "Islamic socialism" or "Buddhist socialism", etc. Where this form of transition is concerned it is essential to undertake an analysis which is not confined to the ideological sphere but which reveals the nature of the transformations that are actually taking place in class relations and production-relations. This also brings up the question of the class nature of the state.

I Present state of theory

Our joint task will be, first, to set to work the practical concepts we possess in order to question with their aid a certain number of the realities of today, with the aim of getting to know these realities better and thereby transforming these concepts of ours into scientific concepts. By this I mean concepts which connect together into a theory which enables us to grasp the inter-connexions of the social realities on which our researches are focused. Our first duty is thus to ascertain what the theoretical situation is that we are at present in, as regards the problems I have just referred to.

In order to do this we must examine the state of the Marxist problematic. In my view, it is thanks to Marx's theory that the transition can be the object of a scientific analysis. It is by applying the conceptual tools and scientific methods that Marx worked out that the problems of transition can be formulated and can be solved correctly.

At this point I must, of course, reply directly to the objection that says that Marx did not merely formulate the problems of transition and provide the conceptual tools by means of which the transition can be thought about, but that he also solved theoretically all this group of problems and thus has already supplied us with the scientific theory of the transition.

The best way of determining the scientific state of our problems will be to try to answer this objection.

In doing this, I shall start from a text which relates directly to our problems, namely, Louis Althusser's *Sur la "moyenne idéale" et les formes de transition* (On the "ideal average" and the forms of transition).[1] Here Althusser formulates some propositions which are of the greatest importance for our subject. I will set them out in the order that seems to me to be significant from the point of view of the problem with which we are concerned, an order which is a little different from that in which Althusser presents them:

First proposition

Althusser recalls that, in *Capital*, Marx sets himself the task of studying the "concept of the specific difference of the capitalist mode of production" and that he is able to do this only "on condition that he studies at the same time *the other modes of production*, as types of specific unity of *Verbindung* (i.e. of combination, C.B.) between the factors of production, and also the *relations between the different modes of production* in the process of constituting modes of production."[2]

Second proposition

Althusser further stresses that Marx's passages on primitive accumulation of capital form at least the materials, if not already the outline, of the theory of the process whereby the capitalist mode of production is constituted, that is to say, of the forms of transition from the feudal mode of production to the capitalist mode of production. This proposition evidently means, among other things, that these passages in Marx (together with those dealing with pre-capitalist modes of production) give us *the outline of a theory (of transition)*, but not yet—since this was not the main purpose of Marx's scientific work—the theory itself.

This situation of the theory is illuminated by Etienne Balibar's contribution to the same volume.[3]

Third proposition

This third proposition is closely linked with the first two.

Marx's theoretical object is the capitalist mode of production in its *Kerngestalt* (i.e., in its "nuclear structure" or "inner structure", C.B.) and the determinations of this *Kerngestalt*. This means that what Marx is studying is not, for example, capitalist England, which he often takes as an *illustration*, but an *ideal object*, defined in terms of cognition, in the abstraction of a concept. This is what Marx is saying when he writes that the "specific character" of the capitalist system "is revealed in all its inner essence".[4]

It is this specific difference that is Marx's theoretical object. This is why the capitalist mode of production he studies is a mode of production with two classes, differing from what we see in the English "illustration", or any other such "illustration" we might find, in which there are actually a much larger number of classes. The specific difference studied by Marx is thus not an empirical average but the concept of the capitalist mode of production, which constitutes that which is essential to it.

Fourth proposition

There is thus a "gap" between the capitalist mode of production in the reality of its concept and the actual economic system of British capitalism, for example. This "gap" constitutes what Althusser calls a "real residue",[5] an "impurity"[6] or, as he also says, what one may "provisionally call a survival" in the midst of the capitalist mode of production which is dominant in Great Britain.[6]

Fifth proposition

This fifth proposition is very directly concerned with our subject of study.

"This alleged 'impurity' is an object belonging to the sphere of the theory of modes of production: in particular, the theory of the transition from one mode of production to another, which merges with the theory of the process whereby a certain mode of production is formed. . . ."[6]

I should now like to offer some observations concerning the content of the fourth and fifth of these propositions:

(1) While it seems to me correct to say that the alleged "impurities", "survivals", etc., form an object belonging to the sphere of the theory of modes of production, I do not think that they can be *the specific object* of the theory of the transition from one mode of production to another. In fact, these "impurities" are always present in reality. They therefore cannot be considered as *the peculiarity of a stage of transition*, or otherwise we should have to say that the real economic world is always made up of economies in

transition, and consequently the concept of "economy of transition" would be deprived of any specific meaning.

If we wish to give the term "economy of transition" a specific meaning—and this seems to me to be essential—we must ask ourselves what these "residues" are that we find so difficult to describe, since we refer to them by means of all sorts of *metaphors*, like "impurities", "survivals", and so on, which is a sign that there is as yet no scientific concept with which to think these objects. Above all, we must, in particular, ask ourselves the following question: is it not rather a specific form of coexistence, or simultaneous presence and interaction of several modes of production, that characterises an economy of transition? And this leads to another question: do not these specific forms of coexistence and interaction of several modes of production constitute specific modes of production?

It is not necessary to work out forthwith the scientific concepts demanded by this way of seeing the problem, but only to offer some considerations which may perhaps help us to find a road that will lead to the establishment of these concepts. This leads me to make a second observation.

(2) What we will for the moment call "survivals" (an expression which makes one think of some legacy from a past which history has not had the time to wipe out) represent, in fact, the *products* of the structures in which these alleged "impurities" are not "survivals", because they are not alien to the real structures in which they exist. On the contrary, they are the result of the totality of the relations which make up these structures, that is to say, of the particular level of development of the productive forces, of the unevennesses of development which characterise these forces, and of the relations of production linked with these unevennesses of development. If we think of these "impurities" as being "survivals" this is because we have not grasped thoroughly enough the interconnexions of the structures that produce them.

When, indeed, we set about studying an actual economy—independently of the very idea of transition—we have to think of this economy as *a complex structure which is "structured in dominance"*. We mentally grasp a structure like this as a specific combination of several modes of production of which one is *dominant*. It is this dominant mode of production that permeates the entire system and *modifies* the conditions in which the subordinate modes of production function and develop.

In other words, by virtue of their very subordination, these "modes of production" are *different* from what they are in their "purity". Marx speaks in this connexion of the "etiolation" of these modes of production.

What is true, however, of the subordinate modes of production is reciprocally true of the dominant mode of production, the features of which are also to some extent modified by the mere fact of its "dominant" role.

Finally, each of these complex structures constitutes not a simple juxtaposition of modes of production, but a complex structure which is *unique*, endowed with its own structural causality. At the same time, this unique structure is subject, in general, to the dominance of a specific structure which corresponds to that of a given mode of production; for example, the capitalist mode of production. This is why it is that while, in a complex structure of this type, like nineteenth-century France, say, we find numerous structural elements belonging to modes of production other than the dominant mode, we are nevertheless justified in saying that this structure corresponds to that of a capitalist economy.

If the simultaneous presence and interaction of several modes of production is a feature of any actual economic structure whatsoever, then it is, of course, a feature of an economy in transition; but an additional element enters in here, namely, the *mode of dominance* and the *methods of eliminating* the non-dominant structures. This is one of the problems we shall have to examine.

I should like to illustrate the observation I have just put forward by taking the example of the situation in the Soviet Union in 1918 and in 1921.

In his report on the tax in kind, dated 9 April, 1921, Lenin said:

"Take a close look at the actual economic relations in Russia. We find at least five different economic systems, or structures, which, from bottom to top, are: first, the patriarchal economy, when the peasant farms produce only for their own needs, or are in a nomadic or semi-nomadic state, and we happen to have any number of these; second, small commodity production, when goods are sold on the market; third, capitalist production, the emergence of capitalists, small private capital; fourth, state capitalism; and fifth, socialism."[7]

Here we have a typical instance of a complex economic structure, but also an example of an economy in transition to socialism, because, as Lenin stresses in this same report, the working class holds state power and also "the factories, transport and foreign trade".[8]

Under these conditions, even a certain development of capitalism, whether in the form of concessions to foreign capital, limited in scope and strictly regulated, or in that of a certain growth of internal capitalism, is incapable of changing the predominant orientation, owing to the working-class nature of the state and of the latter's grasp of what Lenin calls the "commanding heights of the economy".

I now return to the problems set by the analysis of any complex economic structure. In order to analyse such a structure, and especially in order to foresee how it will develop, we can apply the knowledge available to us concerning the way each of these "elementary structures" functions and develops. We must appreciate, however, that this method is only approximative. Its weakness is that it treats as independent modes of production elementary structures which possess no "autonomous" existence except in the idea that we form of them as distinct modes of production, that is, as modes of production which, in their very concepts, are pure structures. This is why the conclusions we can draw from such proceedings are still only approximate. Recognition of the divergences between these conclusions and reality must in the end lead to the conceptual construction of a complex structure, structured in dominance, the structural causality of which will correspond better to that of the actual economic system.

To this I should like to add that the "mixed" character of the actual structures and systems is not merely an "internal" feature of the various national economies but is also, and to an even greater extent, a feature characteristic of the world economy. For the development of the productive forces in every country is to some extent conditioned by *world production-relations*. This can be seen especially in the countries dominated by imperialism but it is also true in the dominating countries. This therefore means that the world economy itself is a complex structure of complex structures. Now, the world economy is the ultimate economic reality. It is in the world economy that are "combined" (in several dimensions) the most diverse *modes and systems of production* and the *various national economies* which form parts of this complex totality.

Thus, when we study the working of a particular national economy in which a certain mode of production seems to be "dominant"—for example, the economy of some country in Latin America in which large-scale land-ownership is dominant on the spot—we ought not, if we want to arrive at meaningful conclusions, consider this economy otherwise than in its *mode of relations with the modes of production which are dominant on the world scale*; because we cannot understand this national economy if we do not grasp that it is a part of world production-relations. It is thus as an integrated structure, for example, as a structure dominated by the American economy, that the specificity of development of this economy can be understood.

Similarly, the transformations of structures and the different stages of transition that a national economy can undergo cannot be analysed in a valid way except by putting these transformations back into the world structural totality. In this way we can understand how it is that the stages of transition of each economy that carries out its socialist revolution can be qualitatively different from the "apparently analogous" stages passed through by the countries which have preceded it on the same road. This is so not merely for reasons internal to each economy, that is, because of the particular level of development of its productive forces and the unevennesses of this level of development, the class characteristics peculiar to this economy, and so on, but also because the world totality has itself been transformed. From this standpoint, the October Revolution marks the beginning of a new age, not only for the Russian economy but also for the world economy, the structure of which was profoundly transformed.

This leads me to formulate the following proposition: with the dividing-up of the world by imperialism, a world economic system was established. The break-up of the unity of this system began with the October Revolution. Since then, world economy has entered a period of transition. The characteristics of this transition, its specific phases, need to be studied as an objective phenomenon with both national and international aspects. Such a study requires the elaboration of specific concepts. For the moment, we possess only practical concepts, and very poor ones at that, such as "coexistence on the world scale" or "the world struggle between the two systems". Such concepts merely point to the existence of a problem, namely, that of the forms and phases of transition on the world scale; they do not as yet enable us to set this problem on the scientific plane. What constitutes the difficulty of the problem is not merely its size or its novelty, it is also the specificity of this world transition which implies political and ideological transformations at the level of the different states, for these are the transformations that, within each state, alter the dominance of a mode of production. These, for example, are what have brought it about that, in the course of a few months, the economy of Cuba ceased to be dominated by American capital and became integrated into the world socialist economy and has taken the road towards the building of socialism. The immediately national character of such transformations often makes us lose sight of the international nature of the process of transition.

After making these general observations, I should like to dwell upon some points of terminology, for through an effort to clarify terminology we may be able to make our way to a more rigorous formulation of the concepts.

II Proposals on terminology

When we speak of the problems of transition, this expression calls up the ideas of passing from one mode of production to another, of the constitution of a mode of production, of the transformation of an economic system, and so on. Each of these expressions in turn may describe different problems. It is therefore necessary to link these concepts together in order to find the road to a theoretical elaboration of the theme. To this end I propose the following terminology:

First of all, I propose that we speak of the theory of the "*constitution*" of a particular mode of production, in order to designate the theory of the formation of certain of the *conditions* for a new mode of production, and so the theory of the origins of this mode of production. It is such a theory that Marx sets forth when, in his analysis of the primitive accumulation of capital, he shows how, *within the womb of the feudal mode of production, the conditions* for the capitalist mode of production were formed, and this through the specific working not only of the economic structures but also through that of the political structures, as, for example, the intervention of the political authority to promulgate and put into effect the enclosure acts in England. The same theoretical necessity demands today that we discover the conditions for the socialist mode of production which are in process of formation within the womb of the capitalist mode of production (in the sense in which Lenin said, for example, that "socialism looks out of all the windows of present-day capitalism").

The theory of the constitution, within one mode of production, of some of the conditions of another mode of production, is thus also that of the transformation and dissolution of the existing production-relations. This dissolution affects the whole social structure, and not merely the structure of production. It is marked by specific forms of intervention in the infra-structure by the superstructure.

In contrast to the theory of the constitution of the conditions for a new mode of production, it must be said that the theory of the passage from one to the other is on a different level of abstraction, because it is specifically concerned with the *ideal* passage from one production-structure to another, and therefore not with an *historical* passage.

This brings us back to the actual theoretical nature of the mode of pro-duction, as a varied combination of the constituent elements of every pos-sible mode (the working people, the means of production), a combination which takes place in accordance with the two relationships (of property and of real appropriation) which are features of the structure of every mode of production·

The *ideal* nature of the modes of production conceived at this level of abstraction has as its consequence that their succession in the realm of ideas may be different from the real transition from one economic system to another. This transition is, indeed, never the succession of one mode of production to another, but always a transition from one complex mode of production, structured in dominance, to another complex mode of produc-tion, structured in dominance.

This kind of succession is not subject to any single-line development because here the different levels of the *entire social structure* react on each other and may create the conditions for a direct transition from one domi-nant mode of production to another, whereas, in the ideal series, these modes of production do not succeed one another. We see that the very complexity of the social structures rules out any unilinear development.

As I recalled just now, this complexity extends to the world scale, since each national economy, which is itself a complex of structures, constitutes a *link*, either dominated or dominating, within world economy, and the contradictions that develop in a given country are not merely "internal" contradictions, but result also from the mode of insertion of the country in question into the world economic and political complex (hence the concept of "the weakest link").

Accordingly, while we can conceive of abstract laws of passage from one mode of production to another, we cannot state that any law of linear succession is historically necessary, as between the dominant modes of pro-duction of the complex social systems. We know, furthermore, that the dissolution of a mode of production creates merely the *conditions* for the appearance of another determinate mode of production. It does not estab-lish the *necessity* of this mode, for this necessity is determined by the con-ditions of transformation of a structure that is much more complex than the economic structure alone, namely, the conditions of transformation of the totality of the social structure and the political and ideological super-structures.

Thus, the dissolution of the capitalist mode of production does not create *all* the conditions for its succession by the socialist mode of production unless the political and ideological conditions for this succession are present as well. This may therefore take place either sooner or later, depending on the *structure of conjunctures* through which every historical social formation passes. So, in the world totality of today, countries which have not developed internally the capitalist mode of production, or have hardly developed it, are able, owing to internal and international contradictions, to experience a *conjuncture* which enables them to do without the development of this mode of production so far as they are concerned, and to pass directly to the building of socialism; the Democratic Republic of Vietnam is an example of such a process.

Here we see that, in addition to a *theory of the origins* of a given mode of production, we need not merely a *theory of (ideal) passage* but also a theory of the *structure of conjuncture* that opens the way to a transition. This conjuncture is usually one marked by the collision of a number of contradictions, which gives a certain moment of history a revolutionary quality and provokes the re-structuring of a social formation, that is, the replacement of one social formation by another. It is then that there opens a period of transition which can itself be the object of the *theory of transition*.

If we look at these matters on the plane of the national economies, we can say that the current period shows us *two main types* of transition:

(1) That from an economy previously dominated by capitalism (even if *internal* capitalism was weak or practically non-existent there) to an economy evolving towards socialism; this transition-in-the-strict-sense implies a preliminary condition—the passing of *state power* to the working class, or to a coalition of formerly-exploited classes within which the working class plays the dominant role.

(2) The second type of transition (transition in the broader sense) is that experienced by an economy which, having been subjected to direct colonial domination, now enters a post-colonial period.

This second type of transition, which does not eliminate the internal forms of exploitation of man by man, implies a much less thoroughgoing breach with the past than occurs in the first type, since, at bottom, the previous domination is not abolished but merely modified. It is not abolished because a system which preserves the exploitation of man by man and in which the state is not in the hands of the working people but in those of the exploiting classes must, in the last resort, seek backing in that part of the world economic and political system which strives to uphold class privileges and is therefore in political solidarity with any and every system of exploitation.

These are, ultimately, the internal economic, social and political conditions that determine the integration of a country either in the world capitalist system or in the world socialist system.

Therefore, the expression "economy of transition", when it is used for the post-colonial economies, seems to be capable of two different meanings:

(1) The expression may simply mean that the previous *form* of domination has been modified without the nature of this domination being altered.

This is the case with a country like India, where state capitalism has been used by the Indian bourgeoisie to reinforce its own power. But the very limits which the existing economic system sets to the development of the Indian economy have in the end obliged the Indian bourgeoisie to stay under the domination of foreign capital.

(2) The expression "economy of transition", when applied to a post-colonial economy in which power has not passed into the hands of the working people, seems capable of being used also to describe a situation of momentary equilibrium between the social classes confronting each other. Such an equilibrium, which may lead to the formation of *class coalitions* (whether formal or not) is eminently *unstable*. It cannot provide the social foundation for an economic situation with specific laws of development. Such a situation of unstable equilibrium was that which Indonesia knew down to September 1965. I consider that in cases like this one ought not to speak of an "economy of transition", but rather of a "situation of transition": a situation of this kind is, moreover, usually marked, in the economic sphere, by an almost total absence of development.

If we accept, provisionally at any rate, the terminology which has just been suggested, we shall say that, at the level of a single country, the theoretical problem of the economy of transition concerns the theory of a complex mode of production *which has just replaced another complex mode of production*, following a rupture in the formerly existing structured totality.

The economy of the transition period is thus the economy of *the period directly after a break,* and this is why the theory of the transition is not a theory of origins but a theory of *beginnings.* In the strict sense of the word it is the theory of the *beginnings of a new mode of production.* One of its objects consists of the initial stage, or rather of the problems of the period of initial instability, of the period preceding what Marx calls the "social stability" of the mode of production.[9]

The initial stage is that in which the fate of the new social formation has not bet been sealed, or in which this fate is still uncertain. In both cases this stage corresponds to the "morning after" a break with a mode of production that was previously dominant, or to a serious shock to the former domination (the case of the period immediately following "de-colonisation" in a formerly colonial country). This "morning after" may, of course, extend in some cases over a number of years.

However, the problems of the economy of transition, as I propose to deal with them here, go beyond this phase of initial instability. They concern, as I have said, not merely the initial stage, as the first stage of the transition period, but the whole of the transition period as the first phase of a period of history. For example, in the case of the Soviet Union, I shall interest myself both in the period immediately following the October Revolution and in the present period.

What, then, constitutes the *"transition phase"* (in the sense of the phase of transition between capitalism and socialism, for example) is no longer the fact of instability or the absence of domination, but the fact of a still relatively great *lack of conformity* between the essentials of the new social relations which are henceforth dominant and the productive forces, a state of affairs which also means a certain type of contradiction between the form of property and the real mode of appropriation. Under these conditions, the new social relations do not yet dominate by their own strength; in other words, the conditions for expanded reproduction of these social relations are not yet given.[10]

When such a situation of lack of conformity between the new social relations and the productive forces exists, the dominance of the new social relations can be ensured only through *mediations*, for example, in the case of the economy in transition to socialism, by having recourse to those two extreme types of mediation, use of the market (as in the example of the N.E.P.), or administrative centralisation (as in the example of the first Five-Year Plans). These mediations testify to the still very great depth of the internal contradictions.

The latter can only be resolved through a development of the productive forces which will bring about conformity between the new social relations and the productive forces themselves: in the case of the socialist economy, this development must lead to an integration and interdependence of the productive forces far-reaching enough for the mechanism of the market and the mechanism of administrative centralisation to be alike discarded and replaced by a co-ordinated management of the economy through original mechanisms, at the centre of which there will be a planning centre of a new type.

The above observations call for additional terminological definitions. It seems right to reserve the term *"phase"* to indicate the *two great moments* in the *development of a social formation,* namely:

(1) that of its *beginnings,* i.e., the transition phase in the strict sense which is also that of a specific non-correspondence between productive forces and production-relations (this is a point to which I shall come back): and,

(2) the phase of *expanded reproduction of the production-structure,* which can be subjected to a synchronic analysis and is marked by a dynamism of its own.

Each of these phases is distinguished by a specific interconnexion between the levels of the social formation and between their contradictions, and so by a certain type of uneven development of these contradictions. In the course of one and the same phase, that which at one moment is a principal contradiction becomes a secondary one, or else a secondary aspect of this contradiction becomes a principal aspect. These shifts in contradictions show the pace of development of the different *stages* of a given phase; they are marked by changes in relations between classes or between the different strata of the same class. It was thus that the Kronstadt revolt and the economic crisis preceding it indicated such a shift and compelled the Bolshevik Party to change its economic policy. Lenin wrote at that time:

"Economics in the spring of 1921 was transformed into politics. 'Kronstadt.' "[11]

Having arrived at this point, we find two kinds of problem coming up:

(1) Is there a typical way of dividing up the transition period into *stages*, with specific features? If so,

(2) what are the relations between these typical stages and the historical periods through which the economies of the socialist countries have passed?

These are the questions which we must try to answer.

III A fundamental feature of the transition period

We must, however, begin by offering at least the beginning of an answer to the following theoretical question: if we are to consider the transition phase as a whole, at the level of a national economy, is there any feature common to the whole of the phase which justifies us in regarding it as *one* phase?

If this question be answered in the affirmative, a further question then arises: if there is a feature *common to the whole* of the phase of transition from one mode of production to another (in the strict sense of the word), can different transition phases also have features in common? In other words, if there is a fundamental feature of the phase of transition from the feudal mode of production to the capitalist mode of production, is a similar feature to be found, in a different form, that is, with other terms, in the phase of transition from the capitalist mode of production to the socialist mode of production?

The point of departure for answering this question is obviously provided by analyses relating to the transition from the feudal mode of production to the capitalist mode of production.

As Etienne Balibar has shown, the phase of *transition to capitalism* was marked by a certain form of *non-correspondence* between the formal mode of appropriation and the real mode.

The *formal* mode of appropriation in the phase of transition to capitalism was already the capitalist form of property, that is, the separation of the worker from his means of production; however, the *real* mode of appropriation was not yet the mode of appropriation specific to capitalism, namely, large-scale industry.

Marx wrote on this subject:

"At first, capital subordinates labour on the bases of the technical conditions in which it historically finds it. It does not, therefore, change immediately the mode of production."[12]

This first phase, this phase of the transition to capitalism is that of *manufacture*. Manufacture thus appears as the *mode of production* of the phase of transition to capitalism. What is characteristic of this mode of production is that manufacture merely radicalises to an extreme degree what was the distinctive feature of handicraft work, namely, the unity of labour-power with the means of labour.

Thus, whereas social production-relations bring about a *formal dissociation* between the worker and his means of production, the labour-process maintains their *unity*. *Non-correspondence* between social production-relations and the labour-process is thus characteristic of the period of transition to capitalism.

This non-correspondence is abolished later on, through the industrial revolution, the development of which was made possible by the formal subjection of labour to capital. The industrial revolution, that is to say, the development of the productive forces which this change implies, breaks up the *unity* of the worker with his means of production. The latter cease to be *individual* and become *collective*. Thenceforth there is *separation* of the worker from his means of work on the plane of the work-process no less than on that of social production-relations. There thus comes about a correspondence, what Etienne Balibar calls an *homology*, between the two forms of appropriation. With large-scale industry, the subjection of labour to capital is no longer merely formal, it is real, as Marx puts it.[13]

As we know, this *homology* has at the same time an underlying *contradiction*, namely, that which counterposes the *private* ownership of the means of production to the *social* character of the productive forces.

To return to the period of transition to capitalism, we see, then, that this is marked by *a certain form of non-correspondence*. The latter also finds expression as a *chronological gap*, between the formation of the different elements in the structure: capital as a "social relation" exists previous to and independent of the "real" subjection of the worker, that is, of the specific form of real appropriation which corresponds to the capitalist mode of production.[14]

The question we now have to answer is the following: is the period of transition to socialism also marked by non-correspondence and a "chronological gap", this gap being itself destined to be closed by the triumph of a new type of industrial revolution, that is, by the predominance of productive forces with characteristics corresponding to the new social production-relations?; and this predominance itself being made possible as a result of the prerequisite appearance of socialist production-relations, that is, as a result of a certain type of "chronological gap"?

I think this question can be answered, in the affirmative, by putting forward the following propositions, which, of course, need to be elaborated. It seems that the form of "non-correspondence" specific to the phase of transition to socialism is the following: the mode of property is formally— so far as the chief means of production are concerned—that of ownership by society as a whole, whereas the real mode of appropriation is still by limited groups of working people, since it is only at the level of these groups that real appropriation of nature takes place.[15]

The chronological gap peculiar to the mode of production of transition to socialism would thus also mean the constitution of a mode of formal appropriation "preceding" the corresponding mode of real appropriation.

The material basis of this non-correspondence thenceforth appears as being constituted by the nature of the productive forces that are set to work within the framework of what is still called the socialist "enterprise", or "firm", that is, of "enterprises" or "firms" which have to be allowed a certain degree of autonomy precisely because they form the framework in which the real appropriation of nature takes place.

From now on, however, the development of the productive forces in certain branches, e.g., in the production of electricity and in the large-scale chemical industry (in the form of big combines) reveals the appearance of a mode of real appropriation which can still be dominated at the level of society as a whole. When this evolution is complete in essentials, that is, when these productive forces of a new type are the dominant productive forces, there will be a state of *homology* between the mode of appropriation and the mode of property, there will be coincidence between juridical power and effective capacity, and the transition phase will be over. It would seem that it can be said straightaway that this presupposes a very far-reaching development of automation, technical integration and remote-control methods of management.

On the basis of the foregoing, we see that what marks the transition phase as a whole is not mainly the instability of the new social order, nor is it the absence of domination by the new production-relations, it is the fact that there is still a relatively large degree of non-correspondence between the new production-relations, henceforth dominant, and the nature of the essential productive forces.

The lower the local level of development of the productive forces in a given country, the higher the degree of non-concordance of which we speak. It was in this sense that Lenin wrote in 1921 that:

"The economic basis of socialism is not yet there."[16]

A gap like this has important consequences as regards the articulation of the different levels of the social structure. This non-correspondence implies, in fact, a specific efficacity of the political level. So long as there is non-concordance between the new production-relations and the nature of the productive forces, the functioning of the economic system can be ensured only by specific mediations. For example, in the case of the economy in transition to socialism, recourse has to be had to such mediations as state capitalism, use of the market (as with the N.E.P.) and strong administrative centralisation (as in the first Five-Year Plans).

This seems to me very important in relation to the study of the political superstructures of the transition period, in particular the forms of democracy and the role of the administrative apparatus. This is precisely why Lenin insisted on the idea of the "economic foundations" for the "withering away of bureaucracy" and the problems of what he called "combating the evils of bureaucracy".[16]

I think that it is by starting from the idea of *non-correspondence* between the formal and the real modes of appropriation, and by taking into account the *extent* and the *specific forms* of this non-correspondence, that we have to proceed in tackling the problems that arise at the different stages of the economy in transition to socialism, and that we can try to construct a theory of these stages. That will enable us to see that, depending on the countries concerned, that is, on the *initial extent* of the non-correspondence and the *specific forms* of this non-correspondence, this transition period can be longer or shorter, and, above all, can be marked by the playing of a radically different role, as between one country and another, by the bureaucratic apparatus, and so by different forms of socialist democracy.

On the economic plane, it is the extent and the specific forms of non-correspondence that must be taken into account in correctly setting the problems of the role played by the market and by money, of the role (now being so much discussed in the Soviet Union) of direct relations between socialist enterprises, of organisational forms in agriculture, of changes to be made in the actual mechanism of planning, and so on.

All these problems are both economic and political. Solving them calls into question the relations between classes or the relations between the different strata of one and the same class, the relations between the "top section" and the "lower ranks", and so on. . . .[17] In other words, it is a matter of bringing to light the contradictions engendered by a certain type of non-correspondence. Such contradictions, if not properly dealt with, may take on an antagonistic character, or from contradictions of the secondary order become principal contradictions. For example, if the problem of small-scale peasant production is not handled correctly, this may lead either to a setback in the productive forces of agriculture (which had occurred before the introduction of N.E.P.) or to such an increased role being played by the market that the development of socialist production relations may be seriously compromised (as has happened in Yugoslavia).

In concluding these observations regarding the period of transition to socialism, a point needs to be made about the dimensions and the nature of the *break* separating the phase of *transition* to socialism from the phase of socialism's further development. It is obvious that this break will be even greater than that separating the transition phase from the last phsae of capitalism. We can see already that this break will mean the end of the separation between manual and mental work and between operative work and management, that is to say, the end of subdivisions which are still important within the working class itself.

After these observations regarding the transition to socialism, I should like to go quickly over some problems relating to economies which have emerged from the colonial period. Here it is important to raise the question of the specific nature of these economies in transition.

One of the specific features of this transition is that the *principal* aspect of their present situation is not a result of the *internal* development of their past economic structure, that is, of an internal evolution of their productive forces which caused them to evolve from one stage to another. On the contrary, the productive forces of these countries were generally in a stagnant condition. Further, their post-colonial situation is dominated by the *breakdown* of a political dependence. This breakdown opens the way to new possibilities, through specific interventions from the political plane into the plane of production-structures.

Just as the encounter between these colonial societies and the Western capitalist societies belonged, according to Balibar's analysis, to the diachrony of these societies, because it brought about a transformation in their mode of production,[18] so the breakdown of their dependence tends to bring about (quickly or slowly) a transformation in their mode of production. As with any transition of this kind, we see a specific mode of intervention by the state, law and political force in the mode of production. The rapid development of state intervention, the promulgation of development plans, the nationalisation of productive enterprises and foreign trade, are examples of these numerous irruptions from above at the level of the economic structures. What marks off these interventions from the transition to socialism is that they do not emanate from a state machine that belongs to the working class, or to an alliance of classes led by the working class, but from a state machine that upholds and defends the privileges of the economically dominant classes; here, what plays the decisive role is the contradiction between the making of certain investments and certain *outside* interests, and not, directly, the contradictions within the given society.

I would further add that, where economies that have emerged from the colonial period are concerned we shall have to study essentially something that, though it looks to us like an initial stage, is perhaps only the last stage of the old mode of production, that is, a dissolution that should then lead on to a *real* transition; where the socialist economies are concerned, on the other hand, we shall have to study several stages of the transition period. This will be the case, in particular, with the Soviet economy, of which the on-going transition phase can already be subdivided into a certain number of specific stages, each with its own distinct social and economic, and therefore political, features.

Accordingly, what I propose to examine are essentially the problems of these two types of economy of transition which are characteristic of the world today:

(1) The problems of the *economies which have carried through a socialist revolution*, that is, in which the problems of building socialism are on the order of the day.

It is not, of course, my aim to examine all these problems. It would certainly be more fruitful to give priority to those among them regarding which there is reason to believe that they present us with the most fundamental questions of theory. Among these there is, in particular, the place of simple commodity production, and even of petty capitalist production, in the first stages of an economy evolving towards socialism. This is one of the questions that were raised very sharply at the time when the N.E.P. was formulated.

Another question is that of the forms of transition from simple commodity production to co-operation. Here we find, notably, the case of the collectivisation of agriculture in the Soviet Union, but it is necessary also to examine other procedures for transforming agriculture, such as those that have been employed in China.

A further question is that of the forms of mediation needed in order to dominate effectively the contradictions that may arise from the non-correspondence between the modes of formal and real appropriation. We must investigate, especially, the progressive role that these contradictions may be capable of playing, that is, the way they can drive the productive forces forward, and the conditions that have to be fulfilled in order that this may actually occur.

The questions raised by the linkage of problems of planning and problems of managing the economy will also have to be looked into, particularly through the experience of Cuba and the discussions that have taken place there.

When these questions are gone into thoroughly, it becomes apparent that they are fundamentally theoretical in character, and it is this content that we must endeavour to bring out, by analysing recent historical processes and the theoretical reflexions already formulated regarding these processes.

(2) The problems of the post-colonial economies. Among the questions raised by the evolution of these countries I will mention that of the role and significance of state capitalism. There is reason, for instance, to analyse the specific differences between *this* state capitalism from that which is developing, on the basis of monopoly capitalism, in the big imperialist countries. There is reason, too, to consider the specific differences between the state capitalism of countries which, like India, are dominated by a powerful industrial bourgeoisie, and the state capitalism established in countries with productive forces that are very little developed or where only a very small-scale bourgeoisie, essentially peasant and mercantile in character, is to be found, as, for instance, in Mali or Cambodia.

Finally, it is essential to study the new structures of capitalism, for the twofold reason that the study of these structures is undoubtedly very instructive for our understanding of certain problems that confront the socialist economies themselves and that on the other hand, the recent evolution of capitalism entails far-reaching repercussions on the potential evolution of the post-colonial economies. Here there arises, especially, the problem referred to by the practical concept of "neo-colonialism".

These are, for the moment, the main themes I propose to deal with. I have others in mind, too, but I think it is better to begin working together on themes that have already been defined, before trying to define more precisely the themes which we shall tackle later, or the order in which these will be tackled.

(Introductory statement to the seminar at the École Normale Supérieure, Paris, on: "The Problems of Transition", December, 1965.)

NOTES TO CHAPTER 1

1   L. Althusser, E. Balibar, R. Establet: *Lire le Capital*, Paris (Maspero), 1965, Vol. 2, pp. 179–85. (Eng. edn: *Reading Capital*, New Left Books, 1970.)

2   *Ibid.*, Vol. 2, pp. 182–3.

3   E. Balibar: *Sur les concepts fondamentaux du matérialisme historique* (On the basic concepts of historical materialism), in *ibid.*, Vol. 2, pp. 187–332.

4   Marx, *Le Capital*, Tome VI, p. 257. (Eng. version from *Capital*, III, F.L.P.H. edn., p. 239.)

5   Althusser et al., *op. cit.*, p. 182.

6   *Ibid.*, p. 183.

7   V. I. Lenin, *Oeuvres complètes*, 4th edn., Moscow, 1962, Vol. 32, p. 313 (Eng. version from *Collected Works*, Vol. 32, pp. 295–6.).

8   *Ibid.*, p. 314 (Eng. version, p. 296).

9   Marx, *op. cit.*, Tome VIII, p. 174 (Eng. version from *Capital*, III, F.L.P.H. edition, p. 774).

10   It is necessary to consider also an opposite situation, in which the old social relations can no longer dominate by their own strength, because henceforth the productive forces overflow, in a sense, the production-relations within which they are supposed to be confined. This situation is that of imperialism in its last stage, compelled to have recourse either to violent measures of coercion or to rapid increase of unproductive expenditure (mainly war expenditure, but also any other form of expenditure aimed at diverting part of the accumulation fund from productive use). This point will have to be examined separately.

11   Lenin, *op. cit.*, Vol. 32, p. 347 (Eng. version, p. 327).

12   Marx, *op. cit.*, Tome I, p. 303 (*Capital*, I, Eng. edn. of 1938, p. 297).

13   Marx, *op. cit.*, Tome I, p. 535 (*Capital*, I, Eng. edn. of 1938, p. 518).

14   Cf. E. Balibar, *op. cit.*, Vol. 2, pp. 228–9.

15   These are points which I have endeavoured to analyse below, in Chapter 2, "The socio-economic framework and the organisation of social planning", and in Chapter 3, "Forms and methods of socialist planning and the level of development of the productive forces".

16   Lenin, *op. cit.*, Vol. 32, p. 346 (Eng. version, p. 325).

17   Lenin, *ibid.*

18   Balibar, *op. cit.*, Vol. 2, p. 314.

2: The socio-economic framework and the organisation of social planning[1]

I   A general survey of the mode of organisation of present-day planned economies

The reality of socialist planned economy is more complex than any picture it was possible to try and form before there had been actual experience of it.

This kind of economy does not merely entail a central authority, the exclusive centre where social decisions are made, and which draws up a plan so highly detailed that the units of production or distribution are reduced to a merely technical function that consists in strictly carrying out the *orders* received from the central authority, which has foreseen everything and calculated everything.

In fact, the plan worked out at the centre, however detailed it may be, lays upon the production units only a limited number of tasks of an obligatory nature (what are often called the obligatory "indices" or "indicators"). A more or less extensive margin of initiative is thus left to the production- and distribution-units.

Consequently, these units are not mere technical subdivisions of what might have been conceived as a "single state trust". This expression, "a single state trust", was, we know, used by Bukharin in his book *The Economy of the Transition Period*, in which he maintained that, in an "organised social economy", there was no place for economic science, but only for direct administration of things. We know, too, that this view was not accepted by the other Soviet leaders: Lenin, in particular, regarded it as utopian and as expressing an "ultra-Left" attitude.[2]

In the practice of present-day planned economy, the units of production are not mere technical units, but *economic subjects*, which as such take *decisions*, and which have had to be accorded a margin of initiative and responsibility that makes of them also *juridical subjects*. These juridical subjects are, as such, sources of rights and obligations. They are subject not only to the obligations imposed on them by the plan but also to the obligations which they themselves undertake.

The products that pass from one economic unit to another are, in general,

not shared out by way of *administrative orders*, but mostly circulate by way
of *purchases and sales*, which give rise to *payments*.

There is thus, in most cases, not a sharing-out of products but a circulation of *commodities*; there is *money* and there are *prices*, that is to say (at
least in appearance), there are *commodity categories*, which in turn mean a
system of accounting in terms of prices, a system of calculation in money,
and differentiated wages, together with a *financial* system and a system of
credit, with a state *banking* network which can make fairly long-term
loans.

This is the description one can give of all the planned economies at
present in being, whether those in which the productive forces are most
highly developed, as in the Soviet Union or in Czechoslovakia, or those in
which agriculture still plays a big part, and where the productive forces
are comparatively undeveloped, as in China or in the Democratic Republic
of Vietnam.

This complex reality, this combination of socialist state property and
social planning, on the one hand, with commodity categories (or at least the
appearance of them), on the other, may seem to contradict some of the
descriptions of socialist society given in advance by Marx or Engels.

II. Some passages from Marx and Engels

I do not intend to speak here about the earliest writings of Marx and
Engels, such as Engels's speech on 15th February 1845, at Elberfeld, when
he declared:

> "In communist society it will be easy to know what is being produced and
> what is being consumed. As we know what each individual needs, on the
> average, it will be easy to calculate what a definite number of individuals
> need, and since production will no longer be in the hands of any private
> producers but in those of the Commune and its administration, it will
> not be at all difficult to regulate production according to needs." (MEGA,
> Erste Abteilung, Band 4, p. 372.)

Such passages as these antedate the working out of scientific socialism.
I shall therefore refer only to certain later passages.

I shall recall, in particular, that in the *Critique of the Gotha Programme*
(written in 1875), Marx wrote, among other things:

> "Within the co-operative society based on common ownership of the
> means of production, the producers do not exchange their products; just
> as little does the labour employed on the products appear here as *the
> value* of these products, as a material quality possessed by them, since
> now, in contrast to capitalist society, individual labour no longer exists
> in an indirect fashion but directly as a component part of the total
> labour." (Quoted from the Editions Sociales, Paris, 1950 edn., p. 23:
> Eng. trans., F.L.P.H. edn., p. 20.)

In this same *Critique of the Gotha Programme*, Marx explains that he has
in mind not developed communist society, but communist society as it has

just emerged from capitalist society. It is for *this* society, that is, for this economy of transition, that he foresees each worker receiving, instead of wages in money, "a certificate from society that he has furnished such and such an amount of labour (after deducting his labour for the common funds), and with this certificate he draws from the social stock of means of consumption as much as costs the same amount of labour." (*Ibid.*, p. 23; Eng. trans., p. 20.)

According to this passage, there will be in socialist society, even at its beginning, neither commodities, nor value, nor money, nor, consequently, prices and wages. This is the same idea which Marx had already formulated in *Capital* and which about a year later Engels took up again in *Anti-Dühring*, especially when he wrote:

"The seizure of the means of production by society puts an end to commodity production. . . ." (Quoted from Costes edn., Vol. III, Paris, 1933, p. 51: Eng. trans., 1934 London edn., p. 311.)

There is thus, at least seemingly, a contradiction between the actual working of the socialist economies which we know today[3] and the analyses made by Marx and Engels.

III. The nature of the problems to be studied

If we accept that the present-day socialist economies, as they really are' correspond to *objective demands* imposed by the working and development of these social formations[4] and not to "distortions" of an "ideal model" (which Marx and Engels always refused to provide), we have to ask ourselves how to explain the contradiction which there at least *seems* to be between this reality and some of the analyses made by Marx and Engels.

It is all the more essential to do this because the good or bad working of the planned economy is obviously affected, in a decisive way, by the forms given to the organisation of this economy, and so by the role assigned to the production units, to exchange between these units, to money, prices, and so on.

On another plane, the role played by commodity categories in the planned economies of today is not without far-reaching influence on behaviour and attitudes, and, more generally, on the ideological superstructures. For this reason, too, one cannot omit to investigate the reasons why commodity categories have been retained, at least in appearance.

Furthermore, the frequent changes in organisation which take place in the various socialist countries (especially, in recent years, in the Soviet Union), the hesitations and fluctuations (towards a greater or lesser degree of centralism, or of autonomy allowed to the enterprises) which these changes reflect, make it plain that the final achievement of the best form of organisation, that is, the best adapted to the level of development and the nature of the present productive forces, as also to the requirements for building socialist society, cannot be regarded as having already been fully attained (though it is through such changes that these requirements make themselves felt).

B

The hesitations in the practical sphere themselves show that what is being gone through at present is a stage of research which involves a substantial element of trial and error. That does not mean, of course, that theoretical considerations play no part in current researches, but the hesitations in the field of practice show us that these theoretical considerations do not yet constitute a body of thought strongly structured enough to be capable of guiding with exactitude the search for the best forms of organisation.

We must therefore also look into the theoretical considerations which are generally accepted, and see to what extent we can carry a little further the analyses which underlie them.

This thought is closely linked with a thought about the structure of the plans and about the means of putting them into effect.

By "structure of the plans" I have in mind the order of the dimensions in which the aims of the plan are laid down (both physical and non-physical dimensions), the degree of detail into which the planners go in laying down these aims, and the nature of the plan-indicators that are made binding on each enterprise.

By "means of putting the plans into effect" I mean the respective parts played by administrative orders, economic calculation and the various instruments that are available for directing the economy. For the moment, of course, I shall deal with these different problems only in their most general aspect.

To begin with, I shall say a few words about the most obvious reasons for the apparent contradiction between the present mode of organisation and functioning of the planned economies and some of the formulations made by Marx and Engels, formulations which they always put forward with the greatest caution and which they always refused to offer as anticipations.

Among the most obvious reasons for the retention of commodity categories within the socialist economies of today we must mention the presence in these economies of several different forms of property.

IV The diversity of forms of property in the means of production

We know that, in *Economic Problems of Socialism in the USSR*, Stalin put forward a refutation of the view according to which there is a contradiction between the existence of commodity production in the USSR and the passage we have quoted from Engels, in which the latter declares that "the seizure of the means of production by society puts an end to commodity production".

Stalin notes that, in this passage, Engels does not make clear whether what is involved is the seizure by society of *all* the means of production, and he rightly observes that, in another passage in *Anti-Dühring*, Engels speaks of society's taking possession of "all means of production". (Costes edn., Vol. III, p. 68: Eng. edn., p. 326.)

Stalin draws the conclusion that, for Engels, the disappearance of commodity production presupposed the expropriation of *all* the means of production in a country (which has not taken place either in the USSR or in any other socialist country). Stalin does not seem sure, moreover, that commodity production would really disappear even if all the means of production were nationalised, at least in countries where foreign trade continues to play a big part.

Indeed, we must take note that, after having remarked that it is only in Britain that, in his view, it would be possible, given the high degree of concentration of agricultural production, to nationalise *all* the means of production and so to eliminate commodity production, Stalin adds, immediately:

"I leave aside in this instance the question of the importance of foreign trade to Britain and the vast part it plays in her national economy. I think that only after an investigation of this question can it be finally decided what would be the future of commodity production in Britain after the proletariat had assumed power and *all* the means of production had been nationalized." (Stalin, *Les Problèmes economiques du socialisme en URSS*, French Communist Party edn., Paris, 1952, p. 12: Eng. edn., F.L.P.H., *Economic Problems of Socialism in the USSR*, pp. 14–15.)

However that may be, Stalin comments (*op. cit.*, p. 13) that Engels did not answer, and moreover did not try to answer, the question of what happens to commodity production in a country where *only part of the means of production* is sufficiently concentrated to be capable of expropriation, while another part, essentially in agriculture, is broken up to such a degree among owner-producers that it is out of the question to contemplate the expropriation of the latter.

After putting this question, Stalin points out that Lenin answered it, in particular in two of his works, that on the tax in kind and that on co-operation.

This is true, even though, in these works, Lenin did not answer the question in exactly the same terms as Stalin.

Here I think it is necessary to insert a parenthesis.

In the summary given by Stalin (*op. cit.*, p. 14) of Lenin's theses on co-operation and on the introduction of the tax in kind (Lenin's report to the 10th Congress of the R.C.P. (B), entitled "Report on the substitution of a tax in kind for the surplus-grain appropriation system", 15th March 1921), the collective farms are indeed put in the centre of the analysis. However:

(1) When Lenin defended the thesis of *commodity exchange*, he was obviously not thinking of the collective farms, which hardly existed at that time, but of the *individual peasants*, and in particular the middle peasants. He says so expressly when he writes: "We must try to satisfy the demands of the middle peasants", and when he adds that this satisfaction cannot be given without "a certain freedom of exchange" (Lenin, *L'alliance de la classe ouvrière et de la paysannerie* (The alliance between the working class

and the peasantry), Moscow, 1957, pp. 742–3) (Eng. version, *Collected Works*, 4th edn., Vol. 32, pp. 217–18.)

(2) When Lenin speaks of co-operation, he has in mind not only, or even mainly, *producer* co-operatives (i.e., collective farms) but also, and especially, *trading* co-operatives (for buying and selling). This emerges clearly from what he says about co-operative stores, and from his declaration that, in order to be a good co-operator one must be "a cultured trader". (*Ibid.*, pp. 828 and 829: Eng. version, *Collected Works*, Vol. 33, p. 470.)[5]

Though the second of these observations is not of fundamental importance for the main subject of our present discussion, I think it is necessary to make it for at least two reasons:

a) Because, since the collectivisation of 1928–9, Lenin's idea of the development of co-operatives has been associated in a one-sided way with the idea of the development of collective farms, which was *not* Lenin's conception—for him the development of co-operatives embraced *all* forms of co-operation—and:

b) Because Lenin ascribed very great importance to co-operatives in the framework of the building of socialism. We know that he wrote: "And given social ownership of the means of production, given the class victory of the proletariat over the bourgeoisie, the system of civilised co-operators is the system of socialism." (*Ibid.*, p. 830: Eng. version, *Collected Works*, Vol. 33, p. 471.)[5]

After this parenthesis, we can return to the essentials of Stalin's argument: if commodity production survives under the dictatorship of the proletariat, this is:

(1) Because not all the means of production have been nationalised (and they have not been nationalised because they are not all ripe for this), and so

(2) Because there exists, alongside state property, *collective-farm* property, and the collective farms do not give up their products otherwise than by way of *exchange*, i.e., as *commodities*.

It must be added, similarly, that the existence of private production carried on by individual craftsmen, and especially by collective-farm peasants on their individual holdings, constitutes another *raison d'être* for commodity production, exchange, money, etc.

All this amounts to saying that, in the planned economies of today, the state has not taken possession of *all* the means of production and this is why the commodity categories survive.

This explanation seems to me correct so far as it goes, but inadequate. It does indeed enable us to understand why there is *commodity production outside the state sector*, and why there is *commodity circulation on the periphery of this sector*, when the state sector sells its products to the other sectors or to the consumers, or when it buys products from the other producers, but this explanation does not enable us to understand *the retention of commodity categories within the state sector*.

Why, within the state sector, do the enterprises make purchases and sales? Why do they dispose of their products at certain prices? Why do they carry out transactions in money? etc. It is these questions that the argument about the co-existence of several forms of property does not seem capable of answering. And this is the problem we must now examine.

V. The commodity categories within the state sector

We will first consider the ways in which the retention of commodity categories within the state sector has been explained. Here again we shall find a particularly well-worked-out formulation of these explanations in Stalin's *Economic Problems. . . .* They can be summed up like this:

1 *The commodity character of part of the production of the state sector*

The state sector actually disposes of some of its products as commodities, and so part of its production continues to be *commodity production*, which continues to be *regulated*, at least within certain limits, by the *law of value*.

a) The chief and primary category of products which thus become commodities are the products intended for personal consumption. Stalin writes:

"As a matter of fact, consumer goods, which are needed to compensate the labour power expended in the process of production, are produced and realised in our country as commodities coming under the operation of the law of value. It is precisely here that the law of value exercises its influence on production." (*Op. cit.*, p. 18: Eng. edn., p. 23.)

b) Secondly, even some means of production continue to be disposed of as commodities, namely, those which are sold abroad (cf. *ibid.*, p. 45). The means of production thus exported actually become commodities.

I have already mentioned that Stalin expressed doubt whether, in a country like Britain, where foreign trade plays a very important role, commodity production might not be retained, even if all the means of production were nationalised.

I will leave aside, for the moment, the problem set by the influence of foreign trade on the retention of commodity production. This is a problem of considerable theoretical importance, since, through it, the following question is being asked: does not the complete disappearance of commodity production presuppose also the achievement of socialism throughout the world, and real international planning?

For the moment it is the commodity character of the production of consumer goods that will occupy our attention.

Let me recall, first, that after having mentioned that objects for personal use are disposed of as commodities, Stalin goes on to say:

"In this connexion, such things as cost accounting and profitableness, production costs, prices, etc., are of actual importance in our enterprises. Consequently, our enterprises cannot, and must not, function without taking the law of value into account." (*Ibid.*, p. 18: Eng. edn., p. 23.)

This argument seems to me to be a weak one. The weakness shows itself in at least two ways:

(1) First of all one ought to explain why consumer goods are *sold* for

money, and not *distributed* in exchange for labour-certificates, as Marx foresaw in his *Critique of the Gotha Programme.* So long as this is not explained, the problem is merely *shifted elsewhere,* not solved.

(2) Secondly, even if for the time being we accept the explanation given for the retention of commodity production by the fact that objects of personal consumption are sold, this does not seem to help us to understand why, *within the state sector,* the means of production are *bought and sold* and bear a price, etc.

Stalin perceived this difficulty, and formulated a second explanation.

2   *The requirements of calculation*

This second explanation is found in the section of *Economic Problems . . .* entitled "Reply to Comrade Aleksandr Ilyich Notkin". In this section, Stalin asks:

"Why . . . do we speak of the value of means of production, their cost of production, their price, etc.?"

And answers:

". . . This is needed for purposes of calculation and settlement, for determining whether enterprises are paying or running at a loss, for checking and controlling the enterprises." (*Op. cit.,* p. 44: Eng. edn., pp. 58–9.)

It is clear that this second explanation is not satisfactory, either, for *the real question is, precisely, why calculations have to be made by means of commodity categories* and why they are not made directly in terms of *labour-time.*

If calculations have to be made in commodity categories, then this must surely be because these categories possess a certain reality. What, indeed, would be the use of calculations carried out with categories that did *not* express a certain reality?

This is the heart of the question, and it is not answered by merely remarking, as Stalin does, that the *content* of the commodity categories is not the same as under the framework of capitalism.

It is indeed obvious that these categories do not relate to the same social relations, but they exist nevertheless, they possess reality, they are not just a "pure form" of accountancy, and it is this fact that they exist that has to be explained.

All the more necessary is it to explain their existence because, on the one hand, this does not seem to have been foreseen by theory, and, on the other, the explanation given will be helpful, as regards principle, in dealing with these categories as the expression of real phenomena, with an objective existence (from which likewise follow objective requirements) and not as "conveniences for calculation" which could therefore be manipulated in an arbitrary fashion.

There is something even more important: discovery of the *raison d'être* of commodity categories in the planned economy of today is *a necessary stage in the establishment of effective conditions for the disappearance of these commodity categories at a later stage,* the stage regarded as the ultimate aim towards which contemporary economic plans have the task of carrying the planned economies.

Before examining what seems to me to form the bases for the existence of commodity categories in the planned economies of today, including their presence within the state sector, I think it will be useful to recall briefly some of the conclusions that have been drawn, or which could be drawn, from the analyses in Stalin's *Economic Problems*. . . . I think it will also be of use to note certain thoughts that are to be found in this work and which may be helpful to us in formulating a reply to the question before us.

3 *The conditions for the disappearance of commodity categories, according to Stalin's "Economic Problems . . ."*

First of all, as regards the conditions for the disappearance of commodity categories, we must note that in Stalin's work the emphasis is laid on the need for the preliminary disappearance of the two main sectors of the present-day socialist economy. Stalin writes:

"Of course, when instead of the two basic production sectors, the state sector and the collective-farm sector, there will be only one all-embracing production sector, with the right to dispose of all the consumer goods produced in the country, commodity circulation, with its 'money economy', will disappear, as being an unnecessary element in the national economy." (*Op. cit.*, p. 16: Eng. edn., p. 20.)

From this Stalin draws the following conclusion, which coincides with that of the founders of Marxism:

"In the second phase of communist society, the amount of labour expended on the production of goods will be measured not in a round-about way, not through value and its forms, as is the case under commodity production, but directly and immediately—by the amount of time, the number of hours, expended on the production of goods. As to the distribution of labour, its distribution among the branches of production will be regulated not by the law of value, which will have ceased to function by that time, but by the growth of society's demand for goods. It will be a society in which production will be regulated by the requirements of society, and computation of the requirements of society will acquire paramount importance for the planning bodies." (*Op. cit.*, pp. 20–1: Eng. edn., pp. 26–7.)

To these two quotations I will add a third, taken from the same same work. In the chapter entitled: "Concerning the Errors of Comrade L. D. Yaroshenko", Stalin sets out what he regards as the "three main preliminary conditions" for the transition to communism.

These conditions are, he considers, a relatively higher rate of expansion of the production of means of production; such a cultural advancement of society as will secure for all its members an all-round development of their physical and mental abilities, and which will put an end to the present division of labour; and the gradual disappearance of collective-farm property, which will be replaced by a form of public property that will make it possible, "by means of gradual transitions, to replace commodity circulation by a system of products-exchange, under which the central government, or some other social-economic centre, might control the whole product of social production in the interests of society". (*Op. cit.,* p. 56: Eng. edn., p. 75.)

4 *Discussion of the preceding theses*

From these quotations there emerge the following ideas concerning the conditions for and consequences of the disappearance of commodity categories:

a) This disappearance is conditional on the disappearance of the division of production between two sectors, the state sector and the collective-farm sector, and the progressive raising of collective-farm property to the level of public property.

b) Nevertheless, this condition, while necessary, is not in itself sufficient; in addition, a "social-economic centre" must appear which can "control the whole product of social production in the interests of society", so effectively that a system of "products exchange" will replace "commodity circulation". (Actually, it would seem preferable, in this connexion, to speak of *a system of products-allotment* rather than a system of products exchange.)

These conditions having been realised, the category of value disappears, for "the amount of labour expended on the production of goods will be measured not in a roundabout way" but directly and immediately. The law of value will thus have "ceased to function", and production will be "regulated by the requirements of society".

This leads us to raise the following questions:

First: if the essential condition for the disappearance of commodity categories is the establishment of a "social-economic centre" capable of disposing of all the products in the interest of society, the disappearance of collective-farm production, while constituting a *necessary* condition for the appearance of such a centre, would not be a *sufficient* condition for this. One may indeed ask whether, in addition, certain conditions would not need to be realised *relating to the functioning of the single public sector as a whole.*

Second: What is the root of the difficulty that prevents accounting in labour-time from being substituted for accounting in terms of value? Is it a technical difficulty? Or is it a social one?

In the latter case, is this difficulty bound up only with the existence of two sectors of production, or is it also, and more profoundly, bound up with the fact that, though the cognition or verification of needs is carried out to a very great extent *a priori,* nevertheless a large proportion of needs is not known except *a posteriori,* and then still very inadequately?

If this is so, it will be appreciated that it is not possible at present to determine *a priori,* in an accurate way, the labour-time *socially-necessary* for the production of various goods.

What can be measured, though not without difficulty, is the labour-time *actually expended*, but this is not automatically the same as the socially-necessary labour-time. The latter depends, on the one hand, on a *correct estimation of needs* (otherwise, part of the labour expended may not correspond to any need) and, on the other, on a *correct choice of production-techniques* (otherwise the labour-time expended may not be socially necessary).

That seems to be where the real problem lies. We are all the more disposed to think so today because the techniques for measuring the labour-time actually expended in various lines of production have made great progress, thanks to the use for this purpose in recent years of tables of inter-sectoral relations. Here must be mentioned, in particular, the pioneer work of the Hungarian economist Csikos-Nagy and, more recently, that of the Soviet economist Ivanov (see his article, "Problems of determining the amount of value", in *Vestnik Statistiki*, 1963, No. 2, and the article translated into German in *Sowjetwissenschaft*, 1963, No. 10).

If one of the ultimate and essential reasons for the retention of commodity production lies not in the problems raised by measuring the amount of labour *actually expended* but in those raised by measuring a priori the labour-time *socially-necessary*, then a social decision-making centre is undoubtedly necessary for this measurement to be effected: but what makes it possible for such a centre to work effectively is that the objective conditions have been realised for *a priori* estimation of the needs of society and the procedures whereby these needs can best be satisfied by society's labour as a whole.

If this is so, we can say that it is when, and because, society has become capable of consciously regulating its production by reference to its needs (that is, of expending social labour-power "consciously", as Marx puts it)[6] that the commodity categories will disappear, and not the other way round, with the disappearance of commodity categories enabling society to regulate production on the basis of needs.

By putting the problem in this way we are therefore led to say:

a) That the root of the retention of commodity production and commodity categories is the absence of a social-economic centre effectively *capable* of disposing of all the products, and strictly regulating production in relation to the needs of society;

b) that the absence of this centre is connected, in the first instance, with the existence of several forms of property;

c) that, beyond this diversity of forms of property (and underlying it), it is *the present level of development of the productive forces*, which is still inadequate, that prevents a social-economic centre from being able effectively to dispose, consciously, of all the products, and really to regulate production according to the needs of society.

Observation of the objective conditions of the functioning of the state sector in the countries with planned economies shows that, *even in this sector, a single centre does not attain to such power to dispose and regulate,* and it is from this that follows the necessity for a certain autonomy of the enterprises, the need to endow these enterprises with certain powers of disposal, a certain freedom of manoeuvre, which in turn results in the rules of business accounting, the money economy within the state sector, the commodity categories, etc.

Having arrived at this point we must, however, raise two questions:

a) In the last formulation we have reached, are we not mistaking *effect* for *cause*? More concretely, is it not because the enterprises have been *given certain powers* that there is no social centre really capable of regulating production by needs?

b) Does not the preceding analysis amount to calling into question the view taken by Marx and Engels that, *when society takes possession of all the means of production, commodity production will cease*?

These two questions are closely linked, and so the answers I am going to try and formulate will likewise be closely linked.

VI *Statisation, socialisation and taking over of the means of production by society*

We must begin with the most fundamental question, which is obviously this: must we cease to accept that commodity production will come to an end when society takes possession of all the means of production?

It seems to me that this question must be answered in the negative.

Commodity production presupposes definite social conditions, namely, producers producing more or less independently of each other. When these social conditions no longer exist, that is, *when society has fully taken possession of all the means of production, there can no longer be any place for commodity production*.

But in that case, it will be asked, how is this assertion to be reconciled with the foregoing analyses? Is there then no lesson to be drawn from the experience of the planned economies? Does no new conclusion emerge from this immense social *praxis* constituted by several decades of planning?

Of course there are conclusions to be drawn from this experience. But these conclusions can only be drawn if the tools appropriate to the analysis of this experience are used, that is to say, correctly worked-out concepts. It is precisely the confrontation of the practical experience of planning with ideas which have not always been defined with sufficient rigour[7] that should enable us to refine our concepts more thoroughly, and thereby to understand better both the experience itself and the true significance of certain analyses made by Marx and Engels.

In the argument which follows I shall not take the excessively long and pointlessly complicated line of presenting first an analysis of the experience of the planned economies and only then, on the basis of this analysis, formulating more rigorously the concepts enabling us to interpret this experience.

I shall confine myself to the second procedure, that is, I shall try to reformulate certain concepts more precisely and then interpret certain passages on the basis of this reformulation: this is how I shall endeavour to take account of practical experience, i.e., through a concrete analysis which I shall not develop here.

Let us begin then, by re-reading certain passages in the light of experience, in order to try and clarify the concepts and establish a unified interpretation of them.

1 *The social implications of state ownership*

It seems to me to be necessary, first and foremost, to set in its context the passage from Engels about "the seizure by society of the means of production", and to illuminate this passage both by means of the context and by reference to practical experience.

Before expounding the idea that with "the seizure by society of the means of production" commodity production comes to an end (*op. cit.*, p. 51). Engels has shown:

a) that the social character of the modern productive forces tends inexorably to their socialisation, that is, to the appearance of social forms of ownership of these productive forces. He notes that, within capitalism itself, these social *forms* of ownership are represented by joint-stock companies and state ownership. Given, however, that the capitalist state, which officially represents society, in fact represents only the ruling class, Engels says, in a passage I have already quoted:

"State ownership of the productive forces is not the solution of the conflict [between the social character of the productive forces and private ownership], but it contains within itself the formal means, the key to the solution." (*Anti-Dühring,* Vol. III, p. 44: Eng. edn., pp. 306–7.)

b) Engels has also shown that when "the proletariat seizes the state power", it "transforms the means of production in the first instance into state property", and he adds (*ibid.,* pp. 46–7: Eng. edn., pp. 308–9): "The first act in which the state really comes forward as the representative of society as a whole—the taking possession of the means of production *in the name of society* (my emphasis, C.B.)—is at the same time its last independent act as a state. The interference of the state power in social relations becomes superfluous in one sphere after another, and then ceases of itself. The government of persons is replaced by the administration of things, and the direction of the processes of production. The state is not abolished, *it withers away.*"

If we think about these passages and try to clarify them in the light of the lessons of social *praxis,* we see that what Engels is saying is that when the state controlled by the proletariat "takes possession of the means of production", it does this "in the name of society", *which is not the same thing as society's taking possession of them.* It is later, in proportion as the state withers away and the administration of things replaces the government of persons, that there really occurs the taking possession of the means of production *by society,* which administers itself.

If we read the passage from Engels in this way we can appreciate that commodity production does not "cease" abruptly, as might be suggested by the interpretation according to which taking possession by the state is equivalent to taking possession by society, but that it withers away as the process of taking possession by society advances, since *this taking possession is a phenomenon that is realised in the course of a period of history, simultaneously with the withering away of the state.*

When we put the problem in these terms, we see that ownership of the means of production by the proletarian state is not yet direct taking possession by society, but the stage that leads to this, on condition that other stages follow (whence the importance, for an entire period of history, of the dictatorship of the proletariat, in order to ensure that the state shall really act in the interests of the working people, and that the retention of the commodity categories, money, and so on, shall not bring about the rebirth, in new forms, of the exploitation of man by man).

This leads us to make a distinction between statisation (even by a workers' state) and socialisation. This is the point I shall now consider.

2 *Statisation, socialisation, domination of the productive forces by society*

The distinction between statisation and socialisation has not always been made with sufficient strictness, and there are a number of passages where one of these words is used instead of the other. Nevertheless, a distinction is needed between, on the one hand, statisation or nationalisation (which are *juridical acts*) and, on the other, socialisation, which implies *a capacity on the part of society* to account for and allot the means of production and their products.

Lenin specially insisted on this distinction in a well-known work, *"Left-wing" childishness and petty-bourgeois ideas* (see *Oeuvres complètes*, Vol. 27, pp. 337 et seq.). In this work Lenin launches a vigorous attack on those Communists who, in May 1918, demanded what they called "a most determined policy of socialisation". This is what Lenin wrote in this connexion:

"Dear 'Left Communists', how determined they are, but how little thinking they display. What do they mean by pursuing 'a most determined policy of socialisation?' One may or may not be determined on the question of nationalisation or confiscation, but the whole point is that even the greatest possible 'determination' in the world is not enough to pass *from* nationalisation and confiscation *to* socialisation. The misfortune of our 'Lefts' is that by their naive, childish combination of the words 'most determined policy of socialisation' they reveal their utter failure to understand the crux of the question, the crux of the 'present' situation. The misfortune of our 'Lefts' is that they have missed the very essence of the 'present situation', the transition from confiscation (the carrying out of which requires above all determination in a politician) to socialisation (the carrying out of which requires a *different* quality in the revolutionary).

Yesterday, the main task of the moment was, as determinedly as possible, to nationalise, confiscate, beat down and crush the bourgeoisie, and put down sabotage. Today, only a blind man could fail to see that we have nationalised, confiscated, beaten down and put down more *than we have had time to count.* The difference between socialisation and simple confiscation is that confiscation can be carried out by 'determination' alone, without the ability to calculate and distribute properly, *whereas socialisation cannot be brought about without this ability."* (*Op. cit.,* pp. 348–9: Eng. edn., Vol. 27, pp. 333–4.)

In this passage Lenin contrasts the juridical form (ownership, property) with the concrete production-relations, which are social relations. It is these relations that may or may not make it possible to pass from statisation to socialisation, depending on whether or not they enable society or its organs to account for and allot in a rational way, that is, efficiently, the means of production and their products.

State ownership is a *necessary condition* for socialisation *on the plane of the state* (which is not yet socialisation directly on the plane of society), but it is not by itself a sufficient condition. In order that there may be socialisation on the plane of the state, the latter must have the *capacity to dispose effectively and efficiently of the means of production and their products.* Without this *capacity,* we have nationalisation without socialisation. Such a capacity results from an *historical development,* it is connected with the actual development of the productive forces (which include men themselves, and the level of their knowledge) and with the correlative transformation of production-relations.

I shall have to come back later to various aspects of the problem of the greater or lesser correspondence between juridical *authority* to dispose of certain means of production and effective *capacity* to dispose of these means of production. We know that what matters, in the last resort, is concrete capacity and not abstract "authority".

It is quite obvious that, on the basis of one and the same state ownership of the means of production (i.e., on the basis of the same juridical form), many degrees of concrete capacity to set these means of production to work are possible. It is therefore only if there is a sufficient level of capacity that there is real domination by society, or by the state acting in the name of society, over the means of production, and thus effective taking possession by society. Only when the taking possession by society of which Engels speaks attains a sufficient degree and level can society allot social labour in a conscious way, and the commodity categories disappear.

The building of socialist society is thus an historical process during which *planning* begins by being *social direction* of the productive forces (through a—more or less complete—effective socialisation of these forces), and becomes *social domination* of them (which leads to the complete disappearance of commodity production).

The fact, explicitly recognised by Lenin, that statisation does not automatically coincide with socialisation, in the sense of effective "social direction" of the statised means of production (and, so, *a fortiori,* in the sense of social domination of these means of production) is fully confirmed by the difficulties encountered in putting plans into application even within the state sectors of the socialist economies of today. The successes achieved in this effective planning, and the difficulties encountered, show precisely that the objective conditions for real social domination over the forces of production are only in the process of coming into being, and this is why it is *necessary* to allow a relative freedom of manoeuvre either to the production units of the state sector or to certain "economic groups" which can be called economic *subjects*.

It must be emphasised at this point that the non-coincidence between nationalisation and effective social direction stands out very clearly when one considers the nationalisation of the land from the standpoint of its consequences in respect of the social direction of the productive forces of agriculture.

In the Soviet Union, for example, the land was nationalised at the time of the October Revolution, but *exploitation of the land* (that is, the practical setting to work of the productive forces of agriculture) was for a long time after that event mainly undertaken by individual peasants.[8]

Twelve years after the October Revolution (on the morrow of the collectivisation carried out during the First Five-Year Plan), the exploitation of the greater part of the land was the responsibility of the collective farms, that is, not of the state or of organs directly dependent on the state, but of groups of working peasants.

The efforts of the Soviet state to direct the productive forces of agriculture have taken, successively or simultaneously, a variety of forms: production-plans of the collective farms, ratified by the state organs, directing role of the Machine and Tractor Stations, plans for commercialisation of agricultural production, use of "economic levers" (i.e., especially, the price system). At present the state uses essentially indirect methods to direct collective-farm agriculture. I shall return to this point in a moment.

Furthermore, even today, the production realised on the peasants' individual holdings is only indirectly or very imperfectly the object of social direction, though the land of these individual holdings is also state property. If this is so, it is not, of course, because the production of the individual holdings is of slight economic interest—on the contrary, the contribution made by these holdings to total consumption is far from negligible—but because *the very nature of the productive forces put to work* on these holdings does not allow of effective and *direct* social direction of their use.

To a lesser extent (that is, with a greater possibility of social direction), this is also true of the productive forces of the collective farms: this is what accounts for the abandonment of attempts, never crowned with success, at *direct* planning of collective-farm production and the attempt to direct it *indirectly*, through plans for commercialisation and the combination of technical and administrative management (to which corresponded the creation, in March 1962 of collective-farm-and-state-farm production managements)[9] and the increasing use of "economic levers" (especially through the revision of the system of agricultural prices, carried out several times since 1953).

Thus we see that what, besides state ownership (which is the starting-point and basis of real planning), is equally necessary for *direct* social direction of the productive forces is *a sufficient development of these forces, resulting in their having a sufficiently social character.* So long as this development is inadequate, state ownership may remain *partly* an empty juridical framework. As Marx puts it in the *Critique of the Gotha Programme*:

"Right can never be higher than the economic structure of society, and its cultural development conditioned thereby." (*Op. cit.*, p. 25: Eng. edn., p. 22.)

This means that if the legal regulations promulgated do not correspond to the economic state of society, these regulations remain, partially or temporarily, without effect, or else their actual effect is not what was expected. We perceive here an aspect of the law of necessary correspondence or non-correspondence between the production-relations and the character of the productive forces.

If this correspondence is ensured, the production-relations do not impede the development of the productive forces. If it is not ensured, if there is a contradiction between the production-relations and the character of the productive forces, the latter do not develop as fast as they technically could, they develop irregularly, through a succession of periods of slow development and other periods of more or less rapid development, and perhaps even periods of stagnation.

One of the essential problems of the development of the planned economy is to ensure the fullest possible correspondence between the production-relations and the character of the productive forces. It is by way of this correspondence, consciously sought for, that the socialist state, which is master of the "commanding heights" of the economy—that is to say, which has eliminated private ownership of the social means of production—is able to ensure the overall direction of the productive forces, expanded reproduction on the scale desired, and *preparation* of the conditions for *complete social domination* of the productive forces, a domination which will be finally ensured by the disappearance of the commodity categories and of the state itself.

3 *Adaptation of property forms to the level of development and the character of the productive forces*

If socialist planning is possible, this is because, basically, the productive forces of modern times are social in character and the socialist state deals with them in accordance with their nature. It was in this sense that Engels wrote:

"This treatment of the productive forces of the present day, on the basis of their real nature at last recognised by society, opens the way to the replacement of the anarchy of social production by a socially planned regulation of production in accordance with the needs both of society and of each individual." (*Anti-Dühring,* Vol. III, p. 45: Eng. edn., pp. 307–8.)

a) *The more or less social nature of the productive forces.*

Treating the productive forces in accordance with their nature means, first, recognising the *degree of actual socialisation* of the various productive forces; and then adapting property-forms and production-relations (i.e., the forms taken by relations between the producers, individually and collectively) to the degree of socialisation, which is constantly increasing, of the productive forces. It thus signifies *recognising certain objective requirements* and conforming to them. Without conforming to them it is not possible to give social direction to the development and utilisation of the productive forces.

The first requirement that has to be met if social planning is to be ensured, the most fundamental requirement of all, is that the state should take possession, in the name of society, of all the means of production and exchange which are really social in character.

The more or less social character of a production process and, therefore, of the means of production employed in it, is essentially linked with two types of evolution:

(1) The increasingly social origin of the means of production which are set to work in the given production-process;

(2) The increasingly social destination of the products which emerge from the given production-process.

By the "increasingly social origin" of the means of production set to work in a given production-process is meant the fact that these means of production come from an increasingly large number of branches of the economy. Thus, in the beginning, agriculture, for example, is more or less self-sufficient; that is, the number of means of production of extra-agricultural origin (or, at the level of the agricultural unit of exploitation, coming from outside this unit) which are employed is very limited. Increasingly, however, agricultural production comes to depend on means of more and more diverse origin: tools, machinery, fuel, electrical equipment, electric power, fertiliser, insecticides, herbicides, etc. The same is true in every branch of industry, starting with the extractive industries and going on to embrace the transformative industries, and in every unit of production.

The increasing socialisation of the productive forces is thus shown in the fact that every branch has recourse to means of production from an ever-greater variety of sources. This process is the other aspect of the increasing division of labour and the increasing specialisation of economic activities. It is this socialisation of labour that forms the objective basis for planning and renders it both possible and necessary, owing to the increasing *inter-dependence* of the various elementary processes of production.

We are now able to measure, more or less accurately, by means of certain coefficients, the degree of socialisation (from the standpoint just explained) of different branches of production in a number of countries.

For example, if we consider the use, direct and indirect, of industrial products by agriculture, we see that for a value of gross production equivalent to 1,000 the consumption of industrial products by agriculture is 61 in Italy, 78·3 in France, 88·8 in the USSR, 89·9 in Britain and 108·7 in the USA.[10] In the case of very advanced agricultural units the industrial in-put coefficients would, of course, be very much higher.

These percentages are, naturally, affected by the comparative levels of industrial and agricultural prices; they are none the less significant, however.

More detailed analysis of the industries that contribute to agriculture's productive consumption also gives interesting results. It emerges that, for a gross production value of 1,000, American agriculture consumes 4·4 products of the engineering industry, while Soviet agriculture consumes 27·8; on the other hand, consumption of products of the chemical industry is 21·1 in the United States, and 7·7 in the Soviet Union, on the same basis.

By "increasingly social destination of the products" is meant the fact that the products arising from a production-process are destined, generally speaking, to be sold to an increasing number of users, either directly or indirectly. This phenomenon has various aspects:

A Each branch of production works, either directly or indirectly, for an increasing number of other branches. This is merely another side of the increasing social division of labour. Thus, the chemical industry which, when it appeared as a distinct sphere of production, worked in the first place only for a small number of other industries, has progressively expanded the field in which its products are used. Today this field is practically universal. It ranges from agriculture through the extractive industries, to the metal-working industries (especially in the treatment of metals), etc. If we take *indirect uses* into account, we see that at the present time every branch of production is virtually working for every other branch, and consequently feels the impact of every fluctuation that may occur in any sector of the economy.

To illustrate the extent to which the products of one branch of industry are distributed through the others, it is possible to use other coefficients besides the foregoing.

For example, one may use for this purpose the "coefficient of productive utilisation" (in the sense of intermediate consumption) of the products of the different branches. In terms of prices at the point of production, we find that 63·5 per cent of Soviet agricultural production is destined for intermediate consumption, as against 71·3 per cent of American, 54·6 per cent of Hungarian and 45·2 per cent of Yugoslav.

For the same purpose of discovering the degree of socialisation of production (in the sense of this word now being considered) we can examine the figures relating to the degree of utilisation by various industries of the products of each industry (see on this point the table on page 832 of the German translation of the article mentioned in note 10).

As Berri and Shvikov write in this article: "A comparison of the structures of production, using inter-sectoral balances, enables us to discover important features in the production-structures of different countries, features which are determined above all by the degree of development of technique and of the social division of labour. . . ." (*Ibid.*, pp. 832–3.)

B The increasingly social destination of the products is also shown in another way, when we examine the *size of the community served by a production-unit*. With the advance of the productive forces this size usually (though not necessarily) grows larger. Thus, it may successively be local, micro-regional, regional, national or international.

The need for state ownership of certain means of production is all the greater because these means of production are used in activities (or in economic units) which are more thoroughly integrated in the social division of labour, either through the very nature of the means of production employed or through the destination of the products.

b) *The degree of socialisation of the productive forces and the levels and forms of ownership of the means of production.*

While state ownership or nationalisation is necessary for social direction of the productive forces, where all those means of production are concerned which are well integrated into the social division of labour, or which serve the needs of a nation-wide or international community, on the other hand, as a general rule, social ownership needs to be established at a lower level in the case of means of production that are less integrated in the social division of labour or which serve the needs of a community less than nation-wide in its scope.

Analysis of the great experiences of the building of socialism shows that these "lower levels of social ownership" of certain means of production may consist of ownership by regional or local organs of the state power, ownership by local politico-administrative authorities (municipal councils, for instance), or, at a still lower level, various forms of co-operative ownership.

When the socialisation of the productive forces is very slight, as in small peasant holdings which are not mechanised, and in handicraft production, going over to social forms of ownership (nationalisation, establishment of craftsmen's co-operatives, etc.) may, if it is carried through without substantial technical changes, correspond to no objective economic necessity. When this is so, a decision to make this change cannot help the productive forces to progress, or even provide a better management or a better current utilisation of them (sometimes, indeed, as a result of going over to forms of ownership that do not correspond to the degree of actual socialisation of the means of production, a setback will be given to the economic efficiency with which these means of production are used).

When decisions have to be taken on changes in property-relations, *economic criteria are not, of course, the only ones that have to be taken into consideration*, especially in periods when class contradictions are assuming acute forms. It may be necessary, for instance, in order to consolidate the social foundations of the socialist state, to nationalise means of production which, from a strictly economic standpoint, do not call for nationalisation.

Political needs then take precedence of economic ones, since the consolidation of the power of the socialist state is, indeed, the essential condition for further economic achievements and the guarantee that these achievements will be socialist in character.

On the other hand, it must be stressed that nationalisation, or lower forms of social ownership, may be indispensable, despite the slight degree to which certain means of production are socialised, if *the requirements for further development of the socialist economy are to be met*. This applies in relation to the following problems:

A *The problem of rapid introduction of new techniques*, especially in agriculture. Peasant holdings do not as a rule offer a favourable framework for mechanisation or the introduction of new measures of agricultural technique. Consequently, the transition to modern agriculture may require as a preliminary measure the introduction of collective forms of ownership; these then form the indispensable framework for the future progress of the productive forces in the direction of socialism.

We must, of course, examine closely the concrete forms of collective ownership which are in fact needed in order that certain techniques may be introduced. Thus, I do not say that collectivisation of the land is in every case the best way of ensuring *collective utilisation of mechanical means of production*.

Also in need of close examination is the problem of the *pace* of transition to collective forms of property: if this pace is much faster than that at which new techniques can *actually* be introduced, there is a risk of establishing a juridical framework that will long remain inappropriate to the nature of the productive forces. The negative economic consequences of such non-correspondence may be numerous.

Besides these economic considerations, social and political considerations are obviously of decisive importance in what may be seen as the right pace for going over to collective forms of ownership. Among such considerations must be mentioned, in particular, the extent to which these new forms are accepted by the persons concerned, the effect that a certain pace of change in property-relations will have on the balance of strength between the classes of society, and so on.

To come back to the more directly economic aspects of the problem, it will be observed that better use of the existing means of production, through specialisation and regrouping of production-units, may also be a determining reason for far-reaching changes in forms of ownership. This can happen, for instance, in the case of transition from individual to co-operative production in handicrafts, or of replacement of small-scale private capitalist production by mixed enterprises, in which means of production contributed by the state are associated with means of production contributed by private capitalists. In other situations, nationalisation may be the only way to ensure that existing means of production are used to the best advantage.

In all these cases, the concrete forms that must be assumed by the new property-relations, and also the procedures for changing from one form of ownership to another, and the pace at which these new property-relations will have to be introduced, can only be decided as a result of very careful consideration of a number of economic, social and political factors.

We know that transition from *private* forms of ownership to *collective* forms can be ensured by other methods besides nationalisation, on the one hand, or forming co-operatives, on the other. In fact, the methods by which the private sector, and above all the capitalist sector, can, over a certain period, be progressively *transformed* into a socialist sector, or absorbed by this sector, are extremely numerous. The various historical experiences that have now been undergone, especially those relating to the different forms of *state capitalism* established in China between 1949 and 1957, are especially rich, and the cycle of such experiences is certainly far from complete.

In general, one may suppose that the increasing role played by the economy of the socialist countries in world economy will make it possible to find fresh and increasingly flexible ways of transforming the private and capitalist sectors and absorbing them into the socialist sector.

B *The mobilisation of a sufficiently large accumulation fund* to ensure the further development of the socialist economy may constitute another reason determining transition at a relatively rapid pace to forms of social ownership that are "ahead" of the social character of the means of production.

In a certain number of instances, nationalisation or collectivisation are *the only possible ways of mobilising the economic surplus* that is formed in some sectors of the economy. Nevertheless, if these changes in property-relations would go too far beyond the degree to which the productive forces are actually social, and if other ways of mobilising the surplus are possible and would be more efficient (such as taxes, the use of prices for redistributing the net product, and even loans, etc.), it may not be advisable to change the property-relations too prematurely, since, by so doing, one may sometimes reduce the efficiency with which the means of production are used and so, in the end, reduce the absolute amount of the economic surplus (to such an extent that, even if a larger *proportion* of it is mobilised, the *absolute amount* available for social purposes may be no greater than before, or may even be smaller, despite a possible reduction in the amount consumed by certain social strata).

C *Full employment of the labour-force* may also demand a transition to social forms of ownership, since this is sometimes the only possible framework for the development of collective work and redistribution of current income in accordance with work done. This was the reason, on the economic plane, for the rapid development of the co-operatives in China in 1956–7, and then that of the people's communes in 1958. In this way the conditions were established for a technical division of labour that was made both necessary and possible by the presence of a *relative* surplus of agricultural labour-power.

To conclude these remarks on changes in property-relations, I think it is very important to stress again the following two points:

(1) Since the productive forces are destined to become more and more social in character as they progress, it is essential that property-relations and the totality of society's juridical rules be such as to ensure that it will be *possible to appropriate these productive forces on an ever higher social plane.*

From this follows the great importance there may be in possibilities for the *merging* of co-operative economic units or the formation of *inter-co-operative units* (such as, for example, mergers between collective farms) which, from a certain point onward, are alone capable of putting to use the modern means of production which the co-operatives have in their charge.

From this follows, above all, the decisive importance that can attach to state ownership, even of means of production which are *not yet* fully social in character, because, as already mentioned, this ownership prepares the framework within which this social character will be able to develop fully, under conditions much better adapted than the co-operative framework to the progress of planning and the eventual withering-away of the commodity categories. The co-operative framework, indeed, permits the survival, or even the strengthening, of ownership in certain means of production by *relatively small groups*: and these groups may come to form an obstacle to respect for *overall social interests*—all the more seriously the more these groups are mainly economic in character, and the larger they are, controlling considerable resources.

Thus, the question of progressively raising co-operative property to the level of public property, or of what has been called "property of the people as a whole", is a question that must inevitably arise at a certain stage of development of the productive forces.

The way this question can best be handled, without arousing useless social contradictions, is not yet clearly settled. It is not certain that the merging together of collective farms, even if this is desirable at the present time, provides a complete answer.

The progressive merging of state organisations and co-operative ones in a single production *complex* may, perhaps, be more likely to furnish the solution. The setting-up in the Soviet Union of collective-farm-and-state-farm directorates may mark a stage towards a solution of this sort, but it must at once be said that this measure was not adopted with that prospect in mind, but merely in order to solve certain urgent problems of Soviet agriculture.

Another line along which the transition may be effected from ownership by limited groups of producers to public property is perhaps that of the Chinese people's communes. Actually, the people's communes are not expanded co-operatives but *political and administrative organs*, that is, *local organs of the state power* which are thus able to transform themselves into local organs of the *national administration of the productive forces*.

In any case, I do not propose, for the time being, to dwell at length on the questions which arise in this connexion. What I want to do is to stress that contradictions are possible, and in some instances inevitable, between ownership by a small group of *producers* and the interests of the national economy as a whole.

A current manifestation of these contradictions can be observed in the sphere of the state organs' policy regarding prices to be paid for the products of the co-operatives. This is a point to which I shall have to return.

A parenthesis can be inserted here, pointing out that a problem similar to that just mentioned may also arise when *rights of disposal or control, of a certain scope,* are accorded to economic groups of limited size (for example, to the group made up of the workers in a particular factory), over *means of production which are entirely social or are destined to become such fairly quickly.*

In fact, when rights of disposal and control are institutionalised in favour of a limited group of producers (as, for example, when a group like this is given power to decide what it will produce, what it will invest, the prices at which it will sell, the amount of income it will consume, and so on), such rights can give rise to the *equivalent* of a kind of ownership by this limited group, even though, in theory, the means of production over which these rights are exercised are public property.

We must keep this problem in mind when we approach the question of councils of management (notably as these exist in Yugoslavia) or other forms of organisation which may engender a *new contradiction* between the social character of certain means of production (which result from the work of many branches of social production and the products of which are in turn destined for a great variety of branches of social production), and the rights of disposal and control over these means of production accorded to the workers (that is to say, the limited groups) who have to operate them.

It must be observed at this point that, with the progress of automation and of electronic techniques, it can happen that means of production which represent a substantial amount of *social* labour are operated by an extremely small group of workers.

(2) On the other hand (and this is the second point to which we have to return), while it is often necessary to establish forms of ownership which "anticipate" to a substantial degree the completely social character, not yet actually realised, of certain productive forces (in order to ensure the development of these forces, or to ensure the socialist character of economic development and thus to make easier the mobilisation of the economic surplus, etc.), it remains none the less true that the result of doing this may be a certain *non-correspondence between the forms of property and their content,* in so far as productive forces which are still not fully social have been taken over either by a group or by the state, in the name of society.

This last point alone requires a fairly detailed analysis. At first glance, at least, such an analysis must deal with the problems of internal organisation of the socialist sector belonging to the state.

Actually, these questions *go beyond* mere problems of organisation. They relate to the *real production-relations,* to the nature of the *economic subjects* which together make up the socialist sector belonging to the state, and they thus oblige us to consider once more, from a different angle, the problem of the role played by the commodity categories within socialist society, at a given stage of its construction or of its development.

We thus come back to the problems we raised earlier, about the nature of the relations established between the producers, or the groups of producers (which constitutes the fundamental aspect of the production-relations),[11] and about the nature of the economic and juridical subjects within the socialist sector belonging to the state.

4 *The production-relations within the state sector of the socialist economy*

At a certain degree of development of the productive forces and the maturation of their social character, the relations between the different production-units cease to be capable of establishing themselves on a day-to-day basis, with the completion of certain production-operations (as still happens today in many sectors of production). Thenceforth, these relations have either to be predetermined, in essentials at least, and therefore conceived in advance and regulated by a *plan*, or else determined currently by a *social decision-making centre*.

In either event, it is no longer necessary or even possible for the production-units to establish merely direct but irregular inter-relationships (through which the social character of the labour performed within each of them manifests itself). Relationships between production-units must henceforth be either predetermined, in which case they will be regulated in advance by the plan, or else decided and programmed at some level which is higher than the production-units themselves. The latter thus become cells in a *technical division* of labour.

Either way, the work done within each production-unit can assume a *directly social* character, in the sense that it corresponds, at the very moment when it is performed, to a social need the dimensions of which have really been calculated in advance.

When this is so, the *destination of the products is predetermined in a socially-conscious way*. The "production-units" are now no longer anything more than technical organs of the division of labour; they are no longer centres of economic decision-making. In other words, the technical division of labour has been raised to a higher level.

When, on the other hand, this is not so, the various production-units continue to provide products the destination and utilisation of which are determined in advance only with a rather large element of uncertainty. This is what makes it necessary to allow these production-units a certain amount of freedom to manoeuvre. This "freedom of manoeuvre" is, in fact, only the other side of an *inadequate degree of social forecasting*. It expresses the *de facto* inability of society, or of its organs, to regulate *the whole* of social production "consciously".

As I have already indicated, it is this situation that, in my view, explains the necessary survival, throughout an entire period, of the commodity categories, and the existence of *distinct economic subjects* even within the state sector of the socialist economy.

Before analysing more closely the bearing of the facts mentioned above, and the objective conditions for them to disappear, we must throw light on the existence, in the socialist economies of today, of three categories of phenomena which seem, as it were, to presage or announce beforehand the ways in which economic subjects possessing a certain amount of autonomy will vanish from the scene.

a) *Planned obligations to buy and to sell.*

The first of these phenomena is to be found on the plane of planning itself. It makes its appearance when the economic plan does not restrict itself to fixing the production *targets* which have to be reached by the various branches of the economy or the various production-units, but lays down for each enterprise not merely the quantitative and qualitative detail of the production tasks to be fulfilled but also, and above all, its sources of supply and the destination of its products.

This latter practice is very widespread in the Soviet Union and in the socialist countries of Europe. Where it prevails, it reduces the part played by contracts between enterprises to that of executive instruments of a plan for allotting products, or that of giving concrete form to certain minor aspects of the obligations laid down by the plan.[12]

In reality, it seems to me, this practice can mean two opposite things:

(1) In some instances, this practice results from a situation of comparative shortage, i.e., of a poor adjustment between resources and needs.

In that sort of situation, the total amount of demand pressing upon current production, as expressed by the using enterprises (whether productive or trading enterprises matters little) at the given price-level, and given their financial resources and the tasks they have to carry out, would tend to exceed supply. When this is so, and if, for some reason or other, no change is made in any of the factors mentioned above (price-level, amount of financial resources, scope of tasks to be carried out), an *administrative share-out* is unavoidable. This sharing-out of the products by administrative methods may be provided for in the plan or it may be effected by administrative decisions which are distinct from the plan in the strict sense, though taken in pursuance of it.

Whatever the procedure followed, the application of an administrative share-out reduces to the minimum the "freedom of manoeuvre" of the production-units and also reduces to small importance the practical bearing of the contracts made between these units. Nevertheless, a situation like this, which itself results from a state of comparative shortage, cannot be seen as presaging the disappearance of economic subjects endowed with a certain degree of autonomy and the correlative disappearance of the commodity categories. This situation is not the consequence of an abundant and harmonious increase in the productive forces but, on the contrary, of a still weak and insufficiently harmonious development of these forces.

(2) In other instances, contrariwise, centralised sharing-out of certain

products does not reflect the inadequacy of the amount of these products available, but results from the fact that only one central authority is in a position to estimate *how to ensure the best social utilisation of the products under consideration.*

One can cite as examples of such cases the centralised allocation of investment resources and of certain capital goods, when this allocation can be done optimally only by taking into account a wide range of factors, such as the *future* pace of development of the various production-units (some of which may belong to an extremely wide variety of branches of production). Another example is that of the calculations required for the optimum *spatial* arrangement of the production-units to be set up. The part to be played by a central authority becomes decisive as soon as it is necessary to take into account factors which are beyond the economic "horizon" of each production-unit taken separately and which therefore cannot be included in economic calculations carried out at the level of one isolated unit.

When this is so, a situation really exists in which the commodity categories and the relative autonomy of the production-units have ceased (at least so far as the operations under consideration are concerned) to be adequate instruments for expressing *social needs*, even indirectly. In such a situation, the needs are, and can only be, grasped directly and expressed without recourse to commodity categories.

All the same, one may ask whether, in a case like this, recourse to the administrative share-out is really the most appropriate method of allotment, or whether it may not rather mean that practices dating from a situation of shortage are being applied to a different situation.

There are, in fact, *other ways of effecting a centralised allotment besides the purely administrative way.* These ways are less rigid than the latter and they are, moreover, often actually used. Without wishing to make too much of this aspect of the matter, I think it may be useful to note the following points:

A centralised allotment of certain means of production can be accomplished, for example, by setting up a *central office for buying and selling* all products of a certain kind. Centralised allotment by this method can be economic rather than administrative. Thus, the central office for buying and selling can be entrusted, under the plan, with:

(1) Conveying orders to the various production-units for the goods which the central office has to "allot", these orders being conveyed in accordance with the plan, as regards both specifications and delivery dates; while, on the other hand,

(2) The production-units which, under the plan, will have to use the products in question, send their orders for these products to the central office.

The central office can thus keep a clear running account of the actual allotment of the products for which it is responsible and, if necessary, can modify the priority in which the users will receive the goods they have ordered, so as to allow for the actual way the situation is evolving, and especially for the real capacity of each particular user to instal a given piece of equipment at a given moment.

In this way the direct link that would otherwise be established between a particular supplier and a particular user can be broken. A direct link of this kind, though it offers great advantages in some cases (fixing of responsibility on definite persons, adaptation of the quality of the products to the users' requirements, etc.), may also offer serious inconveniences from the standpoint of social supervision of the allotment and use of a certain number of products. This type of direct link may, in particular, result in a user who should have been given priority having to put up with delays due to the fact that his supplier has made a quicker delivery to another user. Similarly, this type of direct link may result in a supplier honouring his contract by despatching equipment to a user who is, in practice, not in a position to instal this equipment forthwith.

The existence of central offices for buying and selling does not necessarily mean, of course, that these offices themselves have to take delivery of the actual products they allot: sometimes this may occur, but sometimes the offices may confine themselves, at whatever time they choose, and taking all the circumstances into account, to instructing a particular production-unit with which a contract has been made to supply certain products to a particular using unit.[13] Verification of the quality of the goods delivered can then be ensured by the central office which is responsible to the user for this quality as well as for the honouring of delivery-dates and specifications.

Respect for the norms of allotment which have been laid down centrally may also be ensured through the intervention of the banking system. This is done by assigning to each production-unit which uses certain products *credits that cannot be used except for obtaining these products.* When this is done, the using enterprises can obtain those goods covered by this *credit-appropriation* system only within the limits of the credits assigned to them for this purpose. *This amounts to temporarily depriving part of the money in circulation of its role as universal equivalent.*

(It is to be observed that, in any case, the role of money as universal equivalent is played only to a greatly reduced extent inside the socialist state sector as it operates in the Soviet Union, owing to the fact that use of the circulating funds held in money form by the different enterprises is subordinated to the actual requirements of the economic plan.)

Through the mechanism of "credit-appropriations" the banking system is used as an instrument for carrying out in a relatively flexible way a plan for the allotment of certain products which has been drawn up centrally. In this case, however, the using enterprise can choose its own supplier and fix the delivery date it wants, and also, perhaps, specify some other points in connexion with the order it places. In some circumstances the existence of such freedom of choice for the using enterprises may be essential for efficient management of the economy.

When such freedom of choice is needed, but a centralised method of allotment is arbitrarily imposed instead (the productive forces not yet being ready for such a method), the consequence may be a veritable squandering of resources: products arriving too soon or too late at the using enterprises (which have no way of either refusing to accept products sent them by a central administration or hastening the despatch of goods from the centre), mistakes in specifications, and so on.

It may be noted that the banking system can be used as agent for supervising the execution of a plan of allotment drawn up centrally but carried out in a flexible manner, even when relatively scarce products are being allotted. This is a method which can be very much superior, through its very flexibility, to a purely administrative method. It does in fact make possible, without recourse to price-manipulations (which in some cases would be ineffective), the adjustment of total demand to total supply.

To illustrate the foregoing, let me take as an example a country where, over a certain period, the demand for fertiliser has shown a spontaneous tendency to exceed supply (the latter being restricted by capacities for production and import). The demand could be restricted by several different methods:

(1) By decisions taken on the plane of the commodity categories; for example, by raising the prices at which the fertilisers are sold to the using units.

From a wrongly abstract view of things, this would "always" be the economically most effective method, for it would restrict the use of fertilisers to those users alone who were capable of getting the maximum increase of production from them (i.e., using profitably even very expensive fertilisers). Actually, this is not necessarily so, for the users are far from always capable of *forecasting* in a serious way the increase in yield and receipts they can obtain through using a given quantity of fertiliser. Under these conditions, a rise in the price of fertilisers will restrict the demand from units managed by the most cautious or most timid administrators, while having little effect on the demand from those who do not worry much about profitability. A more efficient use of fertilisers will thus not have been achieved, and, moreover, it may prove necessary, in order to restrict demand sufficiently, to raise prices to levels having no proportion any longer to production-costs. This may happen at the beginning of a period of accelerated development, when a substantial section of the "cadres" are still lacking in any very precise notion of economic calculation and the conditions in which it can be undertaken.

(2) By adopting a centralised allotment procedure which is non-administrative, i.e., which is technico-economic in character. In this case, for example, each production-unit will be assigned (on the basis of a more or less well-founded estimate, economic and technical, such as could be made by a regional management centre or an agrotechnical service which had studied the increases in yield obtained during a recent period in different production-units as a result of their use of fertiliser) credits specially "appropriated" to the purchase of fertilisers, and this under conditions such that the total amount of these credits is equal to the total value of the

fertilisers distributed, at the prices at which they are supplied to the using enterprises.

(3) By adopting an administrative method of allotment. In this case, for example, each production-unit will be required to present a demand in advance to an administrative authority. The latter, after examining these demands, will assign a given amount of fertiliser to each production-unit. This procedure can be effective only if the administration in charge of allotment possesses sufficient technical knowledge to ensure the optimum allotment and if it is in a position to respond rapidly to the demands it receives.

If, however, this is not the case, in other words, if allotment is not ensured by a competent technical organ but by a bureaucratic apparatus, it is likely that administrative semi-paralysis will result, with a multiplicity of authorities bearing responsibility for making decisions. Thus, in Cuba in 1963, demands for fertiliser had to go through seven or eight administrative authorities, and the latter might take eleven months to respond to the demands they received. Naturally, replies made in this way, after consultation with various authorities which were often remote from the using units, might, when they came, no longer bear any relation to the objective needs of these units.

In the various instances in which the allotment of products no longer depends on the users' choice, whether because of "shortage" or for reasons connected with the striving for optimum social allotment of certain products,[14] we see, instead of the allotment of resources by way of the market (a method of allotment which may survive, to a certain extent, even inside the socialist sector, within the limits laid down by the plan, so that this market is no longer a "free" market but one which is under social control), either a technico-economic method of allotment or else an administrative one.

In either of these two instances, the role played by the commodity categories is blunted, together with that of the relative autonomy of the production-units. The link between these two phenomena is thus once again confirmed, while the conditions for their departure from history are made apparent, namely: the appearance of the possibility and necessity of effective social forecasting calculations, that is, of calculations which can cover not merely the total *quantities* of the various products to be supplied during a certain period, but also the *qualities* that these products must possess and the *place* and *time* for their best utilisation.

However, as already said, the cases I have mentioned form only one of the categories of phenomena that presage the disappearance of economic subjects endowed with a certain degree of autonomy, and so also the disappearance of commodity categories as these still manifest themselves within the state sector of the socialist economy.

b) *Centralised economic management of certain branches of production.*

The possibility of effective economic calculation on a relatively high social plane, as contrasted with economic calculation on the plane of a production-unit, is now appearing in certain branches of the economy. This is true of the branches that supply products that are homogeneous or that can be brought under precise specification, especially where these products come *from production-units which are organically interlinked*. In such cases the various production-units can be subjected to management which is largely or even wholly centralised and effected by electronic means. This centralised management, carried out on a technico-economic (and so non-administrative) basis forms one of the ways in which the commodity categories wither away.

The most substantial examples of an evolution of this kind are provided by the centralised management of a network of interconnected electric power stations, like that which operates in the European part of the Soviet Union, or that which has been organised between the electric power stations of Poland, the German Democratic Republic, Czechoslovakia and Hungary. In these two cases, a central electronic machine operates in connexion with a dispatching mechanism which regulates the activity of the various stations. At any given moment the activity of each production-unit is thus *directly* determined by socially recognised needs, within the framework of an optimum economic management of the network. Under present-day conditions, this does not mean that on the plane of the mode of "recognition" of social needs the commodity categories have already disappeared one hundred per cent.

In fact, the *prices* at which the power is sold to consumers, in particular to factories using electricity, may be one of the factors determining the demand for power. However, as these prices are themselves fixed socially, they may, in principle, be such that demand is determined, as a whole and in its structure, by socially recognised needs. Actually, the price mechanism and the behaviour of the economic agents and the consumers are not yet so thoroughly under control that the structure of demand is wholly identical with the structure of what would be socially recognised needs. It may be supposed that when a social authority is really in a position to decide with precision the dimensions of the various social needs, it will no longer be necessary to employ the price-mechanism in order to ensure that these needs are correctly satisfied.

Though the case of the centralised management of a group of electric power stations forms the most substantial example of the disappearance of the relative autonomy of the separate technical production-units, it is not the only one. The centralised economic management of a group of oil refineries or of a park of railway-trucks and locomotives, on the scale of an entire country, provide other instances of management of a large number of technical units (refineries, railway-stations, marshalling-yards, etc.) which have no economic autonomy (precisely because this would prevent efficient management) or which have lost part of this autonomy and so do not take part, from this point of view, in commodity exchange. These units cease, in fact, to participate in commodity exchange as soon as the products they need are *delivered* to them as a result of calculations made centrally (even if, before a delivery is finally decided on, the production-units are consulted by the central authority on the opportuneness of this delivery) and the products they *supply* are also governed by allotment instructions. In such cases there is no longer buying and selling but, instead, circulation of products and currency tokens.[15]

Of course, when products are supplied free of charge by a central authority to production-units dependent upon it, but continue to be "purchased" by this central authority, it is only the level at which commodity exchange is taking place that has been shifted.

Such a change of level may, however, be of considerable importance, and this for several reasons, of which I will mention here only those that seem to me the major ones:

(1) The change in the level at which commodity exchange takes place can result in a reduction, sometimes a drastic one, in the number of participants in these exchanges within the state sector of the socialist economy. When the *quantitative* change reaches a certain scale, it has a *qualitative* significance: it means, in fact, a considerable reduction in the social importance of the commodity categories. In particular, *when in a given branch of activity only one economic subject is left,* this can mean that economic calculation is henceforth carried on only on the plane of that branch, and no longer below that plane.

(2) A change like this in the level of participation in commodity exchange can make possible an extremely exact *ex post* calculation of the quantities of labour *actually* expended per production-unit. This calculation is then, indeed, much easier than that which can be carried out when there are a considerable number of economic subjects in being, all supplying the same sort of products, but themselves supplied under conditions which are various and hard to ascertain.

(3) A change of level like this also makes it possible to cause the labour-time actually expended to coincide more and more closely with what is *socially necessary* for the satisfaction of social needs.

When, in fact, a given product, or category of products, is supplied by *a single economic subject* and, on the other hand, the objective conditions are present for this economic subject really to *dominate* the activity of the technical units which are subordinated to it, this economic subject can make *optimum* use of the production-capacity of the subordinate technical units, to such a degree that it can be said that the labour *actually expended* is virtually equal to that which is *socially necessary.*

This presupposes, of course, a development of the productive forces such that the domination of a single economic subject over the various technical units subordinate to it is a *real* and not merely an *apparent* domination, like that, for example, we see in the case of a bureaucratic administrative "domination". Actually, this latter type of "domination", just because it is not founded upon genuine economic integration, leads to the taking of arbitrary decisions which are the result of unavoidable ignorance of the concrete conditions in which the various subordinate units operate and the requirements that follow from these.

Any attempt by a purely administrative authority to "dominate" the activity of production-units which are not really and organically inter-connected can result only in misuse of the productive forces and therefore in squandering the labour-time required in order to obtain a certain volume of production. In such cases the labour-time actually expended is greater than what is socially-necessary, in consequence of bad organisation, that is, of lack of correspondence between juridical relations and real production-relations.

(4) Finally, and most important, the appearance of a single economic subject at the level of a certain number of important branches of production makes possible *social forecasting calculation* which is much more exact than what can be accomplished when a multitude of production-units exist. Through a development like this we can see the objective conditions coming about for a kind of planning which is no longer restricted to giving social *direction* to the productive forces (which was already a decisive change as compared with a market economy, since it represented a leap from the realm of necessity into that of freedom, as Engels puts it), but which amounts, to an ever-increasing extent, to total social *control* of the productive forces.

Care must be taken, though, and this needs repeating, that the appearance of a single economic subject at the level of a branch of the national economy is based upon the realisation of quite definite *objective* conditions (to which I shall come back again when I analyse the concept of "economic subject"). If one tried to anticipate these objective conditions by setting up a juridical subject which does not correspond to an economic subject, then, far from causing the conditions to arise for control of the productive forces, the risk would be run of losing even the means of giving them direction. In this case, indeed, one would be trying to establish the level at which economic decisions are taken elsewhere than where there is *actual knowledge* both of the conditions under which these decisions can be applied and of the concrete consequences which can result from these decisions. Thus, instead of establishing an organisation capable of acting consciously, there would have been established one doomed to act, to some extent at least, blindly.

Having said this, it is obvious (as I have already pointed out in another context) that some juridical steps may, provided they are accompanied, or followed, by *adequate technical changes*, create conditions which can hasten, in a socially satisfactory way, a reduction in the number of economic subjects, and thus also in the sphere of operation of the commodity categories.

As a general rule, however, the taking of juridical steps, which can speed up a reduction in the number of economic subjects does *not* mean the establishment of a single state enterprise at the level of an entire branch of production *before the objective conditions for this are present*. In Cuba, for example, in the Ministry of Industries, the setting-up of "Consolidados", each managing an entire branch of industry, has given only indifferent results in every case where the conditions were not present for a large number of units to be managed from a single decision-making centre of an economic kind.

Similarly, the powers of *intervention* in the management of production-units which were accorded at one time to the *Soviet trusts* or to the Chief Administrations of the Ministries (*Glavki*) very often had harmful consequences for good economic management, at least whenever the *objective conditions* were not ripe for this centralised management or this central intervention in the current management of the enterprises as a real possibility and an economic necessity, and not a mere administrative measure.[16]

A method which, in some cases, may lead to a progressive reduction in the number of economic subjects is the establishment, at the level of each branch (on the national or the regional scale, depending on the particular case) of a central office for selling the products of this branch.[17]

At an initial stage, an organ of this kind may restrict itself to centralising all orders for the products of the given branch and allotting the fulfilment of these orders among different production-units, taking into account their production-capacity, their labour-costs, their costs of production, their location, and so on. In order to carry out a task like this in a socially useful way, that is, non-bureaucratically, such a central office must not be set up until conditions are present which enable this central office *really to know* the characteristics of the different production-units to which it sends orders, and the circumstances in which these orders will be fulfilled. In practice, this presupposes either that there are only a small number of comparatively homogeneous units[18] or that there are centralised means of electronic recording and calculation, that is to say, generally speaking, a level of development of the productive forces which is already high.

When this is not so, the premature introduction of a form of integration, even of the sort just mentioned, instead of playing a useful economic role, is merely administrative in significance and, far from contributing to the *concentration of responsibilities* and decisions, causes them to be dissipated in a bureaucratic administration. This may render economic calculations very difficult or even impossible, as happens, for example, when the financial autonomy of the production-units is arbitrarily abolished or restricted.

On the other hand, however, when central sales offices have been set up on sound technical foundations, they may become, from a certain moment onward, that is, on the basis of further progress of the productive forces, centres for the supply of raw materials or intermediate products to the units whose activity they co-ordinate. They may then become progressively transformed into *management centres*.

The production-units they manage may eventually cease to be economic subjects and become nothing more than "technical departments" of an integrated complex economic group. If this happens, we have before us a type of *functional centralisation* which is profoundly different from *bureaucratic centralisation*. This functional centralisation may, however, leave, so far as certain decisions are concerned, a relatively wide sphere of initiative to the various "working groups" or "technical departments" that make up this integrated complex economic group. This too is a problem to which I shall come back.

This, then, appears to be one of the lines along which the disappearance of the commodity categories from within the state sector of the socialist economy may be prepared. This line is analogous to "horizontal concentration" in the capitalist economy.[19]

Another line along which the progressive disappearance of the commodity categories can take place is that of vertical integration, also sometimes called "vertical concentration".

c) *Vertical integration of economic activities.*

The socialisation of the productive forces develops in a complex way. It implies that every branch of activity depends to an ever-increasing extent on all the others for its functioning and that, reciprocally, the products of every branch are destined (directly and indirectly) to an ever-increasing extent for all the other branches, or for the national or international collectivity. Each of the branches thus finds itself involved in a more and more extensive and diversified "web" of relations with other branches.

Underlying a course of development like this is a constant intensification of the division of labour. To this corresponds, more often than not, an increasingly thorough *specialisation* of each production-unit.

This specialisation, however, may entail, depending on its degree and form, two apparently contradictory types of consequence.

One of these may be that an economic subject, or even a single physical production-unit (say, a factory), eventually comes to meet the needs of a large collectivity of consumers, whether this is a matter of ultimate consumption or of productive consumption (and it is above all in the production of equipment that specialisation can be carried so far that, even on the world scale, *a single production-unit* is able to supply all of a certain type of equipment: this is so, for example, in the field of the production of certain electronic aggregates, certain rotary printing-presses, locomotives, aeroplanes, etc.). In this case, a single economic subject thus supplies products to a large number of consumers.

Another consequence of specialisation can be, on the contrary, that a physical production-unit specialises to the point that it is meeting the needs of *a single user only*, that is, of one other physical production-unit.[20] When this happens, we have *integration of the activity of the first unit into the activity of the second*. Thenceforth it will be the latter that will completely decide the volume and characteristics of the former's production, so that it tends no longer to be an autonomous economic subject. It becomes increasingly a *technical department* of an integrated *group* which transcends it. At a certain moment, when the integrated group belongs to a single owner, the products coming from the units "up-stream" no longer have to be sold, they flow down towards the using department. The sphere of operation of the commodity categories is thus reduced.

C

The formula of the Soviet "combine" provides an example of a process of vertical integration like this.

In another form, the *Sovnarkhozy* tend towards flexible methods of integration, when they achieve *organic co-operation* between complementary production-units under their authority.

Vertical integration, as is well known, takes place on a large scale in capitalist economy. It goes on in all branches of industry (motor-cars, steelworks integrated with mining, chemicals, and so on). This process is now spreading to agriculture, and is tending to transform in a far-reaching way the relations between agriculture and industry.

Inside capitalist agriculture examples become more and more plentiful of stock-raising units (especially in poultry-farming) which, "up-stream", integrate the breeding of the animals or birds, the production of feeding-stuffs for them and the industrial processing of these feeding-stuffs, and, "down-stream", integrate the slaughterhouses and the treatment of by-products (or else are themselves integrated in these activities). These phenomena of integration have technical foundations which determine their forms and their limits. Thus, for the raising of poultry it is the slaughterhouse that, at the moment, is the "production-unit" which integrates the other activities and to which they are subordinate. It is this unit, too, which by its size determines that of the *integrated group*.

This "technical link" may itself be dominated by a more decisive "economic link". This happens when a group of slaughterhouses (and of the stockraising units which they dominate) is itself dependent on a commercial chain which determines to some extent the volume of consumption and production, by practising a certain policy as regards selling-prices to consumers and buying-prices to producers. The geographical placing of the various "technical links" will then be determined by a particular economic strategy, and will lead to the structuring of the space round about on a technico-economic basis, the distances between each "technical link" and its suppliers being more or less programmed.

Phenomena comparable to this appear also in the canning of milk, fruit, vegetables, and so on. In these activities, the tinning or bottling works tends to structure and dominate a large part of the space surrounding it.

The concrete forms taken by such phenomena of capitalist integration are very diverse. In some cases the units producing "raw materials" belong to the factory where these are processed, which in turn may belong to a chain of distributors. In other cases (at present most frequent), the supply of "raw materials" continues to be ensured by agricultural entrepreneurs who remain juridically independent. Even in this case, though, the *actual management* of the agricultural units is progressively *integrated* in that of the industrial unit. It is the latter that decides in advance the quantity of products that it is to receive, their quality, and the dates and intervals for delivery, and it is also the industrial unit that, very often, delivers to its suppliers the raw materials that they are to process, and which, in general, provides the *technical leadership* of the agricultural units (or at least of the sections of these units which work for it).

There is obviously need to investigate whether the separation between the *ownership* of the agricultural enterprises and the *ownership* of the factory for which they work (a separation which means that what we have here is an *integration of the contractual type*) is a reflexion, on the basis of private property, of certain technical requirements (represented, for instance, by the requirements of crop-rotation), or whether it merely represents a method used by industrial capital to relieve itself of the risks involved in agriculture and to increase its profits by keeping down the prices paid to agricultural enterprises which are made more and more dependent on it.

It is also to be noted that in many tropical countries the sugar refineries form an *organic grouping* with the cane-fields, whether the refineries are the owners of all or part of the fields or whether they are connected with the owners of the cane-fields by crop-contracts. When such organic groups exist, this makes possible a detailed overall "programming" of the production operations.[21]

It also happens, of course (and the ultimate result is technically the same) that a group of agricultural entrepreneurs set up, in the form of a co-operative, an industrial unit for processing their products. In this case we have vertical integration proceeding from "up-stream".

Although, for the time being, vertical integration (organically linking agriculture and industry) has up to now not gone very far in the socialist countries (where, however, the formula of the "agro-industrial combine" has been studied and even tried out in a number of instances),[22] this phenomenon of integration seems to correspond to the requirements of the development of modern productive forces and therefore must also constitute one of the lines along which an increasing number of economic subjects will wither away, with a correlative withering-away of the sphere of operation of the commodity categories.

On the other hand, as I have already mentioned, the *Sovnarkhozy* are endeavouring to promote *organic co-operation* among some of the *industrial* units operating under their authority. Co-operation of this sort may also lead to some form of vertical integration.

Similarly, in the USSR (and in other socialist countries), the horizontal or vertical integration of economic activities can develop on the basis of *agreements made directly between different industrial enterprises*. It may even happen that in some cases such agreements can engender a new juridical personality (this is what has occurred with the so-called "Soviet firm").[23] Such a juridical personality usually corresponds to a new economic subject which tends to re-structure, technically and economically, the activities of the enterprises which have formed it.

Altogether, whatever may be the methods by which the integration of economic activities takes place, this corresponds to a group of economic and technical changes which tend to reduce progressively the number of economic subjects, and, in correlation with this, the sphere of operation of the commodity categories.

Presented in schematic fashion, these changes take place essentially in three forms, which I shall call:

(1) *Unilinear integration*, which means the entry of a production-unit into a "series" within which it loses all economic autonomy. The activity of this unit is then wholly dictated by the needs of the "head" unit (that is, the unit which realises or disposes of the products of the integrated unit).

(2) *Multilinear integration*, which means the affiliation of several production-units to another economic unit. The latter may be responsible either for processing operations, or transport, or distribution, and may be the only one in contact with the "rest" of the economy, either for disposing of the products of the integrated group or else for both disposing of the products and for supplying the integrated group with the products it needs.

This can lead to the establishment of conditions of *management* of the affiliated units based on the "head" unit (or "terminal" unit), whether these affiliated units all supply the same kind of products or whether they each supply complementary products (as happens, for example, with motor-car factories which receive certain items from "suppliers" who are attached to them exclusively).

(3) *Multi-integration*. This means the regular affiliation of a number of production-units to a number of user-units which absorb the whole of their production. This can occur in the case of agricultural units producing a variety of crops and disposing of each category of produce to a different processer, each processer controlling that section of the productive activity of these producers which concerns it.[24]

Rather than talk of "multi-integration", it would perhaps be preferable to use the expression "ramified integration" or "integration by networks", so as to bring out the fact that the integration in question takes place *in several directions* and along lines which *may intersect* at a variety of levels. It is possible that this type of integration "by networks" may be the one that best corresponds, for the moment, to the nature of modern productive forces in certain sectors of the economy.

The sector in which this type of integration seems, at the moment, destined to take an especially important place is that of the chemical industry. In this industry the different production-units necessarily have to maintain close and *reciprocal* inter-relations. To convince oneself of this it is enough to see the dimensions assumed, under capitalism, by the big companies that produce chemicals. There is the well-known example of the Du Pont de Nemours company, in the U.S.A. The turnover of this company is of the order of $2,000,000,000 and it employs about 150,000 people.[25]

In Germany, the three big chemical firms (Bayer, Badische Anilin, Hoechst) each have a turnover of around $600–700,000,000. They each employ about 50,000 people and invest nearly $100,000,000 every year.

In France this form of concentration of the chemical industry is much less advanced, but nevertheless there are two powerful chemical firms: Rhône-Poulenc, with a turnover of more than $200,000,000 and "Produits Chimiques Pechiney-Saint-Gobain", which comes next, with 17 factories and two research centres, the whole employing 11,500 people and supplying, in certain fields (chlorine, sulphuric acid, superphosphates) two-fifths or more of France's total production—even more than half in some branches (e.g., polyvinyl chloride).

The offices and affiliates of big companies of this kind keep up regular relations among themselves and maintain *joint services* for much of their buying and selling.

From the standpoint both of the *current working* of the production units and of their *use of research services* and their investment policy, this amounts to making a huge productive group into *a single economic subject*. Some, of course, of the production-units affiliated to a group like this are less integrated with it than others, and consequently retain a distinct personality, economic and juridical. This is the case, for instance, with the "subsidiary companies" of a certain number of large trusts in the capitalist chemical industry. To some extent the retention of these separate juridical personalities reflects compromises reached between financial groups, the sharing of risks and the seeking of certain advantages in respect of taxation.

In a socialist economy, the reasons for survival of the distinct juridical personality of the production-units integrated in a technico-productive group are obviously less numerous than in a capitalist economy, but it may happen, nevertheless, that such reasons are present, and integration will then be only partial, leaving a certain number of economic subjects each "their own personality", though with reduced functions.

At a further stage of integration, within the framework of the socialist economy, a growing proportion of the production-units are bound to lose their character as *economic subjects*, while retaining a certain economic or social *personality* within the group. This economic or social personality may be marked by the capacity of the production-units to take certain subordinate economic decisions (usually subject to *ratification* by the responsible organs of the overall management of the *integrated complex*).

The various forms of integration, when these develop in a socialist economy, can thus give rise to a relatively small number of "large productive economic complexes" of international, national, regional or local significance, the different sections of which may be governed by *internal technical planning*. This increasingly cuts down the number of units which are in irregular or occasional contact with each other and makes increasingly easy the effecting of *a priori* adjustments of production activities. This raises the plan from the level of *direction* of the productive forces (dealt with as *branches of activity* regarded as *statistical or administrative groups* subdivided into a certain number of *economic subjects*) to the level of *domination* of the productive forces, dealt with as *large economic complexes* of a *functional* nature.

These are the objective bases of the far-reaching changes that take place in production-relations, i.e., in the relations established among the producers.

The increasing *integration* of productive activities carries further the *interdependence* of these activities which is already developing fast under capitalism, and which established the objective basis for the first stage of planning. Within the framework of socialism, this integration goes forward in the state sector and in the co-operative sector, while, little by little, in a variety of ways, whatever of the private sector has managed to survive for a time becomes incorporated in these other sectors.

The juridical "forms" through which the integration of economic activities occurs may be extremely various. It may happen through the forms already referred to, or through others, such as agreements between co-operatives, agreements between co-operatives and state enterprises, mergers between state enterprises, etc. I do not propose to examine these juridical forms in themselves but merely to consider the influence these changes have on planning.

In short, it can be said that, as a result of these changes, when they have taken place on a sufficient scale, economic planning can really become, on the plane of production, *the determining of the current needs of individual consumers, communities and "productive economic complexes"*, and *the assignment of precise tasks corresponding to these needs* to each of the production-complexes.

This assignment of definite tasks cannot, of course, be fully effective unless it is founded on knowledge available centrally of the capacities of these complexes and the conditions under which they work.

When this is present, the irregularity of the relationship between production and consumption (which necessitates unforeseeable adjustments) can disappear completely, and the problem that formerly confronted each economic subject, of finding its "suppliers" or those who would absorb its products, also disappears.

Socialisation of the means of production becomes *complete* when the number of economic subjects is sufficiently reduced for their activity and development to be really subject to *social control*, that is, when society can really use the productive forces as a whole in a conscious way, in order to satisfy needs of which it is aware.

Automation of production and the production and introduction of electronic tools of management provide the material foundation which makes it possible to define, with ever-greater precision and exactness, the *means* that have to be set to work in order to satisfy social needs, but the precise determining of these needs themselves, in so far as they arise outside the sphere of production, implies the attainment of social and institutional conditions that are at present only in process of formation and which it would therefore be premature to try to define in detail as of now.

It is at the moment when society has achieved *full control* of its productive forces, and can completely determine its needs, that the commodity categories will lose all utility: this can be conceived only as the end-result of an historical process consciously conducted towards this culmination.

In the foregoing passages, the terms "economic subjects" and "juridical subjects" have been used. The context itself in which they were used has explained what they mean adequately for the needs of my analysis. Now, however, I must examine these expressions, in order to try and define them more precisely, something that could not be done at an earlier stage.

5 Economic subject and juridical subject

If we accept the analyses made so far, we have to conclude that, at the present level of development of the productive forces, we are still very far from being in a situation in which "the central government or some other social-economic centre" (as Stalin puts it in *Economic Problems of Socialism in the USSR*, henceforth referred to as *E.P.*, p. 56 [Eng. edn., p. 75]) "might control the whole product of social production in the interests of society."

According to the foregoing analyses, this is so not only because, as is widely recognised, different forms of property exist (state, collective-farms, individual holdings, and so on), but because of the *uneven development* of the productive forces in the different centres of production, the *hetero-geneity of the conditions of production* existing in each of these centres, the *still only slight degree of integration* of these centres, the imperfect conditions for the transmission of information from the periphery to the central offices, the complex problems of information, storage, and so on. It is all these facts that explain why it is that, *even within a single state sector*, efficient and therefore socially useful intervention in all decisions by a single "social-economic centre" is still inconceivable.

Under these conditions we can understand that, even within the state sector, juridical subjects have to be formed with power to take a certain number of decisions themselves.

What makes necessary and justified the setting-up of juridical subjects of this kind is that it amounts, in reality, to *acknowledgment of an economic subject*, i.e., *a centre of economic decision-making* such that *no other authority would be capable of taking decisions that would be socially more efficient than those taken by this economic subject.*

On the other hand, if the juridical subject (endowed with certain powers) is not really an economic subject, that is, does not correspond to an authority at whose level effective economic decisions can be taken, it is, as a rule, not socially justified to set it up. When this is the case, the intervention of such a juridical subject will more often than not have the effect of upsetting the process of production, distribution and expanded reproduction. When economic subjects and juridical subjects fail to coincide, the objectives sought by the economic plan or by the economic authorities in general either cannot be achieved or else can be achieved only under conditions of relative inefficiency, that is, at a relatively high social cost and with delays.

The chief problems that arise here are as follows:

a) The problem of determining what the real economic subjects are, so as to ensure that economic subjects and juridical subjects *correspond*.

b) The perfecting of juridical relationships between the economico-juridical subjects so that they match the requirements of the actual production relationships between these subjects and those of planned development of the economy as a whole.

c) The determining of the nature of the decisions that can and must be taken by the various economico-juridical subjects or the different social authorities.

I shall now briefly examine some aspects of these problems.

a) *Determining the economic subjects*

Only concrete analysis can determine what the real economic subjects are. In the course of such an analysis, the concepts themselves can be made more precise, under the dual influence of theoretical study and of testing in the field of social practice.

Analysis must aim, first and foremost, at discovering *the level* at which current economic decisions can be taken most efficiently from the standpoint of the national economy.

At a very low level of development of the social character of the productive forces, the economic subject in the sphere of production may be a single worker—an individual peasant, craftsman, etc.

At a rather more advanced level of development, corresponding to the stage of simple co-operation and the earliest manifestations of the technical division of labour, this link will be determined by the activity of a "working group" which is still not very numerous.

Finally, at a higher level of development, this link may be determined by the activity of a more or less extensive grouping of workers. In the modern economy, it can sometimes embrace thousands or even tens of thousands of workers, grouped in a single economic complex. As a rule, a grouping of enormous size like this is marked by a well-defined *internal structure*.

In the first two cases it is fairly easy to determine the level of the economic subject. It is a different matter, however, in the third case, especially when there are present:

(1) State ownership of a complex set of means of production operated by *many groups of workers* (for then it is necessary to determine what the *combinations of groups* are that correspond to different economic subjects;

(2) A high degree of internal "structuring" of some of these groups, so that sections may appear to be distinct economic subjects;

(3) A high degree of interdependence in the activity of these groups.

This is indeed where the problem arises: "where are the real economic subjects located?" It is this complex case that I will examine.[26]

If we proceed from the foregoing analysis we shall say that the level at which the economic subject is located varies according to the degree of *development* of the productive forces, the *character* of the productive forces set to work, in the different sectors or branches of the economy, and the *nature of the decisions* that have to be taken, since it is the criterion of the possible social efficiency of decisions that will also make it possible to determine what the various real economic subjects are. If we take once again the example of electric power production, we see that this can have a highly developed structure, i.e., can depend on a number of power stations each of which has its own "physical personality", but we also see that centralised management of all the electric power stations of a country, even a large one, can be ensured when these stations are linked together and a system of rapid transmission of information, between the various stations and the centre, has been established, together with a corresponding system of transmission of orders from the centre to the stations.

In a case like this, the *economic subject*, i.e., the "production-complex" at the level of which the most efficient economic decisions can be taken, is the *branch as a whole* which produces and distributes electric power. The separate power-stations are, in relation to this economic subject, merely *technical departments* at the level of which no truly efficient economic decision can be taken, since it is not there but at the centre that it can be decided, on the basis of programming and calculations carried out by electronic instruments, which works should be set in operation at any given moment and which should have their functioning slowed down or suspended.

Similarly, we have seen that the oil-refining industry can also, though to a lesser extent, be managed centrally (on the scale of a large region or a small country). Here again, the most efficient management of the refineries as a whole can be ensured by a centre which takes account of the needs that have to be met in different parts of the country and determines, taking the variable factors into account, the points to which the crude oil should be sent for refining and those to which the refined oil should be distributed. In this case, too, the economic subject may coincide with a given branch of industry.

On the other hand, in activities lacking the characteristics mentioned, it is necessary to decide concretely the level at which the real economic subjects are, that is, *those that are really in a position to use efficiently the given means of production.*

Depending on circumstances, this level will correspond either to an industrial establishment (i.e., a works) or to a group of works which themselves are either *specialised* or else *interlinked in a relatively rigid and permanent way* by the supplies they furnish each other with. An especially important case is that where there is *technical integration* of different production units and, consequently, the appearance, at the level of the "integrated complex" (which, as we have seen, may take the form of a combine, for instance), of a *specific economic subject*.

In the case of agricultural activities, the level at which the real economic subject is located corresponds, in the present state of the productive forces, to a working group which is usually much less extensive than in industry, owing especially to the large number of variables that have to be reckoned with in carrying on effective agricultural production, the range of fluctuations to which these variables are subject, and, last but not least, the still preponderant role played by direct *individual* human action (including at the level of observation) in agricultural production.

The foregoing remarks are essentially intended to *illustrate* the way that the problem presents itself—the problem of deciding the economic subjects on which, at a certain level of development of the productive forces and with certain characteristics of the latter, it is necessary to confer a juridical personality so as to enable these subjects to utilise with maximum efficiency the means of production at their disposal.

What we have to do in fact, is *to work out a theory of the economic subject.* So far, we are a long way from having worked out such a theory, and the decisions taken to endow certain working groups with juridical personality include a large element of empiricism.

In default of a fully-worked-out theory of the economic subject in the production sphere of a socialist economy, it is possible to say, first, that the economic subject constitutes *the place where multiple and irregular relationships with a variety of units of production, of distribution, and (or) of consumption are brought together.* It is the *multiplicity* and *irregularity* of these relations that calls for *economic choices* to be made, and which makes of a group of workers an economic subject.

In other words, the economic subject forms one of the fundamental links in a division of labour which is not yet entirely organic. That is why it is at this level that current *economic decisions* have to be made and the corresponding *obligations* undertaken. That is why it is necessary to endow each economic subject with its own juridical personality and financial resources, so as to enable it to fit itself flexibly (which does not mean independently of the economic plan) into the process of the social division of labour.

The various shortcomings of a system which *mutilates* the economic subject of the functions which alone enable it to undertake in a coherent way the tasks of production and of expanded reproduction in which it is involved have been amply revealed by all the negative experiences resulting from administrative management of the economy.

Administrative management leads to choices being made by an authority different from the economic subject, an authority which lacks the information possessed by the economic subject and which is incapable of assuming effectively the responsibilities incumbent on the latter. It leads to the bureaucratisation of the economy, to an increasingly falsified view of reality. It brings subjective factors into the drawing up of plans, to an extent that increases with the distance between the economic subjects and the level at which choices are made, and this puts more and more obstacles in the way of the formulation of a coherent overall economic policy, let alone its execution.

In the light of these remarks, it is clear that the attribution of certain juridical powers to an economic subject, powers which may make a juridical subject of it, and the nature of these powers, must depend:

(1) On the nature of the decisions to be taken, and, in particular, on the more or less extensive social area they affect.

(2) On the number of technical and economic variables that have to be taken into consideration in order to secure a satisfactory economic solution, from the standpoint of the national economy. The number of these variables must be considered from at least two aspects:

On the one hand, the economic complex to which juridical personality is assigned must not be so extensive that the number of variables or the amount of information that have to be taken into account at the level of this complex are such that, in practice, it is not possible to take a decision based on a correct and adequate study of these variables or this information. It is, in particular, a consideration of this order that may make it necessary to delimit an agricultural economic unit as an economic and juridical subject at a level of size that may be regarded as smaller than the optimum from the standpoint of the use of certain material means of production. Hence, for example, the situation which existed at one time in the USSR, where the comparatively small collective farms had superimposed upon them the Machine and Tractor Stations each of which served several of these farms.

On the other hand the economic complex to which powers of decision-making are assigned must be *large enough for it to have effectively available a sufficient amount of information and decision-making power*,[27] because only on this condition can it manage efficiently, from the standpoint of the national economy, the productive forces that fall within its sphere of action.

In this respect it can be said, for example, that to attribute a distinct decision-making power to each electric power station would create a situation in which the juridical subject would not possess either the information or the power needed for it to use the productive forces in the most efficient way, on the national scale.

Nevertheless, this aspect of the matter can only be taken into consideration if the fact of transferring the decision-making power to a higher level does not give rise to a juridical subject which is incapable of *controlling in practice* all the factors on which it has to rely in taking satisfactory decisions and in *getting them applied* in an effective way. *What, in fact, signalises the existence of an economic subject is precisely its capacity to control a group of productive forces.*

These various observations are already bringing us to perceive the need to accept, in certain cases, the existence of *a hierarchy of economico-juridical subjects, each endowed with distinct powers, depending on the nature of the decisions to be taken.*

Thus, for example, the centralised management of a group of electric power stations can deal only with the problems of supplying these stations and with the scale of their current operations. Decisions affecting investment, however, have to be made at another, higher level, where it is possible to take account of the different requirements of general economic and social development; while, contrariwise, decisions regarding the *internal organisation of labour*, recruitment, maintenance of buildings, and the like, have to be made at the level of each power station taken individually. These last-mentioned decisions will themselves, of course, have to fit into the overall framework of directives and regulations. This therefore leaves surviving at the level of each power station either an "economic subject" with very limited functions or else a working group with a certain "social personality".

1) *Internal structuring of economic subjects and working groups*

The concepts of the "internal structuring" of an economic subject and of the "working group possessing a social personality" also need to be looked at more carefully. To attempt to do this here would divert me from the main purpose of the present study. I will therefore confine myself to mentioning some of the problems to which these concepts give rise.

The problem of "internal structuring" is particularly that of the existence, inside a given economic subject, of different working *groups*.

Some of these groups have a "permanent" technical basis (they retain their social personality so long as the technical process is not changed), as in the case of the different workshops within a factory.

Other working groups have a temporary technical basis, as in the case of teams entrusted with the carrying out of a task which is occasional, momentary or seasonal, and which break up as soon as this task has been accomplished.

The social personality of a group can assert itself only if the task it has to perform lasts for at least a certain minimum period of time. In certain circumstances, this social personality may expand into an "economic personality". This happens when this social personality constitutes *a link in economic and social initiative and control* which is necessary if there is to be efficient division of labour. The fact that a working group has an "economic personality" does not automatically make of it an "economic subject", and this is so, in particular, if the group is not in a situation enabling it to exercise genuine control over certain productive forces, and if its operation merely requires that it carry out *subordinate or secondary choices*, such as those called for in order to realise certain objectives *under conditions determined by a higher authority*.

Without spending a lot of time on this question, I must nevertheless emphasise that the problem of *working groups*, their powers, their capacity for initiative and the nature of the economic and social supervision that can and must be exercised over them for the sake of effective planning, is a problem that is a great deal more complex than may appear at first sight.

In Soviet agriculture, for instance, this question is bound up with that of the *internal structuring of the collective farms*, and, in particular, with the role played by the *work-brigade* and its *optimum size* (a size which must obviously vary in accordance with the *nature of the means of production at the brigade's disposal* and the general degree of development of the productive forces).

The technical basis of the work brigade (which, in certain cases, is organised around a group of tractors) constitutes one of the elements which influence very markedly the actual size of such a working group. But the question also arises of the conditions under which each brigade may have a certain *permanence*, by being (as suggested by D. Muratov) *responsible for a whole year* for certain tracts of land.[28] Finally, the fundamental problem is, it would seem, that of the conditions for *precise responsibility and collective initiative* (on the basis of a certain technique); this problem is located at the level of the *relations between the members of the group* and the relations between the group and other groups, that is, at the level of *concrete production-relations*.

Similar problems obviously arise within the state farms as well. The latter may be divided into "workshops" and "sections" which possess a certain permanence and the "optimum" size of which also has to be determined.

Here again we find a problem of very great complexity, especially in agriculture, namely, the problem of the *"optimum size" of the working groups*.

Theoretical analysis enables us to define the nature of the problems arising here, but the decisive instrument for getting a concrete answer to a concrete question is the carrying out of *economic calculation*. The latter will, of course, give a correct answer only if the problem is first presented in meaningful theoretical terms.

Economic calculation like this must make it possible to compare the *efficiency* of different kinds of organisation. It must be emphasised that the efficiency of a given type of organisation includes a variety of aspects. We must distinguish between short-term efficiency (i.e., efficiency at the level of how economically the available means of production are *currently* being used) and longer-term efficiency. In agriculture, for instance, the latter is shown in the influence exerted by a certain type of organisation on conservation or improvement of soil characteristics. More generally, this efficiency is shown in the influence of the type of organisation on the capacity of the working groups to adapt themselves to innovations or even to promote them, and so on.

The problem is thus much more complex than it seems at first glance.[29]

The problem of optimum size does not, of course, concern only the working groups "at the grass roots" but also the economic subjects made up of several working groups. There too it is in agriculture that the problem appears in its fullest complexity. In industry, the *technical foundations* for the sizes of working groups are determined in a much more obvious way by certain material factors: for example, the optimum size of blast furnaces or of rolling-mills determines very largely the combination of other material factors of production which technically have to be associated with them, and, consequently, the size of the *economic subjects* that will manage a given technical group. As I have already remarked, however, it can happen that what appears to be the optimum size at a purely material level may cause *problems of co-ordination* such that the *economically optimum* size does not coincide with the *technically optimum* size.

In agriculture the question is further complicated by the dispersal of activities in space, the problems of crop-rotation, of adequately intensive employment of machines in seasonal use, etc.

The question of the "cadres" available (and this is obviously true for industry as well, or any other economic activity) may also have an influence on what, *at a given moment*, may constitute the optimum size of certain economic subjects. This is an extremely important aspect of the matter.

Thus, in the Soviet Union, during the ploughing up of the "virgin lands", it was to some extent the problem of agricultural cadres that led to the formation of giant state farms (109,000 hectares was the average in Kazakhstan). Accordingly, as the number of agricultural cadres increased, it was decided to reduce this average size (cf. the discussion in the Central Committee of the Soviet Communist Party, February 1964).

Similarly, in Cuba, the size of the *Granjas del Pueblo*, though too big for efficient management, was dictated by the inadequate number of cadres available. The same reason was invoked for not according financial autonomy to the *Granjas del Pueblo* and confirming it, in 1963, to the *Agrupaciones basicas* (which embrace several *Granjas*). It is intended eventually to confer juridical personality and financial autonomy on every *granja*.[30]

The problems of the internal structuring of the *people's communes* in China are clearly of the same order as those mentioned above. We know that economic and juridical personality was accorded to work-*brigades* (i.e., the former co-operatives) and also to work-*teams* formed within the brigades.

Thus, in an article in the *People's Daily* of 21 December 1960, entitled: "Property on three levels based on brigade property and the fundamental system of the people's communes at the present time", we read:

"In order to develop the spirit of initiative in production and to make full and rational use of land and time, rights of administration and management should belong to the brigade. The production plan of the commune must be based on the production plans of the brigade and the team. The allotment of the different techniques, the targets of production and the technical arrangements must be discussed by the masses and drawn up by the brigade and the team after discussion in common. In short, in this matter the members of the commune are the masters. The commune has only the right to make proposals to the brigades and teams, in accordance with the state plan, and to balance and adjust their plans where necessary. It is forbidden, however, to decide subjectively the areas to be sown to the different crops, to increase the production targets or to fix rigidly the technical arrangements without taking account of the real conditions and asking the brigades and teams for their views."

Commenting on this paragraph from the *People's Daily*, Liu Jo-chin, in a study published in the review *Jingli Yanjiu*, organ of the Economic Institute of the Chinese Academy of Sciences, writes that this passage:

". . . has clarified the relations existing between the plans of the different levels in the people's commune. In other words, the production plan of the people's commune must be based on the brigade plan and the brigade plan must be based on the team plan." [I.e., on the smallest working group, which is closest to concrete and practical problems.]

The plan must be decided on by the *members of the commune* and not by the higher levels, from above and rigidly.

The author adds that the passage:

". . . enables us also to understand that, now, the agricultural plan can be only an indirect plan and not a direct one. Since the commune level can only make proposals to the brigades and must not determine production targets rigidly, it is clear that even less can the state lay down directly for the people's communes a production plan and technical arrangements which are unified and concrete, as it does in the case of enterprises which belong to the whole people. On the contrary, the agricultural plan must be compiled from below upward, that is, by starting with the team, then going up to the brigade and then to the commune, rung by rung; the state plan must be based on the plan of the teams (naturally, the different levels of the commune must organise their production in the light of the state plan and taking into account local and seasonal conditions; at the moment when the plan is drawn up they must take into consideration the state's needs and the tasks laid down by the state). Only thus can the agricultural plan be applied perfectly, only thus can free rein be given to the initiative of the masses and only thus will production make a great bound, realising and surpassing the plan of agricultural production." (Quoted from *Etudes Economiques*, No. 143, p. 63. See also the article by Chou Ti-chin: "The fundamental system of the people's communes at the present stage", in *Etudes Economiques*, No. 134.)

Determining the nature and size of working groups is therefore an important matter for a number of reasons: the efficiency and realism of the plans drawn up at the level of these groups, the efficiency of their application, the degree of initiative shown by the members of the group, the internal social control (i.e., the group's *self-discipline*), and the social control from outside (checking of quantity and quality, and of cost of production).

This brings up, as already mentioned in passing, the problem of *internal economic calculation*, that is, economic calculation at the level of the different working groups. This calculation is obviously not the same thing as the financial autonomy with which *economic subjects* can be endowed. It will doubtless have to continue even after the commodity categories have passed away.[31]

What has been said also brings up the problem of the link between quality of work at the level of the working group and the payment of the group's members.

Thus, in the state farms as at present organised in the USSR, the wages paid to each worker are, as a rule, calculated essentially on the basis of the work done *by the individual,* which since accounting takes place at the level of the state farm as a whole, means that this accounting is very complicated and it is not easy to check concretely on the quality of the work done by each worker. For example, in a report of 25 December 1959, Nikita Khrush-

chev mentioned a state farm where payment of workers required the maintenance of 15,000 cards and documents containing, altogether, 1,800,000
items of information, all of which nevertheless failed, he said, "to ensure
really exact accounting and control".

Payment *at the level of the working group* often corresponds more closely
to the *collective character of the work done*, so that payment made to the group
can subsequently be shared out among individuals in the group in accordance with socially defined standards. This, of course, presupposes that a high
degree of *self-discipline* and *self-checking* has been attained, i.e., a high
degree of political consciousness. If this is not present, then administrative
supervision is inevitable, regardless of its shortcomings.

To conclude these observations on the working groups, it must be stressed
that, when the latter are sufficiently stable and their social personality has
been correctly defined, they can and must constitute (as we have seen from
what has been said above) an *essential level for the preparation of plans and
checking on their implementation*; from which follows the importance of
correct internal structuring of the economic subjects.

These observations thus show us that, inside the production sector of a
socialist economy, the economic subjects are, as a rule, subjects which are
structured internally. (This structuring will probably have to become more
and more complex as the size of the economic subjects grows and integration
progresses). The very existence of this internal structuring often makes it
hard to distinguish between an economic subject and a working group
possessing a social personality.

On this point let me add further that, when the level at which a real
economic subject is situated has to be decided, it is very important to take
into consideration the delays in transmitting information and in arriving
at and notifying decisions. It is necessary to allow, on the one hand, for the
maximum interval that can be permitted to elapse between the appearance
of a problem and the solution that *must* be found for it, and, on the other,
the interval that inevitably elapses, at a certain stage of organisation and
circulation of information, between the moment when this problem appears
and that at which a solution *can* be found for it (this time will obviously
vary with the level at which the decisions are taken).

This amounts to recognising, here once more, that determination of the
economic subject is conditioned in part by the possibilities of transmitting
information, memorising it, and processing it in order to reach decisions,
all of which possibilities are connected with the development of the productive forces. Here, too, experience and economic calculation will provide
concrete answers. It must be noted in this connexion that the use of
simulation techniques can, in some cases, make it possible to avoid excessively
repeated, long-drawn-out and costly experiments.[32]

From this standpoint, the size of the economic subjects, their internal
organisation and their external links appear to be partly subject to the
techniques of collecting, codifying, transmitting, assembling and interpreting information. Included in this "information", of course, are the economic

or technical decisions that may be taken at various levels. This implies that the advances made in the sphere of information techniques may have considerable practical consequences affecting the size of the real economic subjects and the level at which it is possible to take socially useful decisions.

If, at the stage now reached in these reflexions, I were to try to formulate some of the conclusions that can be provisionally drawn, I should say this:

In present-day socialist economy there are units of production or distribution which bear the character of economic subjects. These units are centres for the appropriation of nature by man or for the sharing-out of the products of this appropriation. They form the framework of a systematically organised technical division of labour.

In so far as the different centres of appropriation or distribution are not linked together *organically*, or as a result of decisions that can be taken consciously by a higher economic authority, these units constitute links in a local division of labour and are economic subjects each of which has to determine the conditions of its relations with the others, within the limits laid down by the aims of the plan and by the various regulations imposed in order to ensure good co-ordination of the activity of the economic subjects.[33]

As we have seen, each of these units of production or distribution may be subdivided into "working groups". Relations between the latter are determined by the nature of the techniques being used, in so far as these working groups are not themselves economic subjects.

What, in fact, is the mark of an economic subject (in contrast to the working groups that are not economic subjects) is the fact that the products that result from the production-process carried on within an economic subject can be put to *manifold and optional uses* which cannot be governed by detailed socially useful forecasting, whereas the products that come from a technical unit or working group that is not an economic subject are destined for uses that are determined, or which can be socially determined in advance, in an efficient way.

This is why, as has already been said, the level at which the distinction is made between economic subject and working group varies as time goes by. This level depends on the development of the productive forces, including, of course, the number and competence of the trained personnel, the degree of social consciousness and discipline, the possibilities for collecting and transmitting information, and the possibilities of forward calculation, that are available to the society. The development of the productive forces thus alters the level at which there is or is not complete technical determination, or forward social determination, in a detailed and useful way, of the possible needs for and uses of the various goods emerging from a production-process.

One of the characteristics of an economic subject is that it forms a *working group* (or a complex of working groups) at the level of which economic decisions must be taken.

In contrast to *technical decisions* (required for the efficient use of a *given technique* in order to achieve *given aims*), *economic decisions* determine the nature and scope of the variable relations that may be established between economic units; thereby, economic decisions also determine the *uses* that will actually be made of products with many potential uses.

When the economic subject coincides with a production-unit, the economic decisions that can be taken at its level concern essentially the uses to be made either of the products supplied by other economic subjects and which may enter into the production-process for which this unit is responsible, or of the products emerging from *the production-process dominated by the economic subject in question.*

When, however, the economic subject is responsible essentially for functions of allotment, distribution or management, the economic decisions it can take relate to the uses that will be made of products emerging from a production-process carried on by other economic subjects.

In any case, economic decisions are those which establish, directly or indirectly, relations between economic units, when these relations are not entirely determined by the very nature of the technical processes. Such decisions do not, of course, depend only on the economic subjects.

This leads me to re-emphasise a point made earlier, namely, the need, at a given stage of development of the productive forces, to recognise that there may exist, *in one and the same domain but for different types of decision*, several economic subjects or administrative authorities hierarchically subordinate one to another, the decision of a particular one of these rather than another being preponderant, depending on the nature of the problems to be solved.

2) *Economic hierarchy and administrative or political subordination*

The subordination of one decision-making authority to another may correspond either to a real *technico-economic hierarchy* (as in the case of certain types of vertical integration) or to an *administrative or political subordination.*

According to circumstances, the existence of administrative subordination may give expression either to social necessity or, on the contrary, to a weakness in general economic organisation. In the latter case, it means that an administrative authority has assumed the task of taking economic decisions which it would be better to take at the level of a working group. This can lead to the bureaucratisation of the economy.[34]

The distinction between economic subordination and administrative subordination is not, of course, a matter of legal rules but rather one of the specific features of the authorities concerned. If the higher authority is an integral part of a working group, or a complex of working groups, its domination may express the subordination of the lower authorities to a genuine economic hierarchy; otherwise it is an administrative or political authority.

In a socialist economy, subordination of the economic subjects to administrative or political authorities may result from a variety of situations. Sometimes this subordination corresponds strictly to the requirements of planned development of the economy in the direction of socialism. In this case it expresses the specific conditions in which social priorities are formulated and economic policy applied. This type of subordination may ensure the working out of the decisions which have to be taken at the highest social level. This is so with the main decisions regarding investments, prices, fundamental technical choices and the selection of regions for particular forms of development.

Sometimes this subordination is the only way of ensuring, at least approximately, co-ordination of the current activities of the economic subjects, owing, for example, to the inadequate training of the executives placed at the head of some of the economic subjects.

Sometimes, this subordination merely interferes in decisions that the economic subjects ought to take, because they are better placed to take them. In such cases we have the partial or complete substitution of *administrative management* for *economic management*. This substitution may be rendered inevitable, during a certain period, either by political requirements (need for nationalisation measures taken quickly and on a large scale; an economy unbalanced by the strain of war or by economic attacks), or by mistakes in organisation, or by mistakes in economic policy (e.g., a price policy giving rise to "shortages" that render inevitable an administrative rationing of products).

When administrative management tends to go beyond the objective requirements of planning and the development of the economy, it assumes a *bureaucratic* character. It loses touch with reality. It works slowly, and often in the wrong direction.

When this is the situation, the real economic subjects may react by setting up their own circuits for passing round important information and by following economic rules of conduct which only partly coincide with the decisions taken by the bureaucratic apparatus—to some extent in order to get round the inadequacies and incompetence of the latter.

There may then exist two different pictures of economic life—one which can be seen at the level of the economic subjects themselves and another which is composed at the level of the bureaucratic apparatus and in order to satisfy the requirements of this apparatus. This latter picture may sometimes be so distorted as to constitute nothing but a mirage. When this happens, and this "bureaucratic mirage" serves as the basis for plans, these have less and less effect on real economic evolution.

Even apart from the existence of administrative authorities, the fact that there is a hierarchy of subjects means that certain subjects have to take decisions which interfere directly in the activity of others. Such interference must, in principle, always take place in conditions which ensure that the functions and responsibilities of each subject are clearly delimited. If this is not the case, then the efficiency of the whole and the possibilities of checking what actually happens will be greatly reduced.

3) *Economic subjects, planning authorities and administrative orders*

A fundamental feature of a planned economy is, of course, that the different economic subjects, whatever their level in the hierarchy to which they belong, all have their activities subordinated to the decisions of a *national planning centre*, or of regional, sectoral or functional planning authorities which themselves all depend, in principle, on this national centre.

So far, a centre like this is not a real economic subject, as it does not *directly* control the productive forces as a whole, it merely undertakes, technically, the *social direction* of these forces, in the name of the political authority to which it is itself subordinate.

It is by way of an increasingly complete *socialisation* of the productive forces that this social *direction* can be progressively replaced by *direct social domination*. When that is completed, the planning centre will tend to become, itself, a real economic subject. At that moment, moreover, the ties between working groups will be profoundly altered, because complete and direct social domination of the productive forces will bring about the disappearance of commodity production and tend to transform the relations between the former economic subjects into something analogous to the relations between working groups within an economic subject.

In the present state of things, however, social direction of the productive forces, as undertaken by the planning centre, takes the concrete form of the working out at this centre of a certain number of decisions—the centre does no more, of course, than work them out, since the decisions are actually *taken* by the political authorities.

The decisions worked out at this level are, in principle, those which *determine the entire orientation of the national economy*. They concern the recognition, or estimation, of social needs, and the proportion in which these needs will be satisfied (so far as an *a priori* estimate can play a part here). These decisions also concern the ways in which society's needs are to be satisfied, given the requirements of the overall and sectoral economic balances during future periods of different lengths. They thus concern the chief quantitative and qualitative targets of *production* and the chief *investments*. They also concern the choice of the main techniques and the determining of the system of prices and incomes. This is what, at the present time, forms the basic content of *economic planning*.

Planning decisions, if they are to be effective, must form wholes which are homogeneous and adequately exhaustive. They then constitute *plans*. While it is essential *that the economic subjects take part in the working out of these plans*, in order to ensure that they are realistic, the *subordination of the economic subjects* to the targets laid down by the plans is also essential, in order to ensure that these plans are something more than wishful thinking.

Subordination of economic subjects to the plan is achieved through notification of certain targets to each of them, by economic regulation and by the manipulation of "economic levers". The latter expression means the use of those instruments which the retention of commodity categories makes it still possible to manipulate: prices, money, credit, etc.

It must be strongly emphasised that the decisions taken regarding manipulation of the "economic levers" cannot be arbitrary in character, or, if they are, they will be vain or will render vain some other decisions implicit in the plan, even when these are in principle obligatory. Arbitrary decisions can thus considerably reduce the efficiency of the economic system as a whole. Thus, while in the present state of things a certain number of decisions must, if they are to be adapted to reality, *be the responsibility* of the basic economic subjects (e.g., the production-units), these decisions can themselves only possess real efficacy if the calculations made by these economic subjects are made in "economically significant" prices (the precise meaning of this expression will be considered elsewhere). Consequently, if the prices laid down by the higher authorities are not "economically significant", the efficacy of these decisions taken at the base of the economy will be negated and they may bring about results which were desired neither by the production-units nor by the planning centre.

The subordination of the economic subjects to express *orders* or definite *regulation* results from an *administrative hierarchy*. The latter may be made up either of different levels of the planning organisation (this is so when, besides a central planning organ, there are regional, local, sectoral, etc., organs, which have the responsibility of making the enterprises under their control conform to the planned targets, by making these more exact), or of an economic administration in the strict sense, which is itself responsible to the central authority and the planning organs.

The economic administration may itself be centralised to a greater or lesser degree. It may be made up of economic ministries, organs responsible for allotting certain products, or organs with competence over a certain region (as is the case today in the USSR for part of industry, which is directed by *Sovnarkhozy*, "Councils of National Economy").

As has already been said, if the role played by an economic administration like this extends to tasks that can be undertaken in a socially more efficient way by the economic subjects themselves, there is a risk that the economy will become bureaucratised.

In this connexion it is necessary to avoid the frequent illusion by which the *de-concentration of the organs of economic administration* is seen as meaning the establishment of a *functional hierarchy* of economic subjects. A de-concentration of this sort may well eliminate some of the defects that result from vertical administrative centralisation, but it is not to be confused with a functional economic organisation that locates the essential power of *current management* at the level of the economic subjects.

If seen as a *substitute* for a functional economic organisation, de-concentration of economic administration may often bring the risk of making heavier still the burden of a bureaucratic apparatus, an apparatus which is remote from production and which erects *a screen between the political centre and the economic subjects. When this is the case, the political centre, which ought to be in a position to plan, is doomed to have only a partial, incorrect and even distorted view of real economic life as it actually goes on in the production-units.* The quality of planning can be seriously affected by this.

When the administrative "relay stations" are not merely responsible for tasks of regulation and supervision, but also take *management* decisions, this can result in the setting up of bodies responsible for functions that would be fulfilled better by the economic subjects themselves. The positive role of the administrative authorities is essentially, as a general rule, to supervise, co-ordinate and help the production-units, not to interfere in their activities.

Even when restricted to a supervisory role, however, the activity of the administrative authorities may take on a bureaucratic character, that is, may become remote from the demands of economic and social reality. This frequently happens when these administrative authorities are not themselves subject to strict political and social control. The latter can prevent bureaucratic distortions if it is carried out both by a *ruling political party* inspired by the will to build socialism and by *organs of people's power* which emanate directly from the locality or region within which the main activity of the economic subjects which fall under this control is carried on. When the activities of certain economic subjects are nation-wide in their effect, or even extend beyond the limits of one state, then it is only at the similarly nation-wide or international level that political control can be exercised in a democratic and not a bureaucratic way.

In the foregoing passages I have tried to clarify some of the essential features of economic subjects and also of the *hierarchical* connexions that can be established either between economic subjects themselves or between administrative authorities and economic subjects.

Now I must say a few words about contractual relations between economic subjects.

b) *Contractual relations*

The decisions an economico-juridical subject can take which concern *another independent economic subject* assume the form neither of orders nor of regulations. Such decisions cannot be unilateral, they must be embodied in contracts. Contractual relations, in contrast to relations of subordination, are thus relations which can unite several economico-juridical subjects which are comparatively independent of each other.

The contracts into which economico-juridical subjects enter may be of widely differing content. This is not the place to try and analyse them; I shall therefore confine myself to some very broad indications.

1) *Contracts for buying and selling*

In so far as the various economic subjects (even if they are all parts of the state sector of a socialist economy) have *power to dispose* of certain products, the decisions they take to get rid of these products, or to acquire them, assume, as a rule, the form of contracts (for buying and selling). These contracts give rise to a form of circulation which differs from that resulting from orders to transfer products (such as the orders that ensure the circulation of products within a factory and which are imposed by a higher authority upon a lower one). This form of circulation is the corollary of the relative autonomy of the different economico-juridical subjects.

We have seen, however, that when the plan has laid down in advance the destination, or the source, of certain products, contracts of purchase and sale (which then merely superimpose a contractual obligation upon the obligations arising from the plan) have, to some extent, a formal character: they do not really give expression to the relative autonomy of the economico-juridical subjects. Nevertheless, even when such contracts are made by virtue of the plan, they form, like the payment of the specified price, a *condition* for the alienation of the products sold by one economic subject and acquired by another. These contracts thus reveal the survival of *commodity exchange*. The latter is still necessary because the administrative authorities are unable to formulate with sufficient exactitude, in advance, all the directives relating to the conditions of circulation of the products concerned. What cannot be formulated as directives has to take the form of contracts; for example, matters relating to *specifications*, or *delivery dates*. The combination of planned tasks and contractual obligations thus appears as what are called "planned contracts".

2) *Labour contracts*

Labour contracts are the juridical form by which an economic subject in the sphere of production or distribution decides to employ a worker, and by which the latter undertakes to work for a certain economic subject. In a planned socialist economy, the conditions and consequences of this mutual undertaking are largely laid down by the plan, by regulations and by collective labour agreements (on which I cannot dwell here). An undertaking of this kind constitutes the specific juridical form on the basis of which the workers take part in the sharing among themselves of part of the consumable social product.

In the sector of producer co-operatives there are, of course, no such labour contracts between a co-operative and its members: the leaders of the co-operative assign tasks to each member and decide the conditions governing the share-out of the collective product available.

3) *Credit contracts*

A credit contract is one by which an economic subject (a production-unit, for example) decides to borrow from another economic subject (a nationalised bank, in the socialist planned economies of today). The conditions of this contract are also subject to social regulation and, moreover, *the very purpose of such a contract is often laid down by the plan.*

When this is so, the real *decision* has been taken at a higher level (for example, by the planning authority which in this way allots part of the social accumulation fund). The contract then *essentially gives bodily form to orders* addressed to the two contracting parties; nevertheless, definite obligations arise from this contract, for it provides the framework within which important *particulars* are detailed, concerning the conditions for making the loan and putting it to use.

When, however, what is involved is a loan made "outside of the plan", we have before us a relatively autonomous decision taken by two economic subjects (the one borrowing and the one lending), which operates within

the limits of an overall regulation. The place that can be accorded to this
way of allotting the social accumulation fund has been much discussed. It
is generally agreed that loans "outside the plan" can occupy only a limited
place in a planned economy. The allotment of the accumulation fund does,
indeed, determine to a large extent the pace and even the forms of economic
development, that is, the *fundamental purpose of social planning*.

All the same, if, at the present level of development of the productive
forces, loans "outside the plan" can still be needed, this is due to the
impossibility, at the moment, of foreseeing precisely enough all the technical
changes that will be socially beneficial and which will require the use of a
part of the accumulation fund in order to be implemented. When it is to
the disadvantage of society to wait until a fresh plan has been drawn up
before carrying out certain particularly efficient technical changes, then
recourse is had to the procedure of loans "outside the plan".

It is not without importance to note that the contract by which a production-unit borrows from a bank may bring about partial economic subordination of the former to the latter, since the bank can then exercise control
over the effective conditions for the use of the money.

We may ask whether, during the entire phase of the building of socialism
in which money economy still plays a big role, the *controlling function* of the
state bank does not provide the most flexible means of subordinating
production-units to the decisions of the centre, more efficiently than can be
done by way of a hierarchic economico-administrative apparatus. Here it is
appropriate to recall what Lenin wrote on the matter:

"A single state Bank . . . with branches in every rural district, in every
factory, will constitute as much as nine-tenths of the *socialist* apparatus.
This will be country-wide *book-keeping*, country-wide *accounting* of the
production and distribution of goods, this will be, so to speak, something
in the nature of the *skeleton* of socialist society." (Vol. 21 of Lenin's
Oeuvres complètes, pre-war edition, p. 317. [Eng. version from Lenin,
Collected Works, 4th edn., Vol. 26, p. 106].)

4) *Co-operation contracts*

Finally, the decisions taken by economic subjects and embodied in contracts can also assume, as we have seen (cf., *supra*, note 3), the form of
agreements for co-operation.

It may be thought that the process whereby exchange and the commodity categories will be eliminated will pass, to some extent, by way of
such co-operation agreements between enterprises, which can give rise to
new economic and juridical subjects capable of absorbing the subjects
which have engendered them. However, this process of *contractual integration* can usefully serve the development of the productive forces only if it
reflects real changes in the nature of these forces and in the degree to which
they are socialised.

c) *The nature of the decisions to be taken by the different economic subjects
   and social authorities*

The nature of the decisions that can be taken by the different economico-juridical subjects and by the various social authorities, and which affect other economic subjects and social authorities, is closely bound up with the nature of the relations that have to be established between them.

In so far as the relations established between different working groups, economic subjects or social authorities are relations of *hierarchical subordination*, the decisions taken by the higher authority in relation to the lower are essentially of two types: the regulation and the order.

A *regulation* is a body of decisions which lays down a framework (i.e., limits) for the activities of the subordinate subjects. It implies autonomy of decision-making by the subordinate subject within the limits of the regulation laid down by the higher authority. The further this regulation goes, and the more detailed it is, the less is the autonomy enjoyed by the subject.

Regulation (emanating from the organs responsible for working out the plan, or from the administration responsible for its application) comes into play when forecasting can assume a general form. In such cases it is possible for the higher authority to base itself upon this forecasting in order to decide, once for all (i.e., until conditions change), the *orientation* of certain decisions to be taken by the economic subjects. The same can apply, inside a complex economic subject, with regard to the subordinate economic subjects or working groups.

When forecasting of a general kind is not possible, the higher authority can determine certain actions of the hierarchically subordinate subject by giving it *a specific order*.

Thus, in the planned economies of today, the chief targets to be reached during a certain period by the various economic subjects are laid down by the plan. So far as these economic subjects are concerned, the tasks laid down by the plan constitute orders. It may be that some of the conditions under which these targets have to be reached (e.g., the use of a particular technique) are also laid down by explicit orders. On the other hand, other conditions for attaining these targets, which it would be unhelpful to try to determine from a distance, are governed by decisions taken by each economic subject, within the limits laid down by the regulatory decisions and by the working of the "economic levers" set in operation by virtue of the overall plan.

It is important to recall here that the various working groups or technical units (the workshop, for instance), which together make up an economic subject, essentially receive *orders* coming from an economic authority inside the subject and responsible either for the general direction of the latter or for the direction of one of its constituent links. It is within this framework that the working groups have to take *technical decisions*.

Decisions are called "technical" when they concern a production-process the *purpose* and *nature* of which have already been entirely laid down by the ruling authority.

A working group which has only the right to decide the *material conditions* in which the operations entrusted to it are carried out has no economic personality. Of course, technical conditions do also, as a rule, involve taking *economic efficiency* into consideration but, for every group which can take only technical decisions, the *framework of calculation* of its economic efficiency is wholly and strictly determined from without.

Increasing integration into a complex economic subject of the activities of different production-units (forming parts of the same homogeneous branch or of a chain of units which technically control each other) leads to loss of economic personality by these units, which gradually come to function only in conformity with orders emanating from a central authority, orders which they have to fulfil within the framework of an overall system of regulations. The decisions taken by these units will thus, to an increasing extent, be purely technical decisions.

In a sense, the appearance of economic subjects hierarchically subordinated to each other, when this hierarchical subordination is not arbitrary but corresponds to the nature and degree of development of the productive forces, can be regarded as a transitional phenomenon, the subordinate units being destined to become changed into working groups without any economic personality.

d) *The different types of hierarchy*

A hierarchy will be called "administrative" when the working groups which occupy subordinate places in this hierarchy do not form with the directing authority an organic whole possessing the character of a complex economic subject.

In this case, the directing authority is an administrative or political authority and the subordinate working groups remain economic subjects which thus have, in principle, to take economic decisions that cause them to enter into relations with other subjects.

As has been said, the subordination of the economic subjects in the production or distribution spheres to administrative or political orders corresponds to a necessity of planned economy. It is through this administrative and political subordination that the *priorities of social development* are imposed, along with respect for the *social needs* acknowledged by the plan, and the *a priori co-ordination* of the various activities the interdependence of which may be subject to social forecasting.

On the other hand, when administrative subordination goes beyond what is socially useful and necessary and tends to substitute relations of administrative subordination for economic relations which would be better adapted to the actual exigencies of planned economic development, we see a bureaucratic distortion of the economy and a lowering of efficiency, either at the level of planning or at that of management, or else at both levels.

In extreme cases, an economico-juridical subject may be placed in a situation where it loses *de facto* all its autonomy and is therefore no longer a *real* juridical subject (even if it retains the appearance of one). The only real juridical personality is then that of the higher authority. In cases where the latter is not a true economic subject (this existing at a lower level because it is at this level alone that actual control can be exercised over the productive forces), there can be lack of correspondence between the economic and the juridical conditions in which the group made up of a juridical subject and some economic subjects is functioning.

We have already observed that a lack of correspondence like this between juridical relations and concrete production-relations can cause more or less complete paralysis of the economic subjects, with squandering or under-utilisation of society's resources, and operation by the economic subjects in ways that are in breach of the regulations (which then partly cease to be effective).

In this last-mentioned case, the efforts made by the higher authority with a view to enforcing at all costs a system of regulations which is inappropriate can lead to the proliferation of the bureaucratic apparatus and a control over the economy which is at once more and more detailed and less and less effective (the economy functioning, to some extent, in breach of the rules laid down, and so, in a way, "clandestinely"). Actions performed in breach of the rules are not reported, so that the checking of activities and their results becomes partly illusory; in such circumstances, *forecasting* becomes even more illusory.

When the lack of correspondence between the juridical rules and the actual relations of production goes beyond certain limits, the picture of the economy that the different social authorities form and present to the political authority may be extremely distorted. Thenceforth, the political authority is brought, in so far as it relies on the documents supplied by the social authorities and not on a more direct awareness of reality, to let itself be guided, to use the expression already employed, by a sort of "bureaucratic mirage", which can only result in a grave lack of control over economic reality.

The risks of such a "mirage" being formed are all the greater because the administrative organisation has a vertical structure which is strongly hierarchical, whereas the economy is far from being completely characterised by organic vertical integration. When this is the case, the vertical hierarchy is essentially *bureaucratic*, in the sense that it entails an allotment of *administrative* functions which does not correspond to the allotment of *economic* functions that is needed by the nature and development of the productive forces. Consequently, awareness of economic reality tends to be replaced by an administrative, bureaucratic, subjective and mystificatory "awareness".

When this occurs, indeed, we have a situation in which, on the one hand, there are the real economic subjects, the workers, the constantly changing production-relations, and the real contradictions, while, on the other, there is an administrative apparatus which is busy shuffling papers, reports, figures, statistics. The higher we go in this administrative hierarchy the more synthetic do these papers, these reports and figures, become, and the more abstract, in the bad sense of the word.

Synthesis and abstraction are, of course, necessary for the general direction of the economy, but there are false syntheses and bad abstractions, such as those which select secondary features from a complex reality, instead of selecting the essential features, that is, those which enable one to work effectively upon this reality.

Now, in the progressive ascent of documents and information up through an administrative apparatus structured in accordance with its own logic and not with that of the economy's organisation, the selection that is made among the items of information to hand can easily become determined by what is expected or wanted by the higher authority. The latter, in fact, has to judge the lower authorities by their "achievements", and in an administrative set-up these achievements are mainly "appreciated" through written reports. Thus, the higher this "information" travels, the more thoroughly is it cleared of whatever constitute the negative aspects of the situation reported on, that is, exactly what forms one of the essential elements in it, on which action must be taken if progress is to be made.

When there is a political organisation which is well-structured and well-armed on the theoretical plane, and when this can ensure that another selection of information is made, and another channel provided for its upward transmission, the defects of such a system can to some extent be offset. The defects remain none the less very serious, because it is inevitable that the weight of the "information" selected through a centralised administrative apparatus must tell very heavily upon the nature of the decisions taken, and this is all the more so since administrative organisation is taking the place of the real economic subjects.

From a certain point onward, instead of an effective economic organisation which provides for a proper division between economic tasks and administrative ones, all that is available is a centralised bureaucratic organisation, which contradicts both the needs of economic management (which requires multiple functional relations) and those of genuine democratic centralism (which requires that information, criticisms and suggestions circulate *in both directions*).

Another reason why an administrative apparatus for managing the economy (when it establishes *vertical hierarchical* relations instead of the horizontal economic relations that are needed) can become a constant source of bureaucratic illusions is that this type of organisation leads to *compartmentalisation between production-units*. This compartmentalisation does not, as a rule, correspond to the actual forms of the division of labour, which, on the contrary, usually calls for multilateral links. When the economy is administratively compartmentalised in this way, the units of production are treated as the lowest cogs of a machine which operates vertically and can be controlled from a single centre, whereas, in fact, each of these production-units, in so far as it constitutes an economic subject, is a place where horizontal relations with other production-units must and do intersect. The substitution of administrative and hierarchical relations for direct economic relations thus entails many negative consequences from the standpoint of the apprehension, and so of the control, of reality.

Among the consequences most frequently observed is the greater attention accorded to the physical quantities produced by the different branches of the economy, as compared with the quality of these products, since they are destined for users who are in the sphere of other administrative authorities.

In an economy managed in a predominantly administrative and centralised way, observation confirms that a tendency exists to be concerned mainly with the physical quantities of the various goods to be provided, and very little with the conditions in which these products will be used and the relations that ought to be established between the different production-units in order to ensure satisfactory channelling of the products.

In so far as relations between economic subjects are badly arranged, just because of administrative centralisation, the real *economic effect* of the existence of different physical quantities of products may be quite different from what is expected. What is important is not merely to dispose of definite quantities of fertiliser, insecticide, tractors, spare parts, and so on, but also, and at least to the same extent, to ensure that *each production-unit* receives these various products *at the moment required* and in the *quantity and quality required by it.*

If this does not happen, the economic effect of the possible *overall* availability of the various products may be quite unrelated to the effect anticipated in abstract calculations which take no account of *the concrete conditions under which each production-unit is supplied by the rest.* When these concrete conditions fail to conform to the production requirements of *each separate unit,* but are instead determined by inappropriate bureaucratic cogs, the economic effect of a given overall supply of goods may be nil, or almost nil, or, in any case, insignificant.

In general, lack of correspondence between a hierarchical administrative structure and the orders emanating from this, on the one hand, and, on the other what the economy needs in order to function, can result from failure to recognise the real economic subjects, or from the superimposing on these real economic subjects of a centralised economic administration which is itself unadapted to the real relations between these economic subjects, or from a system of regulation which is too meticulous and bureaucratic, or, on the contrary, from a system of regulation which is insufficiently exact and detailed and leaves to the different juridical subjects a field of decision-making which is bigger than that in which they can operate with full knowledge. This last situation can also lead to both squandering and under-utilisation of resources.

Efficient maximum utilisation of resources can therefore be secured only if there is conformity between organisation and regulation on the one hand and, on the other, the requirements of the economy's functioning.

At the level of each economic subject, this conformity is attained when the economic subject possesses juridical powers which enable it to take decisions within the field where these decisions can be taken *with full knowledge regarding conditions for their application, checks on how they are carried out and forecasting of their future consequences.* The size of this field is mainly determined by the degree of development of the productive forces and of their social character.

Decisions that go beyond the field that can be dominated by an economic subject, and require forward views or measures affecting the future activity of several economic subjects, not yet sufficiently integrated to be dominated by a higher economic subject, must necessarily be either the responsibility of an administrative authority or else be left to the working of the commodity categories.

Thus, when the activities of different subjects *are not integrated* but are only *inter-dependent*, the decisions that have to be taken with regard to these activities belong either to the sphere of direct planning, that is, of *a priori* adjustments (when the forward view can be sufficiently exact) achieved through general regulation or through specific orders, or else to the sphere of commodity relations, when precise forecasting is not a practical proposition. In in-between situations, relating to a field which is wider than that which can be directly dominated by an economic subject, the categories of planning and those of the market will have to be combined, the market categories being subject to manipulation by the planning authorities (this is where the planning of prices and incomes comes in, a subject which will be dealt with in a later chapter).

In the foregoing passages a whole number of problems have been left on one side, connected with the taking of decisions at the level of the economic subjects, or the authorities which supervise them. These problems (which call for extensive analysis in their own right) concern the *mechanisms* which enable an *effective* decision to be made, the consitution of the *organs* responsible for taking decisions within each economic subject or each economic authority, the *mode of appointment* of the members of these organs, and so on.[35] This would take us too far from our main subject, which is the determination of economico-juridical subjects, the nature of the relations that must necessarily be established between them at the present stage of development of the productive forces, and, finally, the effect, on certain aspects of the *working out* and *application* of plans, of the existence of commodity categories and of economic subjects. It is this last point that we must now examine.

6 *Some problems of planning connected with the existence of economic subjects*

The fact that economic subjects exist in the production sphere, endowed with relative autonomy in decision-making, obviously gives rise to a considerable number of problems as regards the drawing up of plans and the implementing of these plans. I will here touch on only some of these problems.

a) *The role played by economic subjects in the drawing up of plans*

In order to see what is involved in plans based on the existence of a large number of economic subjects it is enough to imagine the opposite situation, where there is no *diversity* of economic subjects but only a certain number of technical departments operating inside a single economic subject.

In a situation like that, once the targets for the economic subject have been laid down, the tasks of the various technical departments composing it, and the means necessary for realising these tasks, can essentially be determined *a priori*, provided a certain number of *calculations* are made. In other words, the chief tasks of the technical departments can be *deduced* from the targets of the economic subject, allowing for the technical features, in the strict sense, of the various working groups embraced by this subject.[36]

The position is quite different when an economic subject has to take current economic decisions. These decisions have engendered more or less regular relations between it and a more or less considerable number of other economic subjects. In this situation, the conditions in which the plan can *foresee* the activities of *each* of the economic subjects in question are quite different: *it is not possible to arrive by way of deduction* from the targets to be attained by *a group of economic subjects* at the tasks to be carried out *by each of them*.

In this situation (that is, when there is a plurality of economic subjects), it is necessary, in order to arrive at plans which are both realisable by each economic subject and economically as advantageous as possible, not merely to consult the working groups and arouse their initiative but also to cause the different economic subjects to participate actively in *the actual working out of the plans*.

1) *Procedures for consultation and participation*

It is this situation that confers such importance, weight and significance upon the procedure which consists in preparing centrally a draft plan, sending this "down" to the economic subjects so that they can amend it, and then bringing the amended plan back "up" to the planning centre. This is not merely a *calculation technique*[37] or a way of assembling relevant information, it is *a special way of working out* a plan, dictated by the necessity (for the sake of a high degree of social efficiency) of taking into consideration the *specific* and concrete economic situation of the different subjects.

At a lower level of socialisation of the productive forces than is characteristic of modern industry, that is, in the sectors where this socialisation is relatively less developed, the preparation of the plan cannot yet be undertaken by the "sending down" of draft plans and their return, amended, to the central authority. It has to be done by the drawing up at the centre of a simple *directional framework*, which is handed over to the different economic subjects. The latter then work out, on this basis, *their own draft plans*. These drafts are sent to the central authority, which makes any necessary adjustments, in a continuing dialogue with the economic subjects. As we saw earlier, this is the way in which, in China, the production plans of the work-teams and work-brigades are prepared within the people's communes, as also the plans of the communes themselves.

It must be observed that, in an increasing number of socialist countries, and notably in the Soviet Union itself,[38] the yearly production plans of the industrial enterprises of the state sector itself are to some extent drawn up by this method, that is, starting from drafts prepared *by each of the enterprises*, within the framework of forecasts of general economic development. These general forecasts result either from a prospective development plan or from directives worked out centrally for a period shorter than that covered by the prospective plan.

One may be surprised to find methods of drawing up the plan which assign a more substantial role to the different economic subjects *succeeding* methods which had reduced to little the role played by these subjects. There would seem to be grounds for wondering whether the way the methods of drawing up plans is evolving does not refute the conclusions of the foregoing analyses, since what we see is that when the productive forces of the socialist countries have increased and their social character has been consolidated, a bigger role than before is accorded to the economic subjects in the preparation of the plans.

There are several reasons for this evolution, and they show that it does not contradict the conclusions of the foregoing analysis, despite the fact that it seems to be developing in the opposite way to what would be suggested by a mechanical application of the conclusions of this analysis. On this point I will confine myself to listing briefly some of the reasons that account for this type of evolution:

(1) The rapid transition from one mode of production to another, the imbalance and economic tensions caused by it, and by the great efforts made to accumulate, have, during a certain period, created a situation that rendered temporarily impossible the granting to each economic subject of all the margins of initiative, decision-making or suggestion that corresponded to the actual level of development of the productive forces;   (2) The lack of experience of the managers of enterprises, trained personnel and workers likewise made impossible, for an entire period, wider initiative on the part of the economic subjects and wider participation by them in the working out of the plan targets;

(3) What was a necessity at a certain transitional stage (a necessity which, true, was sometimes interpreted excessively), was later looked upon as a mode of organisation appropriate to the level of the productive forces already attained, so that, for a certain period, there was a tendency to treat the productive forces as though they had reached a higher degree of socialisation than was really the case.

In fact, as soon as the problems of the first transitional phase had been overcome, the far-reaching inconveniences of methods of working out the plan which were not appropriate to the level of development of the productive forces (even after these had progressed) made necessary a revision of these methods, in the direction of more extensive autonomy, and a greater measure of initiative and power of suggestion being accorded to the economic subjects.

This process will certainly have to be reversed later on, in consequence of the ever-higher socialisation of the productive forces. However, if we accept the foregoing analyses, we have also to accept that this reversal of the process will have to be carried out essentially through reduction in the number of economic subjects and transformation of a considerable quantity of them into mere technical departments of complex economic subjects.

2) *Some factors influencing the content of the draft plan prepared by an enterprise*

It must be observed that the content of the first draft of the plan of an enterprise (which will have a very important bearing on the plan ultimately adopted) is much influenced by the *criteria* that will subsequently serve to measure the efficiency of the management of the enterprise and also, perhaps, to determine the amount of part of the payment made to the management, the specialist personnel and the workers.

For example, if bonuses to enterprises or to specialist personnel are awarded on the basis of (or taking into account) the proportion in which the plan of each enterprise has been fulfilled or surpassed, it is almost inevitable (in so far as the motivation of those who are responsible for preparing the plan of the enterprise is based on considerations of material gain, or even of prestige) that the first draft of the plan of the enterprise will assume a "sub-optimum" level, because this is what will enable the enterprise to surpass its own plan without difficulty. Since the yardstick, or criterion, of *surpassing the plan* has often been, and still is, one of the criteria by which the quality of management is estimated, this is a very frequent phenomenon, resulting in the existence within the enterprises of unused "reserves" of production-capacity.

Similarly, as regards costs of production, if bonuses are to some extent awarded on the basis of the achievement by an enterprise of costs of production lower than those foreseen by the plan, the enterprise will tend, when the first draft of its plan is drawn up, to estimate its production-costs as planned at a level higher than is really necessary.

For these reasons it has sometimes been proposed that bonuses be awarded, in part, not on the basis of *surpassing the plan* but on the basis of the *progress proposed by the plan of the enterprise in comparison with the results of the previous year* on condition, of course, that the plan thus put forward is duly realised (this is the gist of one of Liberman's proposals regarding the award of bonuses on the basis of *planned profits*, as proposed by an enterprise itself). The disadvantage of this might be that in the course of a given year each economic subject might restrict itself to achieving the targets it had laid down in advance, even though it could surpass them, so as to keep in hand, so to speak, a sort of "reserve" of proposals for planned advances for use in the subsequent year.

This shows that the margin of initiative and freedom of manoeuvre which has to be allowed to each economic subject (precisely because it alone can know its own production-capacities) is such as to give rise to contradictions between the interest of the economic subject and the collective interest. These are objective contradictions the scope of which one must try to restrict not only by organisational measures but also by develop-

D

ing that political consciousness which alone can make every group feel that the interests of society must take precedence over those of a limited group.

In practice, it is the task of the social authorities standing higher than the economic subjects to check—though this is no easy task—on the extent to which the initiatives or proposals emanating from the economic subjects conform or fail to conform to the general social interest.

In the Soviet Union, when the first draft of the plan of an enterprise is sent up to the *Sovnarkhoz*, the latter has to check whether the economic subject has kept back hidden "reserves" enabling it to surpass the plan. Naturally, when it makes this investigation, the *Sovnarkhoz* tends as a rule to start from the results achieved in the previous year and to raise them more or less mechanically by a certain percentage, so that the total figures of the enterprise plans come up to the targets set for the region or the whole country. This way of proceeding, which is officially disapproved of, entails a number of disadvantages; it tends to make the plan of the enterprise the result not of an objective evaluation of its potentialities but rather of a compromise between its own estimate, usually a modest one, and the more ambitious estimate, which is not necessarily better founded, of the higher social authority.

   b) *The degree of exactness and the more or less obligatory character of enter-
       prise plans*

The existence of economic subjects necessarily endowed with a certain autonomy must obviously reduce the *degree of exactness* that can be achieved in the forecasts embodied in plans.

Accordingly, in so far as the activity of an economic subject is partly determined by the activities of the other economic subjects, it is pointless to try and define in detail, exactly, all aspects of the future activity of each economic subject.

The situation is clearly different where *the figures for overall targets* are concerned: here a fairly high degree of precision can be attained. What is difficult, at the present level of development of the productive forces, is the endeavour to allot *a priori*, with precision, all these targets *among the different economic* subjects. Under present conditions, an *a priori* allotment like this is very unlikely to be the optimum allotment.[39]

Furthermore, even at the level of the working out of overall plans, that is, of overall targets, certain *qualitative aspects* of production must today still be left on one side. For example, the plan may well lay down the number of pairs of shoes to be produced during a year; it cannot foresee, in a socially useful way, the styles of shoes that ought to be produced, and still less the number of pairs of each style and the allotment of this specific production among the different factories. Any attempt to go into such details results inevitably in the manufacture of products which are not those most in demand, and so in a waste of social labour. It would be the same if the attempt were made to forecast in a very detailed way the production of different types of equipment. When the latter is highly diversified, corresponding to a wide variety of conditions of production and use, it is necessary to leave to agreements between enterprises an important role in the specification and destination of what they produce.

The targets and tasks laid down by the plan for each enterprise at the present time in the Soviet Union are essentially the following (so far as industrial enterprises are concerned):

Total amount produced, measured in physical units (by broad categories of products) or in value, at current prices.

Total amount invested, with destination of investments: new building and equipment, modernisation, large-scale repairs.

Principal technical changes (these being *minimum* targets): machinery to be installed, new processes to be introduced, etc.

Technical norms relating to use of materials and power, and reduction in the consumption of intermediate products (these norms represent *maxima* in the sense that the quality of the management of an enterprise is estimated by reference to its success in reducing this consumption as compared with the forecasts).

Number of workers and office staff, in broad categories, and total amount of wages to be paid: these estimates are *maxima* which the enterprise must strive not to exceed, and, if possible, not even to attain; individual wage-rates are, of course, fixed on the basis of official scales.

Cost of production per unit of the products (*maximum* targets).

Selling prices of products. These are compulsory; the prices actually charged must be neither higher nor lower than those laid down. The only exceptions are made for certain products which are new, or are being made in small quantities or even in single specimens. The prices laid down in these cases must be calculated in accordance with certain rules and must be approved by an administrative authority.

Minimum profit, resulting from the difference between cost of production and selling price, and corresponding, in general, to a margin of between 2 and 5 per cent, calculated on the basis of the cost of production.

As will be seen, some of the targets thus laid down by the plan are absolutely *obligatory*, as, generally speaking, with selling prices; others, on the contrary, are *minimum* values to be reached and, if possible, surpassed, as with production figures and technical improvements; while yet others are *maxima* which the enterprise must try, if it can, *not* to attain, as with the technical norms of consumption of intermediate products and the norms of employment of labour per unit product.

The fact that some targets are *maxima* or *minima* that must not be exceeded or must not be attained corresponds to the existence of *limits* within which the enterprise can operate, something which to some extent gives concrete form to its freedom of manoeuvre.

An essential problem is obviously that of fixing these limits in such a way that within them the enterprise can work out an optimum production-programme.

Another problem is to ensure that the optimum programme in question is optimum not only for the particular enterprise but also for society as a whole. These are problems which depend especially on the conditions of economic calculation and planning at the level of the enterprise.

It must, however, be pointed out at once that the freedom of manoeuvre which is necessarily accorded to the economic subject gives rise to important problems in connexion with price policy.

As Oskar Lange observed, in an article published in 1957: [40]

"At the present time there is often a conflict between the profitability of the production of a certain range of goods and the social need for these goods. The enterprises show, to varying degrees, a tendency to produce the goods which are most profitable, even though socially less necessary. This contradiction results from a mistaken policy of price-formation which runs counter to the law of value. Given a suitable price-policy, the goods which are socially most needed would also be the most profitable. If this were so, the socialist enterprise, aiming at profitability of production, would automatically fulfil at the same time its social and economic tasks."

This quotation raises a number of problems regarding price policy which I do not at the moment intend to discuss.[41]

The interest of the quotation so far as our theme is concerned is, in particular, that it shows how it is possible to try and solve one of the *contradictions which can arise between the different tasks of the plan,* by operating a certain price-policy, that which is proposed in this passage, so as in principle to give the enterprise the directive to seek first and foremost to produce the most profitable goods, the prices of goods being determined in consideration of the social priorities themselves.

In connexion with the foregoing, it is also necessary to make certain observations regarding, on the one hand, the proposals that have been made in the Soviet Union to reduce the number of obligatory tasks laid down in the plan and, on the other, certain contradictions or weaknesses that are at present to be found in business accounting and planning at the level of the enterprise.

One of the disadvantages that appear when too many obligatory tasks are laid upon a particular enterprise is, as has already been shown, the *contradiction* that may arise between the fulfilment of different tasks.

It is in order to reduce to the minimum such possibilities of contradiction that the Soviet economist Liberman has proposed the following changes regarding the laying down of plans at enterprise level.[42]

(1) That the plans for individual enterprises, after agreement and approval of targets concerning *amount and range of goods* to be produced, *shall be entirely determined by the enterprises themselves,* which will thus be allowed to choose for themselves the means of reaching their targets.

(2) In order to ensure that the enterprises maintain a conscientious attitude towards the state and have a material interest in producing as efficiently as possible; that a single fund be established from which payment of all categories of "material incentives" shall be made, the amount of this fund

depending on *profitability*, that is, on the profits in relation to the production funds of the given enterprise.

(3) That long-term norms be laid down by the centre to provide a scale of incentives, these incentives being related to the degree of profitability attained by the various branches of production and groups of enterprises which operate in approximately the same natural and technical conditions.

(4) That centralised planning be reinforced and improved by not laying down certain obligatory tasks (control figures) except for the *Sovnarkhozy* alone. That the practice of allotment of tasks among various enterprises by the *Sovnarkhozy* in accordance with the "level reached" by these enterprises be abolished. That the *Sovnarkhozy* be obliged, on the basis of *economic analysis*, to check, evaluate and improve the plans drawn up by the enterprises themselves, without, however, altering the scales of profitability which serve as the basis for awarding incentive bonuses to the enterprises.

(*Note:* These last two categories of proposals aim, on the one hand, at working out a differential system of profitability, on the national scale, taking into account the situations of the different enterprises or groups of enterprises, and, on the other, at not awarding bonuses to enterprises unless they achieve *both* their norm of *profitability* and the *targets* of their plan, targets revised on an objective basis by the *Sovnarkhozy*.)

(5) That methods of using the bonus funds supplied by the profits of an enterprise be laid down in such a way as to expand the rights of the enterprises to use these funds for purposes of individual and group incentive.

(*Note:* This no longer relates, therefore, to the methods of *awarding* bonuses but to the methods of *using* them. It is at this level that "material interest" really makes itself felt, whereas up to this point what has been involved is rather the indices that make it possible to "measure the efficiency" of the management.)

(6) That the principle be established that the prices of new goods be fixed in a flexible way, so that the most profitable products may be profitable both for the producers and for the consumers, that is, may be profitable on the scale of the economy as a whole.[43]

(*Note:* The last proposal aims at helping technical progress to make its way by favouring, as regards profitability, the enterprises that are manufacturing new products, which are more advantageous for the national economy. It is indeed obvious that if the profitability of new products remains the same as that of old-established products, while the management of enterprises is evaluated, and bonuses awarded on the basis of profitability, then enterprises will usually have no interest in introducing new products because at first the launching of a new product can give rise to many difficulties and cause a temporary fall in profitability.)

    c) *Some contradictions or weaknesses in the present practice of business accounting and planning at enterprise level.*

    1) *Investments without security*

Present-day Soviet practice includes the granting *without security* to each economic subject of the resources it needs for its new investments. In other words, when investments are provided for in the plan, in order to achieve certain targets, the enterprise or the economic subject receives from the banking system the funds needed for the realisation of these investments, *without any obligation to repay or to pay any interest to the bank* (this does not apply, in principle, when investments are undertaken "outside the plan").

This practice brings a certain contradiction into the functioning of the enterprise, considered as an economic subject endowed with a relative autonomy of management.

Whereas, indeed, each enterprise has to *buy* the raw materials and inter-mediate products it needs, and, as a result, its purchases enter into its costs of production (which must, at least in principle, encourage it to avoid any waste of intermediate products), it receives its investment funds, so to speak, "free of charge".[44] This may result (and often has resulted) in encouraging the enterprise to ask for investment funds larger than it really needs. It may, in particular, be led to do this in order to build up future "reserves" of increase in production or reduction in cost of production.

Under these conditions, investment is not subject to the same rules of business accounting as current management, something which does not tend to ensure that, at the level of each enterprise, the investment funds are used in the most satisfactory way.

The control exercised over each economic subject by the higher social authorities should, of course, in principle avoid the wasting of investment funds.

To the extent, however, that there is *lack of conformity* between the rules determining the operation of the economic subject, at the level of the use of *current resources*, and those which determine its operation at the level of the use of *investment funds*, and that only the former correspond to its quality as an economic subject, whereas the latter treat it as a mere technical depart-ment, distortion and waste seem to be more or less inevitable.

For this reason it is being more and more frequently proposed, in the Soviet Union and in other socialist countries, that the principle of gratuitous granting of investment funds to enterprises be abandoned, as contrary to the principles of autonomous management. If this proposal were adopted, it would mean that the enterprise would have to repay the investment funds granted to it, and perhaps also (this is, at any rate, one of Academician Nemchinov's proposals) would have to pay to the state treasury a certain sum representing *a definite percentage of the value of the investment funds tied up in it*. This payment would enter into the costs of production of the given enterprise. The justification of this proceeding would be that the present concept of cost (that is, of costs of production without any "capital" charge) is a "category" of simple reproduction, since it includes only current expenses, depreciation and a small "profit". According to Academi-cian Nemchinov (*E.G.*, in Russian, 27th April 1963), each enterprise should be able to re-create, on an expanded scale, its own conditions of work, thanks to a sufficient degree of "profitability" of its investments.

This presents important problems of business accounting at enterprise level, problems which will have to be discussed in another context.

2) *The annual character of the plans*

Another contradiction results from the present practice of working out *annual* plans for an enterprise. The annual character of the plan can actually hinder technical progress. It has been pointed out that an enterprise which introduces innovations that will be fruitful after a lapse of several years may, during the first few years of the installation of these innovations, give a mediocre performance that will evoke disapproving opinions of its current management.

Discussions now going on in the socialist countries show that this constitutes a serious restraint on the introduction of innovations in the enterprises. It is now proposed that this restraint be removed by bringing in ways of estimating the quality of management which will not be confined to the one-year-at-a-time framework.

3) *The quantitative indices*

Finally, another shortcoming of present-day practice results from the essentially quantitative character of the targets. Quantitative targets are obviously easier to measure, but pursuit of them may lead to neglect of the qualitative aspects of production. Thus, enterprises which want to attain a certain volume of production, and which find this difficult, are often tempted to permit a lowering in the quality of their products, so as to increase, so to speak, artificially (or rather, in appearance), the productivity of their work. Under these conditions, society may receive from the given enterprise only services which are in fact inferior to those that would be represented by a volume of production which was smaller but of better quality (either because some of the products are unusable or because they are less durable).

It has often been suggested, in order to remedy this state of affairs, that those cases should be made more frequent in which direct contacts are made between the supplying and the using enterprises, the latter being, in principle, the parties most interested in checking on the quality of the products supplied to them. Not only should direct links be formed in this way, it is suggested, but they should be subject to cancellation by the using enterprise in the event of standards of quality being disregarded by the supplier. The using enterprise would then get in touch with other suppliers who might be able to provide goods of better quality.

It may be that advantages that are unreal are ascribed to this kind of "flexibility" in relations between enterprises. On the one hand, it may not be that the using enterprise will always prove able to spot in good time the inadequate quality of the goods supplied to it, and, on the other, in a situation in which every enterprise is working at full capacity, it is not easy for a using enterprise to find a new supplier.[45]

Actually, it would probably be preferable to entrust a *social authority* with the task of checking the quality of products, by laying down qualitative standards which, if not respected, would result in certain products, though supplied in the material sense, having no economic value, or only reduced value. (This raises the problem of a system of price-fixing which would take account of the *social usefulness* of products—a problem which deserves treatment on its own.)

d) *Methods used by the planning organs to lay down production-targets*

The methods which are used by the planning organs in order to lay down even *overall* targets for production are also affected by the existence of economic subjects.

Owing to the fact that economic subjects exist, endowed with a certain degree of autonomy; to the fact, consequent upon this one, that the commodity categories exist; and also to the fact that the part of the national income which is consumable on an individual basis is allotted by means of money, the central planning organs are obliged, in order to lay down the targets for production-plans, to employ a great variety of methods.

In practice, as I have already indicated, once the basic targets of economic activity for a given period have been decided on in an overall and provisional way by the central planning organs, the targets for the current production plans have to be determined progressively by these same central organs (or their regional or sectoral extensions) on the basis of the following methods:

(1) Working-out of overall forecasts in increasing detail, making use of economic and technical projections and being guided by political and social choices.

(2) Collation, and adjustment to the basic targets, of the forecasts or proposals *of the economic subjects and social groups.*

If these forecasts and proposals have been worked out within the framework of the basic targets, it should be possible to make the adjustments without altering too radically the draft proposals initially composed by the planning organs, but nevertheless it is clear that these adjustments must result in incorporating in the overall targets themselves certain proposals that have been worked out in a decentralised way.

These proposals and forecasts emanate both from the economic subjects responsible for tasks of production or distribution (trade organs) and from social groups responsible for various sectors of collective consumption.

The role of the planning organs is clearly not confined to adding together these proposals and forecasts but consists rather of comparing and *adjusting* them. These adjustments, which are in principle determined by social priorities, are carried out through a continuous dialogue with the various economic subjects.

Experience shows, moreover, that the capacity of the economic subjects to forecast their future needs, even over a relatively short period, is not always sufficient for the draft plans they produce to be really useful. This is especially true when a planning policy is beginning to be put into effect, when those who stand at the head of the various economic subjects are still relatively inexperienced. When this is so, the central organs have to undertake the preparation of overall forecasts covering the needs of the economic and technical subjects, making use of technical coefficients and tables of inter-sectoral relations.

It must again be stressed that the overall statistical forecasts may often be more significant than the forecasts made at the level of each economic subject taken separately. The tendency, frequently observed, to ask each economic subject for a very large number of forecasts regarding its future needs may result in the central planning organs being pointlessly snowed under with a mass of "information" of little interest, or even lacking in any real meaning: this can prove to be the source of serious mistakes, or at least of substantial losses, when attempts are made to use this "information" or these proposals.

For example, in certain socialist countries at certain periods, the various state farms have been asked to forecast from one year to the next what their needs would be in spare parts, small agricultural implements, and even screws and nails. More often than not, forecasts made and added up in this way turned out to be much more remote from reality than those resulting from the application of statistical norms. True, the latter do not enable one to forecast how many nails or screws each state farm will need individually, but that is of no importance so long as the necessary screws and nails are available in the country and each economic subject possesses the *financial means* to buy them, within the limits of its real needs, from state trading organs which themselves operate with a certain degree of flexibility.

(3) Finally, in a certain number of cases the forecasts of the planning organs can be worked out on the basis of *detailed statistical soundings (polls)* carried out among a certain number of economic subjects or social groups or even individual consumers. Investigations by means of well-chosen samples often bring in information of much greater significance than long questionnaires circulated among thousands of production-units, who complete them with varying degrees of adequacy.

e) *Method of carrying out the plans*

Methods of carrying out the plans are of course very closely bound up with the existence of economic subjects endowed with a certain degree of autonomy. There is a fundamental difference between the methods whereby the internal production- programme of an economic subject is carried out and the methods whereby relatively autonomous economic subjects carry out national plans.

From the theoretical standpoint what is important to stress is that, on the plane of the methods of carrying out the plans, account has to be taken of the fact that the existence of economic subjects, endowed with relative autonomy, implies the superimposing of *macro-decisions* taken at the level of the central authorities, upon economic *micro-decisions* taken at the level of the economic subjects.

To the extent that the micro-decisions taken by an economic subject affect *another economic subject*, they cannot by their very nature be realised by means of orders,[46] so that an important role has inevitably to be played by *contracts concluded between the economic subjects*.

Here again we may quote from the article by Oskar Lange previously mentioned, where he writes:

"The relations between different socialist enterprises ought, in principle, to be based on a system of direct contracts concluded between them, this replacing the present system of allotment from above. The latter method should be retained only in exceptional cases, where shortages of certain goods, especially raw materials, cannot be eliminated through raising prices because the implementation of the economic plan demands more selective methods than a mere price policy."[47]

These conclusions of Oskar Lange's nevertheless call for a complementary observation. This relates to the fact that the very development of structured economic subjects results in the extension of *forms of allotment which are internal to these subjects*. These forms are neither administrative nor contractual, but technical.

I must add, too, that contractual ties between economic subjects cannot be as flexible as they need to be unless an adequate number of *trading organs* are set up within the stated sector, with responsibility for *managing stocks* of intermediate products and finished products.

Indeed, if each economic subject is to decide the moment at which it will proceed to purchase certain products, and also the specifications of these products, it is essential, to ensure the continuity of the production-process, that there be adequate social stocks of the various categories of product. On the other hand, it is equally essential for correct use of social accumulation that the available stocks should not exceed the real needs. This brings up the problem of the correct management of stocks. It is very important to solve this problem: it conditions, to a large extent, the efficient current functioning of the economic system as a whole.

In the socialist countries they have made attempts to solve the problem of stock management by laying down "norms" for stocks. These norms are made obligatory for the enterprises, which must neither exceed certain quantities nor allow their stocks to fall below a certain minimum level.

In fact, the fixing of these norms usually lacks flexibility. It is seldom possible to determine in this way the volume of stocks that genuine economic subjects may need (the situation is different where what are involved are technical departments functioning within an economic subject).

Optimum management of social stocks is a specific economic problem, the solution of which requires exact calculations and the employment of methods of programming. In order to carry out such tasks there will frequently be need for co-operation by either a trading department within a complex economic subject or else a state trading organ responsible for managing particular products.

Though there is no time to go thoroughly into the problem, it is useful to stress that the way stocks are managed has an impact on the pace at which production plans are accomplished. Here arise a number of problems connected with what can be called the "programming of the carrying-out of the plan", problems which cannot be examined immediately because this would take us too far away from the centre of our present concerns.

Conclusion

To sum up, according to the foregoing analyses, the retention of the role played by the *commodity categories* within the state sector of the socialist economy and the *existence of distinct economic subjects* within this sector are connected with the present level of development of the productive forces and the greater or lesser degree of socialisation of these forces, as between one branch and another of the economy, and even, inside the various branches, between the production-units.

If the existence of distinct economic subjects is an objective existence, rooted in a certain level of development of the productive forces and merely *confirmed* by law (which itself can *create* only juridical subjects), it will be realised that *exchange can and must* take place between the economic subjects which together make up the state sector of the socialist sector.

It will also be realised that, on the other hand, with the advance in the social character of the productive forces, an increasing number of production-units are destined to become mere technical units among which products can circulate in conformity with a pre-established plan and without, consequently, any exchange of commodities.

It is in this sense that, in *Economic Problems of Socialism in the USSR*, Stalin was able to speak of the need, "by means of gradual transitions, to replace commodity circulation by a system of products-exchange" (*op. cit.*, p. 56: Eng. edn., p. 75).

When the number of economic subjects surviving in the production sphere is sufficiently small and the conditions in which they operate are sufficiently regularised for it to be possible to forecast, with sufficient precision, their need for products supplied by other economic subjects, the movement of these products from one economic subject to another can really be effected in a socially organised way and in conformity with a pre-conceived plan. Henceforth, the economic subjects progressively become the socially controlled organs of a division of labour which is at once technical and social. Ultimately, the economic subjects cease to be subjects and are no longer anything but non-autonomous cogs in the division of labour.

Thus, the existence of commodity categories within the state sector of the socialist economy is bound up with the fact that, with the productive forces at their present level of development, the economico-juridical subjects must be allowed a certain margin of initiative if the economic system as a whole is to function efficiently.

More precisely, it is necessary, at this level of development, that the initiatives taken by certain working groups shall correspond not merely to *technical* decisions but also to *economic* ones. In other words, some of these decisions must bear, to some extent, upon the purposes for which the means of production at the disposal of the economic subjects are used, and upon the relations that the economic subjects establish among themselves in order to acquire or to alienate certain means of production or certain products, so as to accomplish the plan under the best possible conditions.

It is therefore because it is necessary for the efficient working of the economy that certain working groups may be able to take economic decisions that these groups constitute *economic subjects*. This very necessity means that in the planned economy of today, as has already been mentioned not only do economic macro-decisions have to be superimposed on technical micro-decisions, but also technical macro-decisions on economic micro-decisions.

With the productive forces at their present level, this necessity is bound up with the still considerable limitations on the possibility of *estimating social needs in advance*, especially needs which arise in the production-sphere itself, and with the still very great imperfection of *a priori* estimation of the labour-time that *should* be devoted to the obtaining of the different varieties of product.

It is, in particular, these limitations and imperfections that make it impossible to forecast within the framework of the overall economic plan the precise allotment of the labour-force that would be most efficient, the exact quantities of goods that will actually be available and the detailed way in which these goods should be allotted.

These, then, are the reasons why a margin of initiative must be left to the different economic subjects. This amounts to saying that within certain limits, laid down by the plan itself and by the various juridical authorities, the different economic subjects must necessarily behave, up to a point, like more or less "independent" producers.

In other words, as things are at present, what Marx called "the inter-connexion of social labour" takes effect not only through the plan but also, still, up to a point, through the exchanging of the products of labour. (The expression "interconnexion of social labour" is used by Marx in his well-known letter to Kugelmann of 11th July 1868.)

If economic subjects exist and have necessarily, as such, to be endowed with a certain margin of economic initiative, this means that, at the present level of development of the productive forces, the initiatives taken by certain working groups affect not only the use made by the economic subjects of the means of production that are assigned to them for the accomplishment of certain definite purposes, but also the use or non-use, by way of acquisition, of certain means of production, especially of certain items of equipment.

Satisfactory determination of the juridical conditions in which economic subjects of the production sphere operate presupposes an effort to ascertain what the economic bases are for the right of these subjects to use or not to use certain means of production, and the economic bases of their right to dispose of the products obtained: only in this way will it be possible to decide in conformity with social interests the extent and the necessary limits of these rights.

We know, for example, that when Stalin published his work on *Economic Problems of Socialism in the USSR* he noted that despite the fact that the *means of production* at the disposal of the collective farms at that time (land

and machinery) *belonged to the state,* the product of collective-farm production was the *property* of the different collective farms. It was so, said Stalin, because the land was used by the collective farms "as if" it were their own property, even though the collective farms had no right to sell it, buy it, rent it out or mortgage it. In practice, in the situation that existed at that time (and which has changed since in the direction of an increase in the powers of the collective farms, through the sale to them of the machinery which they use), the collective farms possessed only a sort of *right to productive use* of the means of production, whereas they were *owners* of the products.

As regards the state enterprises in the USSR, they also possess a *right to productive use* of the means of production which are assigned to them. This right of productive use is very much more limited in its effects than that which is enjoyed by the collective farms, for these enterprises themselves belong to the state and their integration in the social division of labour is much more complete than is the case with the collective farms.

The point that must be stressed in this conclusion is that the nature and scope of the rights "to productive use" that are enjoyed by the collective farms and the state enterprises cannot be determined arbitrarily, if it be desired that these rights shall effectively serve the progress of planned socialist economy. The nature and scope of these rights must follow from the need to ensure *conformity between juridical powers over certain means of production and practical capacities to operate these means of production.* This is a point I have developed at greater length in "Forms and methods of socialist planning and the level of development of the productive forces" (the next chapter of this book).

As I have indicated in this article, the attribution to certain social authorities of *juridical powers of disposal* may eventually find expression in the existence of *different forms and levels of state socialist property.*

Whereas, for example, the Soviet state is the owner of certain enterprises, these may themselves be, in a sense, "owners" of their means of production and their products, in so far as they enjoy at one and the same time certain juridical powers *and* effective capacities to dispose of things which conform to these powers. In this way, the "oneness" of a right of ownership which is characteristic of a certain phase of capitalist development is finally broken up.[48]

The scope of the "right of disposal" possessed by the state enterprises is, of course, strictly limited by the fact that these enterprises themselves belong to the state and that the latter allows them rights over the means of production it assigns to them *only to the extent that these rights are used for realising the plan and are necessary* for doing this under good conditions of social efficiency.

Here we find again, on the plane of juridical categories, a conclusion to which we had come on the plane of economic categories: the existence of commodity categories inside the state sector of the socialist economy is not merely an "accounting device" or a convenience for calculations. The existence of these categories expresses, simultaneously:

(1) The survival, to a certain degree and within certain limits, of ex-

changes which take place on the basis of economic decisions taken in a relatively autonomous way by working groups (the autonomy of these groups is *relative*, because they enjoy it only so as to be able to contribute more effectively to the fulfilment of the targets of the plan), and

(2) The existence, required by this relative autonomy itself, of powers of disposal and rights of usage, powers to alienate and acquire, which have been accorded to the economic subjects, rights which can constitute subordinate forms of property.

If this analysis is accepted, then one is led to consider likewise that money plays, within the state sector of the socialist economy, not merely the role of a *unit of account* but also a *real economic role*. And this role is, to make it possible, to a certain extent, for the different economic subjects *to get rid of* their products, or *to provide themselves* with products, *on the basis of their own initiatives*.

If the plan could foresee the exact quantities of products that each working group would provide, and of those that would be required by each group, and if it were in a position to ensure at the desired moment the full satisfaction of the needs of each group, it would also be able to decide *where the products should come from* to meet each group's needs and the direction in which the goods provided by each group should be sent. Under these conditions, the products could be dealt with by means of socially efficient allotment orders, and there would be no further need either for purchases or for sales; nor, therefore, for money.

On the other hand, since such forecasting and such a balance, *a priori*, between supplies and needs are not yet possible (with a few exceptions), and, especially, since they cannot be effected with sufficient precision (from the standpoint of the time and place at which supplies must be produced and despatched), it is necessary to allow a sufficient margin of initiative to a certain number of working groups; this is what, basically, makes it necessary to use money for *buying and selling*.[49]

In the socialist economy of today, money thus plays not merely an accounting role but also a real one (on the economic and juridical plane). There are, for this reason, in the planned economies of today, side by side, a *material plan* and a *financial plan*. Only with the disappearance of the commodity categories within the state sector of the socialist economy will it be possible for the financial plan to disappear also, *giving place to material planning alone* (which will also, of course, include planning and accounting of *labour expenditure*).

(Paper published in *Problèmes de Planification*,
duplicated "Cahier" No. 5.
Centre d'Etudes de Planification Socialiste,
Ecole Pratique des Hautes Etudes (VIe Section),
Paris [Sorbonne], 1965.)

NOTES TO CHAPTER 2

1 This paper has been written on the basis of notes for and reflexions on a series of lectures the author gave in 1963-4 at the Ecole Pratique des Hautes Etudes (VIᵉ Section), Paris (Sorbonne).

The following abbreviations have been used: V.E. = *Voprosy Ekonomiki*, S.W. = *Sowjetwissenschaft*, E.P. = *Economic Problems of Socialism in the USSR*, E.G. = *Ekonomicheskaya Gazeta*, S.N.Kh. = *Soviet Narodnogo Khozyaistva* (*Sovnarkhoz*, or Council of National Economy).

2 In a note written in the margin of Bukharin's book Lenin remarks that the definition the author gives of political economy (the science of a social economy based on production of *commodities*, i.e., science of an unorganised social economy) makes us take "a step back as compared with Engels", who, as we know, defined political economy in the broad sense as the "science of the conditions and forms under which the various human societies have produced and exchanged and, on this basis, have distributed their products".

For our subject, this aspect of the discussion to which Bukharin's book gave rise is obviously of great importance. The views expressed by Lenin about this book were not all, incidentally, so negative as certain commentators were to allege some years later. Some of Lenin's comments will be found in *Zamechaniya na Knigu N. Bukharina "Ekonomika Perekhodnogo Perioda"*, 2nd edn., Moscow, 1932 (see also Vol. XI of the 1928 edn. of Lenin's works).

A commentary on this discussion and its continuations (which therefore gives many other references) will be found in A. Kaufman, "The origin of the Political Economy of Socialism", in *Soviet Studies*, January 1953, pp. 243 et seq. See also Ronald L. Meek, *Studies in the Labour Theory of Value*, London, 1956, especially pp. 256–67.

3 While the idea that commodity categories were destined to disappear in the first phase of socialist society was generally accepted by Marxists before the October Revolution, we know that Lenin was one of the first to renounce this conception and stress the importance of economic calculation even at the level of production-units (cf., particularly, his "Report to the 9th All-Russia Congress of Soviets, December 1921", *Collected Works*, Russian 4th edn., Vol. 33, pp. 160–1).

4 This is exactly what I do accept.

5 Quotations taken from Lenin's article "On Co-operation" (1923).

6 *Le Capital*, Costes edn., Vol. I, p. 65. (Eng. edn. of 1938, pp. 50–1.) The German reads *"selbst bewusst"*.

7 Doubtless because they could not be, without reference to social *praxis*.

8 The superimposing of collective or communal ownership over individual (family) or personal production can be observed, of course, in a number of economic systems in course of transition, e.g., when primitive communal forms are evolving into exploitation by separate families.

9   960 in March 1962, about 1,500 after November 1962.

10   These figures refer to different years in the decade 1950–60. They are quoted from the article by L. Berri and Y. Shvikov entitled: "A comparison between production-structures in the USSR and in other countries (on the basis of inter-sectoral balances)", in *V.E.*, 1963, No. 1, trans. in *S.W.*, 1963, No. 8, pp. 818 et seq.; figures taken from p. 826.

11   The expression "production-relations" is used here in the general sense in which Marx used it when he considered "the distribution of the members of society among the various kinds of production" as "the subjection of individuals to certain relations of production" (cf. Marx, *Contribution à la Critique de l'Economie Politique* (Contribution to the Critique of Political Economy), Giard edn., 1928, p. 327: American and Indian edns., p. 286).

12   An account (in French) of the conditions governing the conclusion and execution of contracts in Bulgaria, at the level of the socialist trading organisations, will be found in the article by Dr. Ivan Vlahov (Sofia): "Le système des contrats des organisations commerciales socialistes", in *Bulletin du Centre National pour l'étude des Etats de l'Est*, 1963, No. 3 (Brussels), pp. 229 et seq.:

13   Dr. Vlahov, in the article already mentioned, calls this "transport in transit". Describing the similar role assumed by the wholesale trading enterprises of the socialist sector as intermediaries between the producers and the retailers, he writes: "In the contractual relations between the producing enterprises and the trading ones, a big part is played by transport in transit, as it is not necessary actually to deliver the goods to the depots of the wholesale trading organisations. The latter present the producing enterprises with lists showing how the goods are to be allotted, stating quantities, varieties and delivery dates for each receiver, and the minimum norms for transport in transit." (*Op. cit.*, p. 238.)

14   The first instance implies a temporary degeneration of some of the functions of money, while the second shows that the social use of money has been transcended, that is, it has begun to wither away.

15   The significance of this circulation of currency tokens becomes apparent, over and above the field we are studying at the moment, when the economic authority which has received these tokens is able to use them as money, that is, to undertake purchases which do not strictly result from decisions taken at a different level.

16   On the Soviet trusts and the *Glavki*, see my book *L'Economie Soviétique* (Paris, 1950, pp. 122 and 126).

17   This type of organisation corresponds to some extent to the "*Sbyta*" and "*Prombazy*" of the USSR (cf. *op cit.*, pp. 230–2).

18   This type of integration is being effected at present in the USSR, at the regional level, through the formation of "Soviet firms" embracing a certain number of enterprises of the same type, the most important of which takes on the leadership of the whole group. Generally speaking, the constitution of such a "firm" is submitted for approval by the *Sovnarkhoz* to which the enterprises are subject. The integration thus achieved is more complete

in some cases than in others. It may even lead to the birth of a new economic and juridical subject, taking the place of the separate enterprises which previously existed. The "firm" so constituted may, finally, take on the functions that were formerly the responsibility of a Branch Department of the *Sovnarkhoz*. When this happens, an economico-technical hierarchy has replaced an administrative one. On the "Soviet firms", see V. Kamenetsky's article "The Soviet firms, results and prospects", in *V.E.*, 1964, No. 5, p. 62.

19 Within the capitalist economy this line is marked by the *merging* of enterprises, with the appearance of buying and selling agencies and management centres. However, capitalist ownership and the contradictory interests of the private owners continually set limits to evolution in this direction, or else, when it does take place, this happens for the exclusive advantage of one particularly powerful financial group, and not necessarily on an economically efficient scale.

20 From the standpoint of the relations that a production-unit enjoys with the "rest" of the economy (relations which, on the basis of state ownership, are of decisive importance for the retention or disappearance of the commodity categories) the fact that a production-unit disposes of all its products to *one single* central sales office may, provided that this organisation is not artificial, have consequences that come very close to the integration of one production-unit into another.

21 The break-up of such organic wholes which took place in Cuba immediately after the Revolution was one of the factors in the fall in sugar production. Since 1963 there has been a move to re-establish organisational unity through a National Sugar Commission and regional and local commissions.

22 In Romania such agro-industrial combines now exist, integrating into a complex economic unit cultivation, stockraising, tinning-plant, factories making animal foodstuffs, and even shops for distributing the products.

23 See note 17.

24 A problem which, though important, I cannot deal with for the moment, is that of the limits set to the integration of activities in a particular productive economic complex. A quick observation that can be made, however, is that *economic* integration takes place only in so far as all the activities integrated satisfy a single economic and technical function and complement each other. In other words, the limit to economic integration is determined by the specific nature of the functions to be carried out, and the relevant test is the cost incurred by a particular activity. It is therefore necessary to know whether or not an integrated function is carried out at a lower cost than a non-integrated one. The idea of economic integration leads on to the idea of the "master of the operation": this role is played, in an integrated economic group, by the *essential functional link* in this group, i.e., the activity to which all the others are subordinate.

The integration of a certain number of activities in an *economic complex* makes the latter collectively responsible, within a socialist economy, for the fulfilment of a group of tasks. What the plan lays down are the tasks of this complex and the general external conditions for their accomplishment, while the internal conditions are the business of the management of the complex; this management may be carried out through a functional hierarchy of responsibilities.

25   This is not enough to situate this company among the very largest American companies from the standpoint of turnover and numbers employed. Thus, General Motors' turnover in 1963 was $16,500,000,000, and in that year it employed 640,000 people and invested $647,000,000 in plant. The net value of the firm's plant on 31 December 1963 was estimated at $3,000,000,000 and its net working capital at $3,700,000,000.

26   It must be stressed that private property relations often hinder the appearance of an economic subject when the productive forces are ready for it. This is particularly noticeable in the capitalist setting, where the *limits of enterprises* are determined by *property-relations*, so that enterprises belonging to different owners (joint-stock companies, for instance), but which *potentially form a single economic subject*, continue to function independently of each other. "Mergers" between enterprises sometimes put an end to this type of situation. The presence of the same directors on the boards of different companies which form together a potential single economic subject may also constitute an *attempt* to overcome the difficulties resulting from the obstacles put by private property in the way of the appearance of an economic subject (this cross-membership, these "personal links", may also, of course, be due to reasons quite other than those mentioned here).

In other cases, nationalisation, within the framework of capitalism, may be the only way of overcoming the obstacles caused by private property and preventing the formation of a single economic subject, though the latter is objectively necessary; in the case of the French economy, the formation of the S.N.C.F. (state railways), E.D.F. (state electricity), Gaz de France (state gas) and Houillères de France (state coal-mines) apparently reflects a situation like this.

Under socialism, too, juridical rules may for a time obstruct the appearance of an economic subject. This happened in the Soviet Union, when factories that ought to have been operating in an integrated way, e.g., within a framework of organic co-operation, were dependent on different central ministries which opposed such co-operation. This is what has been called the problem of "administrative compartmentalisation". It must be added that the reorganisation on territorial lines undertaken with the establishment of the *Sovnarkhozy* has given rise to a certain number of cases of "regional compartmentalisation".

27   It should be observed in passing that this requirement implies that, for a given level of economic interdependence it is not possible usefully to go below a certain level of decentralisation. This is connected with the impossibility of "condensing" all the information needed for socially useful decisions in a system of prices such that all the micro-economic decisions

taken always coincide with the macro-economic ones. This is the other side of the fact that the consequences of certain decisions depend strictly on *other decisions* which have to be taken *simultaneously* (the complementary character of certain decisions). This is a complex problem to which I shall come back when I discuss the role of prices in a planned economy.

28   Cf. *V.E.*, February 1962, pp. 114 et seq.

29   In his book called *Sovkhoz, Kolkhoz ou le problématique du communisme*, Paris, Editions du Seuil, 1964, René Dumont, who declares in favour of the organising within the collective farms of small, individualised work-brigades, endowed with permanent means of production and financial autonomy, writes on this subject:

"If . . . the workers were directly interested in the overall economic results achieved by their little groups, they would strive to combine immediate efficiency of their work with reduction in its arduousness, and the most rapidly productive detail investments.

The betterment of the many hand-tools, from the improved hoe to the wheelbarrow, and that of handling and digging work, would not be so neglected as it is. On every work-site, the links in the work-chain where productivity was very low would be studied by the persons them-selves involved. They would strive to ensure the harmonious development of the equipment as a whole, instead of concentrating on the mechanisa-tion of some parts at the expense of the rest, which in the end proves more expensive." (*Op. cit.*, p. 242.)

René Dumont's proposal amounts to attributing to small work-brigades the status of "economic subjects". The degree of control over the means of production which is possible at such a level does not seem, however, to be sufficient for the brigade to be regarded as a real economic subject. On the other hand, it can certainly possess an "economic personality" and constitute, as we shall see later, *a rung in the ladder of economic accounting*. In any case, recourse to economic calculation and to various experiments is needed in order to decide the level at which the economic personality of a working group is located and that at which the economic subjects are located, as well as the optimum size of both the former and the latter.

In general, the problem of the *resistance to innovation* offered by present-day forms of organisation, both in industry and in agriculture, is causing an important discussion in the Soviet Union at the present time; the February 1964 issue of *Planovoye Khozyaistvo* provides an echo of this discussion.

30   On these questions, see the article by Carlos Rafael Rodriguez, "El nuevo camino de la agricultura cubana", *Cuba Socialista*, November 1963, pp. 71–98.

31   It is well known that internal economic calculation ("business accounting") has been practised for a long time now within Soviet industry. A decision of the Central Committee of the CPSU (B) dated 5 December 1929 emphasised, for the first time officially, the importance of internal economic calculation at the level of workshops and departments of industrial enterprises. Internal economic calculation is, of course, accompanied by the

drawing up of *internal plans* for the workshops and departments in question.

The perfecting of the practical forms in which internal economic calculation can be carried out is an extremely complex matter. This is clearly to be
seen when we analyse the discussions which have taken place on this
subject in the Soviet Union. Thus, in the manual entitled *Ekonomika
sotsialisticheskikh promyshlennikh predpriyatii* (Moscow, 1956), we read:

"It is necessary to mention the 'mistaken' attempts that have been made to
introduce mechanically, at the level of the departments of enterprises,
the same content and forms of business accounting relationships that
prevail between enterprises.

The experience of industrial enterprises shows that the forms of
business accounting *within the factory* must be clearly distinguished from
those of *business accounting by the enterprise itself*. Workshops, departments, divisions and brigades are merely subdivisions of the enterprise,
participating in the total production process of the enterprise, and this
is why they cannot appear as independent units in business accounting.
They do not figure in economic relationships with other enterprises,
banks, financial organs . . . and therefore, so far as workshops, divisions
and brigades are concerned, it is not necessary to make business agreements with other enterprises, have a separate bank account, buy raw
materials and sell finished products, obtain bank credits and allotments
from the budget, or keep accounts of their activity in the form of a
departmental balance-sheet showing profits and losses." (*Op. cit.*, p. 314.)

(On the problems of internal business accounting in factories, see also
Ya. I. Kokhan, *The Organisation of Business Accounting in Factories* (in
Russian), Moscow, 1964.)

As regards the capitalist enterprise, we know that, even if the technical
departments are not accorded financial autonomy, the forms of management tend towards the keeping of *internal balance-sheets for both forecasting
and checking-up*.

It should also be noted that, in a socialist economy, when a certain *level
at which business accounting is to take place* is decided on, this may not always
necessarily correspond to a permanent working group. Thus, in Cuba, the
attempt was made, in certain *Granjas* (*Granja Unidad*, in Havana province)
to keep account of receipts and payments for each *field*, though no working
group was assigned permanently to any one field.

32　The use of simulation techniques and electronic devices for this purpose will clearly assume increasing importance in the years to come. It will
make possible the taking of efficient decisions on problems involving a very
large number of variables, without having to undertake actual experiments,
using "simulated" experience instead.

To illustrate the sort of problems that simulation techniques can help
solve, I will quote the case of the organisation of air traffic. The establishment of a simulator air-traffic control for the whole of Western Europe is
at present being considered. It will be given the task of laying down the
courses that, in 1970, will have to be followed by the six-hundred-odd

aeroplanes which will then be moving regularly across the West-European sky, and of fixing the locations of the relevant ground installations, together with the procedures for ensuring take-off and landing by this air-fleet. The simulator will make it possible to trace the effects of the various possible combinations of ground-installations and the relations between these and the aircraft in flight. A simulator capable of doing this necessitates an electronic brain equipped with over 100,000 transistors.

33 The problem of the organs responsible for this co-ordination will be dealt with a little later.

34 It is clear that bureaucratic distortion of the economy can also occur when, *inside a complex economic subject*, the responsibility for taking certain decisions is entrusted to economic authorities which are uselessly high up in the hierarchy and less well placed than authorities lower down for taking completely effective decisions.

Contrariwise, if the responsibility for taking decisions is entrusted to authorities which are not sufficiently high up the ladder to be able to take account of all the necessary information, together with the complementary nature of certain decisions (cf. note 27), a certain "economic dislocation" will result.

Economic dislocation and bureaucratisation of the economy alike result in a loss of efficiency (in comparison with what could be achieved under other conditions), i.e., in *poor co-ordination* between decisions, or poor adaptation of means to ends.

35 A point here which is essential and which must never be lost sight of seems to me that, within the framework of a planned economy, every economico-juridical subject in the production sphere is merely a *link* in the division of labour, and a link *destined to be subordinated to an increasing extent to a larger subject* (in proportion as the socialisation of the productive forces progresses) of which it thus tends to become, little by little, a mere technical department.

This being so, the setting-up of elected decision-making organs at the level of each production-unit can, as a rule, only be a measure that holds back the complete socialisation of the means of production and even sets an obstacle in its way, emptying of its content the *public* ownership of these means of production and replacing it, *de facto*, with ownership by a *limited group* of workers. When this occurs, we are not on the road to the building of socialism but on the road to the degeneration of the very conditions essential for social planning.

It must further be stressed that when the aim of production is no longer profit but consumption, the social control of productive activity which is essential would seem to need to be exercised more and more at the level of *consumption*, i.e., of the evaluation of social needs. This being so, proposals aimed at setting up a form of control wielded mainly by the producers *as such* can only hold back the adapting of production to its final aim, namely, social needs.

This does not, of course, rule out control by producers over the conditions of production and their active participation in improving the latter. But this improvement means nothing except in relation to *social needs to be satisfied*, so that it is essential that the functioning of the different production-units be conditioned by the size and nature of socially recognised needs.

It must be added, moreover, that with the very development of the productive forces, the time devoted by everyone to productive activity will get less, while the time devoted to consumption and leisure will increase. This, too, points to the conclusion that it is at the level of the organisation of consumption that new forms of social control over production itself must be developed.

Consequently, inside the state sector of the socialist economy, appointment by an authority representing society as a whole of a "director" responsible for managing each economico-juridical subject seems to be the method best adapted to the needs of increasing socialisation of the productive forces, since this socialisation makes every economic subject a mere cog in a division of labour destined to satisfy the needs of society as a whole.

Of course, the fact that each economic subject is headed by a responsible director, appointed by the state power or by whatever other social authority has general oversight of the development and use of the productive forces does not in the least mean that the workers of each economic unit should not be consulted on all the decisions that affect them, that they should not be fully informed about the progress of the unit in which they work, or that they should not have every opportunity to make all possible suggestions and proposals regarding the plan of this production-unit; but the *decision-making power* must not be *atomised*, if the very foundations for the building of socialism and for planning are not to be destroyed.

In very large production-units like, for example, a chemical combine or an iron-and-steel combine, employing tens of thousands of workers, controlling mines, blast-furnaces, rolling-mills, foundries, internal means of transport, and so on, it seems to be essentially at the level of the *basic working groups* that participation by the workers in the drawing up of the plan and in making useful suggestions for its implementation can take place most effectively. At this level it is also possible to set up production committees, committees for introducing innovations, and so on, in which the manual workers, the technical cadres and the managerial personnel all take part.

In production-units where the localisation of the productive forces is still on a very narrow basis, where production cannot be precisely determined by the plan, and in which, consequently, the socialisation of labour is still realised mainly through exchange (as in the case of producer co-operatives), the situation is different from what it is in the big production-units of the state sector. In units like this, appointment of the manager of the co-operative enterprise by the workers' collective does not involve risk that it may prevent the strict subordination of the activity of these units to the targets of the plan, since, in any event, this subordination can only be partial.

To come back to the production-units that belong to the state sector, it must be said that the control that the producers should exercise over these production-units is a control that belongs to *the producers as a whole* and not merely the narrow groups of workers who produce within each of these production-units considered in isolation. This control by all the producers over all the production-units of the state sector raises the problem of political democracy, and so of the democratic structure of the state. This is quite a different problem from that of the internal organisation of the different production-units, and we should be going too far beyond our present task if we were to try to study it here.

In any case, democratic functioning of the state and of the ruling party constitutes the condition for genuine socialist planning which must subordinate both the aims of the plan and the means of achieving it to the overall interests of the workers and of society.

36 Naturally, a thorough knowledge of these characteristics and the potentialities inherent in them is only possible given close consultation with the members of these groups and stimulation of their initiative. Thus L. M. Gatovsky, summing up the work of a seminar devoted to "Cybernetics and Planning" (cf. *V.E.*, 1964, No. 6) is justified in stressing that "no centralised optimisation of the plan and no automisation of management detracts from the importance of local initiative . . ." (p. 95).

37 As in the system of planning at two levels proposed by Kornai and Liptak.

38 Cf. J. Vernes, "Plans, bénéfices et primes en URSS" (Plans, profits and bonuses in the USSR), *Economie et Politique*, December 1963, pp. 48 et seq.

39 Of course, as a result of advances in the productive forces themselves and also of the use of electronic methods of calculation, there are grounds for supposing that these difficulties will be overcome in the not too distant future, at least so far as certain branches of activity in the more highly industrialised socialist countries are concerned, but this means that when that time comes, the character of "economic subject" attaching to the production-units functioning in those branches of activity will already be on the way out.

40 Oskar Lange, "How do I visualise the Polish economic model?" (in German), in *Polen von Heute*, 1st February 1957.

41 Though these problems have been for several years the subject of special attention in the Soviet Union, they are far from having been solved. Thus, when, at a meeting of the Council of National Economy of the USSR in spring of 1964, the activities of the *Sovnarkhozy* of the Kharkov and Central Volga areas were examined, it was noted that, though the industrial enterprises of these areas had surpassed, in overall terms, their production plans and other targets laid down in the form of technico-economic indicators (norms of consumption of intermediate products, productivity, etc.), more than 40 per cent of them had failed to fulfil their tasks as regards the particular goods produced, and thereby "the national economy has failed to obtain large quantities of electrical machines, superchargers, goods trucks, spare parts and mining equipment" (cf. *V.E.*, 1964, No. 6, p. 94).

42   Cf. the article by J. Vernes (see note 38).

43   These were Liberman's proposals put forward in *Pravda* of 9 September 1962.

44   It is only through "depreciation norms" (which are usually low) that the immobilisation of investment funds by an enterprise may lead to a certain increase in its costs of production.

45   The objection that to authorise this practice would upset the plan forecast is, in the main, of formal validity only, since it is failure to respect qualitative standards (even if this be not measured) that *really* upsets the plan forecasts.

46   Of course, micro-decisions which affect only one economic subject by itself can take the form of orders emanating from the management of this subject, or from the organ which manages part of this subject, and addressed to a working group or even to a particular worker, but these are orders that concern the *internal* functioning of the subject and are thus of a technical nature.

47   Article in *Polen von Heute* referred to in note 40, p. 11.

48   It will be observed that, with the development of joint-stock companies, as well as other factors, this "oneness" is already tending to break up: the shareholders are the joint owners of the joint-stock company in which they have invested their capital, but the company is the "owner" of its means of production. The general meeting of the shareholders having, in principle, defined the purpose of the company's activity, it is under the responsibility of the managing director, who is not necessarily a shareholder, that the means of production are put to current use and that some of them may even be bought or sold (in so far as these purchases and sales do not alter the purpose of the company's activity). More important economic decisions (extension of activity, new investments, etc.) are taken by the board of directors, whereas the shareholders' general meeting theoretically takes the decisions with a larger bearing; actually, these decisions are more often than not prepared by the permanent staff of the management under conditions such that the general meeting can do nothing but rubber-stamp them.

This brings out how, in this instance, there is a *lack of conformity* between the juridical power and the effective capacity of the shareholders' general meeting. What has happened is that the social character of the productive forces has burst some of the limitations imposed by the private ownership of these forces, though this takes place to the advantage not of society as a whole but to that of a small number of especially powerful shareholders.

49   If the impossibility of an exact forecast were confined to the sphere of *individual consumption*, it would only be in this sphere that the commodity categories had a role to play; so it is not impossible that the commodity categories may cease to exist in the production sphere while continuing to some extent in that of consumption. It is not out of the question, however, that commodity categories may, on the contrary, disappear *first* in the consumption sphere and only later in that of production. These are problems that, for the time being, can only be mentioned in passing.

3: Forms and methods of socialist planning and the level of development of the productive forces

The following paper originated as reflexions on the theoretical aspects of some of the problems now being faced by the economy of Cuba. As these problems are of the kind that necessarily arise in any country that takes the path of building socialism, it has seemed to me that it might be of interest to publish the paper in its original form, with only a few minor changes. It is true that in my paper a number of important questions relating to the building of socialism are not dealt with, because they were not immediately relevant to the Cuban economy. Some of these questions will be tackled elsewhere in this work.

As will be seen, I am leaving aside here the specific historical conditions of Cuba and the USSR, as well as problems other than economic ones, though these must, of course, be taken into consideration when a concrete solution is decided on.

This paper is, then, a paper on economic theory. The latter is an indispensable instrument for the working out of a correct solution of economic problems, even though it is not, of course, sufficient in itself to furnish complete answers to all the questions posed by practical planning and the organisation of a socialist economy.

In order to solve as correctly as possible the problems now facing the Cuban economy, it is necessary to analyse them theoretically. Only on the basis of such analysis can one discover the economic strategy and tactics appropriate to the needs of the present stage, taking into account the specific concrete features of this stage and of the present level of development of the productive forces. Only an analysis like this enables one to define the forms of organisation and methods of work that correspond to the economic strategy and tactics adopted.

While theoretical analysis is objectively necessary, it is also necessary subjectively, for it alone can provide the correct scientific view which is essential in order to guide the actions of the leaders of the Revolution, the political cadres and the working masses themselves. A scientific view is essential, too, for the practical implementation of the general line adopted.

Among other things, this should enable them:

(a) To overcome the hesitations that may legitimately be felt before replacing familiar methods of work and forms of organisation by new methods and forms;

(b) To avoid the feeling that they are retreating, on the plane of economic organisation, when they are only renouncing organisational forms that are either outgrown or premature, that is, in either case, inappropriate;

(c) To escape the temptation to imitate methods or forms of organisation which may have produced positive results in different objective conditions, where priorities other than those which prevail today in the Cuban economy had to be observed.

On the theoretical plane, as we know, the fundamental problem consists in treating the productive forces in conformity with their nature. If one acts otherwise, it is impossible to master the productive forces, and so to direct their development effectively.

Similarly, on the theoretical plane, it is essential to analyse men's behaviour not as if this were ultimately determined by the *idea* they have of their relations between themselves and of their respective roles (which would imply that it is enough to change this idea, through education, to achieve a change in their behaviour in the desired direction—an idealistic view of the way things happen), but as a consequence of the actual places men occupy in the technical and social division of labour and in a given process of production and reproduction (which also reproduces their needs, while gradually changing them), a process which is itself basically determined by the level of development of the productive forces.

An analysis of this kind enables us to understand that the decisive lever for changing men's behaviour consists in changes effected in production and the way it is organised. Education's role is essentially one of eliminating attitudes and forms of conduct inherited as survivals from the past, and apprenticing people to the new forms of behaviour imposed by the actual development of the productive forces.

It is on the basis of these rules of general analysis, the rules of historical materialism, that we have to solve the theoretical problems set by the evolution of the production-relations, as a result of the progress of the productive forces, together with the problems of delimiting the different forms of property, of the organisation of the socialist sector, of the organisation of exchange, of the distribution of income, and of planning.

I Delimiting the socialist sector from the private sector under the dictatorship of the proletariat

We know that Marx and Engels showed that the development of capitalist economy is accompanied by the appearance of forms of production that are increasingly social, and that it is this increasingly social character of the productive forces that makes *socialisation* of the means of production an *objective* necessity.[1] We know, too, that the founders of scientific socialism showed that the social character of the productive forces is more or less strongly marked, depending on the type of economic activity and the nature of the techniques employed.

From these analyses, and his further developments of them, Lenin drew practical conclusions about the delimitation between the socialist and private sectors of the economy during the first phase of the dictatorship of the proletariat, and about the conditions needed for the withering away of the private sector and the integration into the socialist sector of activities at first carried on by the private sector.

Lenin emphasised especially that it is not possible to solve the problems of small and middle-peasant economy without reorganising the economy as a whole, without "a transition from individual, disunited petty commodity production to large-scale social production". And he adds:

"This transition must of necessity be extremely protracted. It may only be delayed and complicated by hasty and incautious administrative and legislative measures. It can be accelerated only by affording such assistance to the peasant as will enable him to effect an immense improvement in his whole farming technique, to reform it radically."[2]

Lenin thus stresses, in this passage written in 1919, the technical foundations needed for the changes to be carried out in agriculture, the great length of the transition period, and the assistance to be afforded to the peasant during this protracted transition period.

In 1921, in his well-known report on the substitution of a tax in kind for the requisition system, Lenin returned at some length to these same notions:

"Any Communist who thought the economic basis, the economic roots, of small farming could be reshaped in three years was, of course, a dreamer . . ."

"It will take generations to remould the small farmer, and recast his mentality and habits. The only way to solve this problem of the small farmer—to improve, so to speak, his mentality—is through the material basis, technical equipment, the extensive use of tractors and other farm machinery, and electrification on a mass scale . . ."[3]

Lenin, as we know, drew all the practical consequences from this analysis: since the individual peasants, of both the poor and middle categories, are destined to survive as such for a long time,

"We must try to satisfy the demands of the peasants."[4]

And he adds:

"How is the peasant to be satisfied and what does satisfying him mean? . . . If we go into this, we shall see at once that it will take essentially two things to satisfy the small farmer. The first is a certain freedom of exchange, freedom for the small private proprietor, and the second is the need to obtain commodities and products. What indeed would free exchange amount to if there was nothing to exchange, and freedom of trade, if there was nothing to trade with!"[5]

If Lenin eventually insisted on the need to maintain individual agricultural production during a transition period[6] (so long as the technical basis for social agricultural production had not been established, on a scale sufficient to cope with the needs of society as a whole), and on what this implied as regards freedom of local exchange, this was because agricultural production is the hardest branch of the economy to transform technically, both in respect of material conditions and of production-practices; and also because the peasantry is a particularly important class, whose alliance with the working class is essential to the dictatorship of the proletariat. What is true, however, of individual agricultural production is true also of the crafts and of small-scale industrial production, so long as these have not yet developed a high-level technical foundation.

II The organisation of the socialist sector

While the question of how the productive forces should be allocated between the private sector and the socialist sector has long since been the subject of theoretical consideration, this is not true, at least to the same degree, and however surprising it may seem, of the problems posed by the internal organisation of the socialist sector. For this reason, the working out of principles to govern the organisation of this sector in countries taking the socialist road calls for very special attention. The historical experience of the other socialist countries in this sphere needs to be analysed theoretically in order to be fully utilised.

Historically, down to recent years, the internal organisation of the socialist sector in the Soviet Union has been conceived essentially from the standpoint of confronting the most urgent problems, under pressure from particularly difficult and complex conditions, in situations that were often extremely tense (war communism, reconstruction after the civil war, working out and revising the Five-Year Plans while Fascism was advancing in Germany and a new world war threatened, the war itself, then the reconstruction following that). It was therefore not always possible to adapt this organisation systematically to the requirements of the level of development of the productive forces: it had to be adapted empirically to rapidly changing circumstances.

This resulted in relatively frequent changes in organisation, as regards both the production-units, with their juridical powers, and the nature of the authorities to which these production-units were attached, their decision-making powers and so on. The solutions given to these problems obviously have a big effect on the good or bad functioning of the socialist sector, its speed of development, its profitability, its capacity for adaptation to technical progress, and so on.

Since, over a long period, the changes made in the organisation of the socialist sector of the Soviet economy were due above all to immediate practical considerations, they were not at all the outcome of profound theoretical analysis. Only fairly recently have the Soviet authorities begun to proceed differently and tried to take account, in the actual organisation of the socialist sector, of the requirements of the law of necessary conformity between production-relations and the character of the productive forces.[7]

In view of the great importance (for the building of socialism in Cuba or any other country taking the socialist road) of finding a correct solution to the problems of organisation, and in view also of the reference it is essential to make, in this field as in others, to the experience of the most advanced socialist countries, we must give some attention to at least a few of the reasons why these problems have still received, even in the Soviet Union, only a partial and not altogether satisfactory treatment.

Some of these reasons are purely practical. The most decisive of them seems to be the mainly administrative form that Soviet planning necessarily assumed over a long period, owing to the very high priority that had to be given to the development of the economic infrastructure, especially to heavy industry.

The Soviet Union was, in fact, an economically backward country where the material foundations of socialist expanded production had to be laid down quickly, by devoting exceptional efforts to the development of Department I of the economy and, more particularly, to the development of the basic industries. In these circumstances, the need for maximum economic efficiency, which ought to be fundamental to organisational work, had rather often to be neglected, if not on the strategic plane, where it was usually respected, then at least on the tactical plane, where it was often relegated to secondary importance, and not only as regards economic organisation.

Other reasons besides this historical one relate to the stage reached in the theoretical elaboration of decisive points of doctrine, and these deserve close attention.

1 *Economic laws and socialism*

One of the most important of these reasons appears to have been an appreciation by certain Marxists which was inadequate, and sometimes even wrong, of the problem of economic laws and contradictions in socialist economy and society.

An extreme instance of a wrong appreciation of this kind is provided by Rosa Luxemburg who, in a "leftist" view of the future, thought that there would no longer be any economic laws in socialist society and political economy would therefore be deprived of its function.[8]

The same appreciation was made by Nikolai Bukharin in his book on the political economy of the transition period, especially where he writes:

"As soon as we have to deal with an organised national economy, all the basic 'problems' of political economy, such as value, price, profit, etc., simply disappear. . . . This is why there can be a place here for a certain descriptive system and also for a pattern of norms, but none for a science investigating the 'blind laws' of the market, since the market will have ceased to exist. Thus, the end of capitalist-commodity society will also be the end of political economy."[9]

We know how this opinion put forward by Bukharin (who was then defending "ultra-leftist" views) was refuted by Lenin.[10]

For our purpose we shall note two essential aspects of the mistakes made by Bukharin, namely:

(a) Confusion between "economic law" and "law of the market" (which amounts to reducing political economy to a "science of exchange" and not recognising its nature as the "science of social production");

(b) Confusion between the free working of laws and their objective nature.

Mistakes like these obviously make it impossible, too, to understand the conditions under which the law of value operates in the different phases of development of socialist society. It was with regard to the operation of the law of value in socialist society that the wrong theoretical views I have recalled were combated soonest, most vigorously and most systematically. With regard to the practical matter of the internal organisation of the socialist sector, however, the consequences of mistakes like this, or of the same nature, only gradually came to be combated.

It was in his *Economic Problems of Socialism in the USSR* that Stalin emphasised most strongly that objective economic laws exist in a socialist economy,[11] and that he showed, though without deducing all the consequences, that these laws also have a bearing on the way socialist society is organised, that is, on the forms that have to be given to the production-relations and the technical and social organisation of production. These forms need to be modified gradually, so as to adapt them to the actual development of the productive forces, failing which, instead of helping the progress of these forces, they become a fetter upon it.

In this way, the idea of a possible "contradiction" between productive forces and organisational forms in the socialist sector is put forward, while at the same time the non-antagonistic nature of this contradiction is stressed, since there is no group in society possessing sufficient means to resist the necessary changes—which does not mean that certain social strata (such as a bureaucratic stratum, say) may not be interested in opposing changes even though these are necessary.

Mao Tse-tung, too, has emphasised the contradictions that may develop in socialist society, and the need to resolve these contradictions correctly. "Many people," he said, "refuse to admit that contradictions still exist in a socialist society. . . . They do not understand that socialist society grows more united and consolidated precisely through the ceaseless process of correctly dealing with and resolving contradictions . . . The basic contradictions in a socialist society are still those between the relations of production and the productive forces, and between the superstructure and the economic base. . . ."[12]

The fact that only ten years ago it was necessary to refute the thesis that there are no objective economic laws under socialism, and that it was necessary to recall with emphasis the existence in socialist society of contradictions between production-relations and productive forces, shows how backward theoretical thought had become in this sphere, and explains why the problem of the organisation of the socialist sector was posed in scientific terms only belatedly and partially.

2 Property and production-relations

Another theoretical root of the situation described above, and one which is both deeper and even less studied, is the inadequacy, and sometimes the falsity, of the analyses that have been made of the concepts "production-relations" and "property".

We know that, for Marx, production-relations are the relations that men establish among themselves in the process of social production, and that these relations change with the development of the material productive forces.[13]

The nature of the production-relations is thus determined by the productive forces themselves and by their degree of development. Property in (or ownership of) the means of production is the juridical and abstract expression of some of the production-relations, an expression which has to be changed when the productive forces change, and along with them the corresponding production-relations.[14]

The connexion between productive forces, production-relations and forms of property is far from having always been grasped correctly. We see this, for instance, in Professor Oskar Lange's *Traité d'Economie Politique*. Like many other economists, Lange regards ownership of the means of production as the "basis" of production-relations.[15]

Actually, it is the level of development of the productive forces that determines the nature of the production-relations, relations which may find more or less adequate juridical expression in a given form of property in (ownership of) the means of production. Marx emphasised on several occasions this aspect of the link between production-relations and forms of property.[16]

If we regard as the "basis" of the production-relations what is only a more or less adequate juridical expression and form of them, we are easily drawn into making false conclusions. Such a conception, indeed, prevents us from grasping the real content of socialist property and its different forms. Similarly, it stands in the way of a clear and concrete analysis of socialist appropriation and of the roots of the retention of commodity exchange and the law of value during the first historical period of socialist society. It is essential to spend a little time on these points.

The mistake that consists in confusing the juridical form of property with *effective appropriation* is a mistake that has often been made, and which Lenin had to protest against already in his own time. In his well-known article "Against 'Left-Wing' childishness and the petty-bourgeois mentality", he contrasts the juridical act of *nationalisation* with the *socialisation* that implies the effective capacity of society to account and allot,[17] a capacity which is itself bound up with a certain development of the productive forces (which embrace men themselves, with their level of knowledge).

Here, Lenin is contrasting the juridical form with the concrete production-relations. He is emphasising that this juridical form is empty when these relations are such that they do not enable the form to be adequately filled, because *capacity to deal effectively with the means of production and their products* does not coincide with formal ownership.

This brings us back, after a seeming detour, to the problem of the internal organisation of the socialist sector. This organisation is, in reality, only effective if the juridical power to dispose of certain means of production or certain products coincides with the capacity to employ these means of production and these products in an efficient way. The social level at which this capacity is to be found at any given moment obviously does not depend on men's "goodwill" but on the development of the productive forces.

When juridical power and effective capacity do not coincide, when the juridical subject is not really an economic subject, there is a divorce between, on the one hand, *the real process of production and distribution,* and, on the other, *the process aimed at* by those who wield political power without possessing effective capacity. This divorce results in a more or less serious absence of real direction of the economic process by those who are supposed to be directing it, and it usually engenders an overgrowth of regulations and an excessive expansion of the bureaucratic apparatus. These harmful phenomena are themselves bound up with the vain effort being made to try and bridge the gulf separating the formal juridical framework from the actual production-relations, which fail to fill this framework adequately.

Analysed in this way, the problem of the internal organisation of the socialist sector and of the different forms of socialist property can be seen in its full significance.

For example, in the Soviet Union, the collective-farm form of socialist property is better adapted to the level of development of the productive forces at the disposal of the collective farms than the state form would be. This means that, at the present level of development of these forces, socialisation of the production-process is more real within the collective-farm framework than it could be if formal ownership of these productive forces were transferred to the state. The latter would then be obliged either to direct more or less centrally a production-process which, in the present state of things, can only be directed and controlled effectively on the spot, or else to delegate its powers of decision-making to a "director" appointed by the state, who would thus take upon himself the functions that are carried out at present by the collective-farm community and its organs. In fact, such a transfer would cause a setback to socialisation (that is, to control by the community over the production-process) rather than advancing it further. When one speaks of the "higher" forms of socialist property, meaning state ownership, this has only (in relation to production-processes which are not yet ripe for this type of ownership) a strictly *historical* significance, as a provisional view of future development, and has no immediate relevance to the actual level of development of the productive forces. This is the very reason why it is necessary to retain the so-called "lower" forms. Their existence is thus not to be explained, as some would have it, by the "conservative mentality" of the peasants but by the reality of the actual production-relations.

The sale to the collective farms of the agricultural machinery at the disposal of the Machine and Tractor Stations in the Soviet Union provides us with an example of transition from state property to collective-farm property, something that from the formal standpoint implies a "setback" to the degree of socialisation of these means of production. This "setback", however, may signify in reality a step forward in effective socialisation, if it entails, in practice, an advance in the economic efficiency with which society uses the means of production thus transferred.[18]

It is always a matter, when one wants to ensure maximum conformity between juridical authority and capacity to use, of deciding what type of group has the right to control and direct certain production-processes, and this is something that cannot be done correctly without taking account of the nature of the productive forces involved in the particular process.

The same principle, of course, has to govern the allotment of juridical powers, over particular means of production or particular products, among the various governmental organs of the socialist state or the various economic authorities of this state. (Thus, in the Soviet Union, the *Sovnarkhozy* are regional authorities of the state power, whereas a Soviet enterprise is a state *economic* authority.)

The assignment of juridical powers to certain social authorities may be expressed in the existence of different forms and levels of state socialist property.

Thus, while the Soviet state owns certain enterprises, the latter may themselves own their means of production and their products, in so far as they at the same time possess certain juridical powers and the corresponding effective capacity to dispose. The "oneness" of property-right which is characteristic of bourgeois law is thus broken up. It is important to realise that things may, and indeed must, be so during a whole phase of development of socialist society—not only from the standpoint of the organisation of the socialist sector but also from that of understanding what socialist trade is and what role the law of value plays. I shall come back to this point later.

It follows from what has been said above that if juridical power to dispose of certain means of production is granted to an authority which does not possess, at the given level of development of the productive forces, effective capacity to dispose of them, then this arrangement will mean that there is insufficient social control over these productive forces. This is what has happened in Cuba in those branches of industry where the essential juridical power to dispose has been entrusted to the *Consolidados*, whereas the production-units alone constitute genuine economic subjects enjoying effective capacity to dispose.

What can rightly be called a "production-unit" (and what constitutes a genuine economic subject) varies, of course, depending on the level of development of the productive forces. In certain branches of production,

E

where the integration of activities is sufficiently advanced, it is the branch itself that may constitute a "production-unit". This may be so, for instance, in the case of the electrical industry, on the basis of the interconnexion that exists between power stations, since this makes possible centralised direction of the entire branch.

It must further be observed that, depending on the type of use that is made of certain means of production, effective capacity to dispose of the latter may be possessed by different authorities, whence also the possibility of superposition of different juridical powers over the same means of production.

These are the various considerations that have to be kept in mind in defining the place of each of the different forms of socialist property, the rights of the enterprises, their ties with the central economic organs, the ways in which current economic management is carried on, the forms and rules of economic planning, and so on.

III The organisation of exchange

The organisation of exchange, and consequently of the distribution of products, may appear to be dominated by the way production is organised technically. Actually, the organisation of exchange is an integral part of the organisation of the social reproduction process, which consists at once of production, consumption, circulation and exchange of products and activities.

In a socialist economy which includes, at one and the same time, both petty individual production and social production, the organisation of exchange must necessarily assume a different form depending on the type of production. Theoretical study is also needed here of the question of how to organise exchange in the way best adapted to the relations established between the development of the productive forces and the satisfaction of recognised social needs.

1 Individual production and exchange

That the existence of individual production under the dictatorship of the proletariat necessarily entails the retention of the categories "commodity" and "money" is nowadays universally accepted. That the existence of these categories necessitates also the existence of a market and of a certain degree of freedom of exchange is, however, sometimes denied. This is so at the present time in Cuba, and it was also the case in the Soviet Union at the end of the "War Communism" period, during which circumstances had obliged the Soviet power to abolish freedom of exchange and reduce the functions of money to the minimum. At that time there were quite a few Communists in the Soviet Union who believed that abolition of freedom of exchange was compatible with the retention, which was then unavoidable, of individual production, and that this would not hinder the development of the productive forces, and so the consolidation of the dictatorship of the proletariat.

We know how Lenin answered those who thought in this way and how he declared that a certain degree of freedom of exchange was necessary, given the existence of individual production—a measure of freedom that should be controlled and limited so that it would serve the interests of the dictatorship of the proletariat and not affect the latter adversely.

Lenin said that, given the basis of individual production,

". . . here you cannot avoid local free exchange . . ."[19]

and added, as the consequence following from this:

"We can allow free local exchange to an appreciable extent, without destroying, but actually strengthening, the political power of the proletariat."[20]

That a certain freedom of local exchange is necessary not only as a mere temporary measure but for a whole historical period is shown by the fact that a collective-farm market still exists today in the Soviet Union. Its continued existence confirms the need for a local agricultural market as corollary to the existence of private agricultural production—a form of production which, as regards certain important foodstuffs, is responsible for meeting a far from negligible proportion of consumption in the Soviet Union today.

Similarly, the recent experience of People's China has shown that the re-establishment of some individual agricultural production has had to be accompanied by the re-establishment of local markets, and that this has contributed substantially to a marked improvement in the supply of food to the towns and a new rise in industrial production.[21]

Thus, theory and practice alike confirm the need for a certain degree of freedom of exchange as a corollary of the existence of individual production.

The concrete problems which it is of the highest importance to resolve correctly concern the limits to be set to this exchange and how to subordinate it to the interests of the development of socialist society. These problems can be settled only through studying the international experience of the socialist countries, and through day-to-day practical experience,[22] analysed in accordance with the methods of dialectical materialism.

The foregoing remarks and references show, in any case, that the problem of re-establishing in Cuba a local market for agricultural produce results, so far as a certain historical period is concerned, from the nature of the present productive forces of Cuban agriculture.

This is the perspective, too, in which should be conceived the transition of private agriculture towards socialist forms of production, principally by way of co-operative organisation in the countryside.

While the organisation of exchange of goods resulting from individual production gives rise mainly to problems of a *concrete* character, this is not the case with the organisation of exchange of goods produced by the socialist sector, or circulating within this sector, for important *theoretical* questions arise in this field.

2   *Socialist production and exchange*

Here, indeed, the very nature of the problems has often been obscured by a mistaken view of things which has centred analysis not upon the real production-relations but upon abstract juridical categories like the concept of "uniform state ownership", or the general concept of "social ownership".

If to such abstract categories there already corresponded concrete production-relations such that an ultimate and single social authority, that is, a single and solitary juridical subject, was effectively capable of disposing effectively of all the means of production, deciding how they should be used and what should become of their products, then the latter would have completely ceased to be commodities, all the commodity categories (money, prices, etc.) would have disappeared, and there would be no disadvantage in using the concept of social ownership in order to express the complete domination of society over its products and the correlative disappearance of the commodity categories.

In fact, however, such disappearance of the commodity categories presupposes a degree of socialisation of the process of social reproduction much more advanced than exists today. Only on the basis of this more advanced socialisation of the reproduction process will it be possible for the different forms of social ownership that exist today in all the socialist countries to give place to full and complete ownership by society as a whole, which alone will permit the commodity categories to wither away.

We know that, as regards present-day collective-farm production, Stalin analysed this withering-away of the commodity categories in terms of raising collective-farm property to the level of public property and the gradual replacement of commodity-circulation by "a system of products-exchange, so that the central government, or some other social-economic centre, might control the whole product of social production in the interests of society".[23]

The idea of the capacity of a social-economic centre to handle all the products in the interests of society is here seen as decisive. However, society's evolution towards communism absolutely rules out for the future that this social and economic centre be formed by *the state* (or, *a fortiori*, by an economic subject like Bukharin's "single state trust"). This centre will be society itself, functioning through its central directing economic organ—which does not, of course, mean that this centre would act without "relay stations", where very many decisions would have to be taken. In a situation like this, with integration of the process of social reproduction, and organic co-ordination of its various phases, the commodity categories will thus have vanished—which will not mean, however, that objective economic laws will have vanished, but only the laws of commodity economy.

In any case, at the present time, even in the most advanced socialist countries, the process of social production and expanded reproduction is not yet a process which has been completely integrated and organically co-ordinated, with the different parts of it strictly governing each other, and therefore capable of being fully dominated by society.

The development of the productive forces has indeed brought about an increasing *interdependence* between the various economic activities, the different elementary processes of production. It is precisely this interdependence, this *beginning of integration*, that has made socialist economic planning (the only real planning) necessary, and has given its true content to social ownership of the means of production (without which no economic planning is possible).

However, the process of integration of the various elementary processes of production is only at its beginning. Each of these processes is still developing in a relatively independent way. The appropriation of nature by man is therefore taking place in centres (production-units) which are distinct and separate, and between which complex, manifold and more or less regular relations are established. Each of these production-units constitutes, therefore, a centre for the appropriation of nature which has its specific character, its own reality.

While the interdependence of these centres reflects the social character of production and as already noted, gives real content to the social ownership of the means of production, the separate and distinct character of these centres determines the juridical form of the ownership of the means of production assigned to each of them.

Under these conditions, reasoning which starts only from the general concept of "state ownership", to designate the various higher forms of socialist property, and which seeks to reduce the latter to a uniform reality, comes up against insuperable difficulties, especially when analysing the circulation of commodities within the state socialist sector, socialist trade, the role played by money, and so on.

An example of these difficulties is provided by some of Stalin's analyses in his work, already quoted, on *Economic Problems of Socialism in the USSR*. Here, as we know, Stalin tries to explain the need for commodity relations within Soviet socialist society on the basis of the existence of two forms of socialist property: property of the whole people (that is, of the state) and property of more limited groups (essentially, collective-farm property).[24]

By starting from the juridical sphere and analysing the problem on this basis, Stalin is led to deny the essentially commodity character, at the present time, of exchange between state socialist enterprises, and to render incomprehensible theoretically the nature of the buying and selling carried on between state enterprises, the nature, in this economy of money, prices, business accounting, financial autonomy, etc. These categories are thus deprived of all real social content, and appear as abstract forms or technical procedures which are more or less arbitrary, and not as the expression of those objective economic laws the necessity of which is at the same time stressed by Stalin himself.[25]

Here we see once more what a theoretical cul-de-sac one can get into when, in analysing a social process, one starts not from the concrete production-relations but from a juridical concept treated abstractly, and, *a fortiori*, when one makes this concept the "basis" of the production-relations.

In reality, the method of dialectical materialism requires that the starting-point for analysis be the social relations that constitute the other side of the process whereby man appropriates nature (that is, the production-relations and the actual modes of appropriation). If we approach the matter this way, and take into account that at the present level of development of the productive forces, in even the most advanced socialist society, this appropriation-process is *not yet a single process*, wholly dominated by society, but is still a multiform and fragmented process, divided between a number of centres of activity and a number of elementary appropriation-processes which it is only beginning to be possible to co-ordinate on the scale of society (through socialist planning), then we realise thereby the inevitability of exchange between these centres of activity, and the actual social and economic content of the different forms of socialist property, of socialist commodity exchange, the role played by money inside the socialist sector, and so on.

When an analysis is made on these lines, the different forms of socialist property no longer appear as the reason that can "explain" the existence of commodity relations in the socialist sector (which would amount to explaining economic categories by a certain juridical superstructure). On the contrary, it is the existence of certain production-relations that explains the commodity relations and the juridical form they have to assume.[26]

From that point onward we also realise that in proportion as the development of the productive forces leads to an *effective integration* of the production-processes, an *organic co-ordination* of these processes, which increasingly become a single process, the field of commodity relations shrinks, and the sphere of activity of the commodity categories withers away. When this evolution is complete, the planning and management of the economy can be directed by a single social authority (which does not necessarily mean a single juridical subject).

So long as this stage has not been reached, socialist planning takes charge of the conscious direction of all the increasingly numerous processes of social reproduction which are beginning to be co-ordinated (because objectively they control each other), while socialist economic management takes charge of the conscious direction of the various processes that are the responsibility of the different economic subjects. The latter are thus linked together both by the plan, in so far as they objectively control each other, and by commodity relations, in so far as they are still relatively independent.

In recent years the increasingly complex character of the Soviet economy and the other socialist economies has made it clear that the idea of a rapid withering away of the commodity categories and of socialist commodity exchange was premature, and this is why more attention has had to be given to these categories, to the relative autonomy of each socialist enterprise, and so on. At the same time, the increasing integration of the production-processes *in the technically most highly developed branches* has created new possibilities of managing these branches by electronic means. This enables us to understand better the ways by which it will be possible to develop the *a priori* co-ordination of economic activities, thus bringing about the final disappearance of the commodity categories.[27]

The consequences or implications of the foregoing analysis are many. I shall mention here only those which seem the most important in relation to the planning and organisation of the socialist economy.

(a) In connexion with what has been said, it will be realised that, with the present level of development of the productive forces and integration of the elementary processes of production, the labour expended in production cannot yet be, in its entirety, *directly social* labour.

In other words, though the plan lays down the amount of labour to be expended in the different branches of production, it can still do this only approximately, and it is only after the event that it is possible to know to what extent the labour expended on the different kinds of production was, actually and wholly, *socially necessary labour*.

The existence of commodity categories and money inside the socialist sector means, in fact, that it is still to some extent through the market that the *socialisation of labour* is effected.

The socialist market which serves as controller and medium of the socialisation of labour is already very much modified, in the way it works, by the development of socialist production-relations. Thanks to these socialist relations, the producers are no longer linked together *only* through their products (which, in a pure commodity society, meant the domination of the producers by their products, commodity-fetishism, and so on), they also maintain *direct* links, as *associated* producers. As such, they endeavour to co-ordinate their efforts in advance, and they are able to achieve this co-ordination, to some extent, through the economic plan. The latter lays down the fundamental targets of economic and social development and therefore leaves only a subordinate role to be played by the market. This is possible because, over and beyond the elementary processes of appropriating nature (processes which are still separate from each other, and which therefore continue to oppose the producers to each other to some extent), a beginning has already been made in integrating the process of social production. With the elimination of private ownership of the means of production and the introduction of planning, this social process which is becoming integrated is no longer broken up, no longer fragmented as it is under capitalist conditions, which maintain in being relations of production and of property which have been outgrown by the development of the productive forces.

(b) What has been said means, too, that at the present stage of development of the productive forces, even in the most advanced socialist countries, society is not yet able fully to know the state of *social needs* (including the needs that arise in the sphere of material production itself) and to determine politically in a fairly exact way those needs that will be accorded recognition in the future.

What follows from this is that it is impossible to proceed in a satisfactory, that is, an efficient, way to carry out an allotment of the means of production, or of products in general, *in advance*, and that there is need for *socialist trade* and state commercial organisations. Hence, further, the role of money within the socialist sector itself, the role of the law of value and of a price-system that cannot reflect *only* the social cost of the different products but has *also* to express the ratio between the supply of and demand for these products, and perhaps to ensure a balance between supply and demand, when the plan has not been able to ensure this in advance and to use administrative measures to achieve this equilibrium would compromise the development of the productive forces.

(c) The foregoing also means that each production-unit (that is, each social link within which an elementary production-process is going on) has to be allowed a certain *freedom of manoeuvre*. This must enable each production-unit to cope with whatever has not been foreseen, to make the best use, for the good of society, of the resources under its control, since these resources can be properly used only to serve society's real needs, and the latter are not necessarily those that the plan has sought to foresee. This freedom of manoeuvre must, at the present stage of development of the productive forces, relate both to some elements in the programme of activity of each production-unit and to some of the means to be employed in carrying out this programme.

The practical problem is to lay down limits to this freedom of manoeuvre which will ensure that it *serves* the real aims of the plan (the building of socialism, the harmonious development of the productive forces and the satisfaction of society's needs). This practical problem can be solved correctly only by experience, interpreted by theory.

Here it is important to stress that if adequate freedom of manoeuvre is *not* allowed to each production-unit, and an attempt is made to determine in advance, in a detailed way, the activity that each is to carry on, together with the conditions of this activity, the result, in the present state of things, will be an enormous wastage of labour-power and products.

Often, in fact, in planned economies where the necessary freedom of manoeuvre has not been granted to the production-units, this wastage is limited to some extent through the *exchange* effected by the production units among themselves, formally in violation of the plan but actually, more often than not, in order to achieve the real aims of the plan. This is how the objective necessity of economic laws makes itself felt. What is bad in such cases is that, instead of these laws being used con-sciously, which is the principle of the plan, they are allowed to operate spontaneously.

(d) It is this combination of the retention, for an historical period, of the commodity categories, even inside the socialist sector, with the freedom of manoeuvre that has to be allowed, within certain limits, to each production-unit, that gives meaning to the *accounting autonomy* of each production-unit, the *"business accounting"* that takes place in each production-unit and the possibilities of *self-financing* that each unit should possess. These categories, rules and possibilities are bound up with a particular stage of the productive forces. They reflect the conditions and objective requirements for the working of the socialist economy at its present stage of development. Failure to respect them can only hinder the proper functioning of the economy and put difficulties in the way of planning itself.

IV *The organisation of distribution*

It is a commonplace of Marxist analysis to recognise that the relations and modes of distribution are determined by the actual organisation of production.[28] From this it may be concluded that if commodity relations still survive within the socialist sector, at the present level of development of the productive forces, these commodity relations must also still permeate the production-relations. This is ultimately one of the reasons why, at the present time, in all the socialist economies, this distribution also takes place by way of the commodity categories (money and wages).

This is a phenomenon that Marx did not foresee, as is shown, for instance, by the analysis he makes in connexion with his *Critique of the Gotha Programme*. In the passage referred to, Marx envisages an allotment of products by means of "labour certificates", and not through the mediation of a true currency. If Marx imagined the problem of distribution being solved like this in the first phase of socialist society, this was doubtless because at the time when he wrote, it seemed easier for society to dominate in an integrated way the entire social process of production and reproduction than was really the case, or than is still the case today.

Marx's realism was not at fault, however, when he foresaw that, in the initial phase of socialist society, goods would have to be allotted in accordance with work done and not in accordance with needs. Nevertheless, what then appeared to Marx as a requirement essentially bound up with the "survival" of certain norms of bourgeois right can be understood today, in the light of experience, as a consequence of the retention of commodity categories.

Since, however, the producers in socialist society are not related *merely* through their products, but also maintain direct human relations, as associated producers striving to co-ordinate their efforts in advance, and able to do this better and better thanks to the socialisation of the productive forces, the commodity categories no longer dominate either society or the individuals composing it, and the content of these categories is profoundly modified.

Thus, wages in socialist society are no longer the "price of labour-power" (since the producers are no longer separated from their means of production but, on the contrary, are their collective owners), but the way in which part of the social product is allotted. At the same time, this allotment continues to be carried out through the category "wages" because the labour contributed by each individual is not yet directly social labour.

Nevertheless, society's increasing mastery over its productive forces enables it to distribute an ever larger share of the social product no longer in proportion to work done, but in proportion to needs, and not through money categories but in kind. The gradual disappearance of the norms of bourgeois right from the sphere of distribution has thus already begun, and it will proceed faster and faster with man's increasing domination of the process of social reproduction and the extinction of commodity relations and categories.

While the retention of commodity relations and categories, and of all the superstructures connected with this retention, explains the need to relate the payment made to each individual to the quantity and quality of his labour (what is called the "system of material incentives"), the transformation of these relations and categories, and their gradual extinction, which is already under way, with the correlative superstructural changes, explain the increasingly important role given to behaviour inspired by economically disinterested motives.

The respective places occupied by the different kinds of incentive is thus not to be determined arbitrarily, in the name of some moral vision or some ideal of socialist society—it has to be related to the level of development of the productive forces, among which men themselves are included, along with their knowledge, their education, and, in general, their culture.

January, 1964.

NOTES TO CHAPTER 3

1   In general, the bond that links the level of development of the productive forces with the character of the production-relations and the property-relations corresponding to them is referred to nowadays by the expression: "the economic law that the relations of production must necessarily conform with the character of the productive forces". This expression, which was formulated for the first time by J. V. Stalin, was used by him in his book *Economic Problems of Socialism in the USSR* (page 8: Eng. edn., pp. 9–10).

2   V. I. Lenin, "Economics and Politics under the Dictatorship of the Proletariat", quoted from *L'Alliance de la Classe Ouvrière et de la Paysannerie*, Moscow, 1957, p. 675. (Eng. version from *Collected Works*, Vol. 30, pp. 112–13.)

3   *Ibid.*, pp. 742–3 (Eng. version in *Collected Works*, Vol. 32, pp. 216–17).

4   *Ibid.*, p. 742 (Eng. version, *ibid.*, p. 217).

5   *Ibid.*, p. 743 (Eng. version, *ibid.*, pp. 217–18).

6   We know that Lenin recognised this necessity not only in the case of the backward economy of Russia in 1921 but also in that of the "advanced

capitalist countries" (cf. "Preliminary Draft Theses on the Agrarian Question", a paper prepared for the Second Congress of the Communist International, *ibid.*, pp. 728–30: Eng. version in *Collected Works*, Vol. 31, pp. 158–61).

7 It is worth emphasising here the evolution of Stalin's thinking on this question. In 1938 he wrote, about socialist society:

"Here the relations of production fully correspond to the state of the productive forces, for the social character of the process of production is reinforced by the social ownership of the means of production." (J. V. Stalin, *Matérialisme dialectique et matérialisme historique*, p. 27 of the French edn. of 1956, Editions Sociales: Eng. version from *Short Course of History of the CPSU (B)*, 1938, p. 126.)

In his work *Economic Problems of Socialism in the USSR* (1952), however, Stalin wrote:

"But it would be wrong to rest easy at that and to think that there are no contradictions between our productive forces and the relations of production. There certainly are, and will be, contradictions, seeing that the development of the relations of production lags, and will lag, behind the development of the productive forces. Given a correct policy on the part of the directing bodies, these contradictions cannot grow into antagonisms, and there is no chance of matters coming to a conflict between the relations of production and the productive forces of society. It would be a different matter if we were to conduct a wrong policy. . . . In that case conflict would be inevitable, and our relations of production might become a serious brake on the further development of the productive forces." (*Op. cit.*, pp. 56–7: Eng. edn., p. 75.)

8 Thus, Rosa Luxemburg wrote:

". . . political economy, as a science, has completed its role from the moment when the anarchical economy of capitalism gives place to a planned economy, consciously organised and directed by the working community as a whole. The victory of the working-class of our time and the achievement of socialism thus signify the end of political economy as a science." (*Einführung in die Nationalökonomie, Ausgewählte Reden und Schriften*, Berlin, 1951, Vol. I, p. 491.)

9 Quoted from the German translation of Bukharin's book (*Ökonomik der Transformationsperiode*, Hamburg, 1922, p. 2).

10 See note 2 to Chapter 2 of this book.

11 ". . . the laws of political economy under socialism are objective laws." (Stalin, *op. cit.*, p. 10: Eng. edn., p. 12.)

12 Mao Tse-tung, *De la contradiction au sein du peuple* (On the correct handling of contradictions among the people), Peking, 1957.

13 Thus, Marx wrote:

"In the social production which men carry on they enter into definite relations that are indispensable and independent of their will; these relations of production correspond to a definite stage of development of their material powers of production." (Marx, *Contribution à la critique de l'économie politique* (Contribution to the critique of political economy), trans. Laura Lafargue, Editions Marcel Giard, 1928, pp. 4–5: Eng. version from New York and Calcutta edns., p. 11.)

14   Thus, immediately after the passage quoted above, Marx goes on: "The sum total of these relations of production constitutes the economic structure of society—the real foundation on which rise legal and political superstructures and to which correspond definite forms of social consciousness. . . . At a certain stage of their development, the material forces of production in society come in conflict with the existing relations of production or—what is but a legal expression for the same thing— with the property relations within which they had been at work before." (*Ibid.*, p. 5: Eng. version, *ibid.*, pp. 11–12.)

15   Cf. Oskar Lange, *Economie Politique*, Vol. I ("General problems"), Paris, 1962, p. 18.

16   See, in particular, his *Introduction to the critique of political economy*, pp. 326–30 of the translation by Laura Lafargue of the *Contribution*. See also the draft of Marx's letter to Vera Zasulich in which Marx stresses that it is the need for collective work in the primitive community that underlies the common ownership of the land, and not the other way round (Vol. XXVII of the Russian edn. of the works of Marx and Engels, p. 681).

17   Cf. Lenin, *Oeuvres complètes*, 4th edn., Vol. 27, pp. 300–1.

18   It should not, of course, be concluded from these observations that the ways in which the means of production are allocated, with the corresponding property-forms, must be determined *exclusively*, in the period when socialism is being built, by considerations related to efficiency in the use of the various means of production.

In order to ensure the building of socialism, immediate economic efficiency is clearly not the only thing that has to be kept in mind—far from that, since:

". . . politics must take precedence over economics. To argue otherwise is to forget the ABC of Marxism." (Cf. Lenin, "Once again on the Trade Unions, the current situation, and the mistakes of Trotsky and Bukharin", *Works* (in Russian), 3rd edn., Moscow, 1937, p. 126: Eng. version from *Collected Works*, 4th edn., Vol. 32, p. 83.)

It is because nationalisation, under the dictatorship of the proletariat, means the ending of the control exercised by the capitalists over the means of production thus nationalised, that, in certain circumstances, imperfect utilisation of some means of production by the proletarian state (through lack of sufficient conformity between the juridical authority possessed by this state and its real capacity) may be preferable (or even unavoidable), from the standpoint of the building of socialism, as compared with utilisation of these same means of production by another social class, though this may, at the given moment, be more efficient.

Similarly, a relatively less efficient utilisation (from the immediate standpoint) of the means of production controlled by the Machine and Tractor Stations was regarded as preferable to handing over these means of production to the collective farms, in the early years of collectivisation.

In general, it can occur that the degree of social development of the productive forces of a particular industry, or a particular industrial enterprise, may not "justify" their nationalisation, so far as immediate economic efficiency is concerned, and yet this may be *fully justified* from the standpoint of reinforcing the dictatorship of the proletariat when the latter requires that the economic basis of the power of the hostile classes be broken.

Conversely, when the dictatorship of the proletariat is sufficiently firm not to need to nationalise productive forces which are not yet highly socialised, there may be no justification for carrying out such nationalisations, especially when the proletarian power has sufficient levers at its disposal to compel these means of production to serve the purposes of the building of socialism, while retaining what are still, for the time being, the most efficient conditions for the utilising of these means of production.

19   Lenin *L'Alliance de la classe ouvrière et de la paysannerie*, p. 745 (Eng. version, *Collected Works*, Vol. 32, p. 219).

20   *Ibid.*, p. 746 (Eng. version, *ibid.*, p. 220).

21   *Pékin Information*, 2nd September 1963, pp. 16–17.

22   In his report to the Tenth Congress, Lenin refused to lay down what should be the limits to freedom of exchange. He declared that it was necessary to establish the principle that there must be limits, but beyond that he would not go, saying:

"Try one thing and another, study things in practice, through experience, then share your experience with us, and let us know what you have managed to do. . . ." (*Op. cit.*, p. 749: Eng. version, *Collected Works*, Vol. 32, p. 222.)

23   Stalin, *Economic Problems of Socialism in the USSR*, p. 56 (Eng. edn., p. 75).

24   This explanation is set out at length in Point 2 of the "Remarks on economic questions connected with the November 1951 discussion", the one entitled: "Commodity production under socialism". Stalin's attempt at an explanation which is offered here refers essentially to the attitude of the collective farms. Thus, he writes:

"The collective farms are unwilling to alienate their products except in the form of commodities, in exchange for which they desire to receive the commodities they need. At present the collective farms will not recognise any other economic relation with the town except the commodity relation-exchange through purchase and sale. Because of this, commodity production and trade are as much a necessity with us today as they were thirty years ago, say, when Lenin spoke of the necessity of developing trade to the utmost." (*Op. cit.*, p. 16: Eng. edn., pp. 19–20.)

25   The difficulties resulting from this way of tackling the problem stand out very clearly in the section of *Economic problems* . . . entitled "Reply to Comrade Alexander Ilyich Notkin". In this passage Stalin asks:

"Why . . . do we speak of the value of means of production, their cost of production, their price, etc.?"

and he answers:

"For two reasons. Firstly, this is needed for purposes of calculation and settlement, for determining whether enterprises are paying or running at a loss, for checking and controlling the enterprises. But that is only the formal aspect of the matter. Secondly, it is needed in order, in the interests of our foreign trade, to conduct sales of means of production to foreign countries. Here, in the sphere of foreign trade, but *only in this sphere*, our means of production really are commodities, and really are sold (in the direct meaning of the term)." (*Op. cit.*, pp. 44–5: Eng. edn., pp. 58–9.)

It is clear that the second part of this reply does not in the least explain why "we speak of the value of means of production" *inside* the Soviet Union: nor does the first part provide any explanation, since what we want to know is, precisely, *why* "this is needed for purposes of calculation".

26   This analysis coincides to some extent with that made by O. Sik in his book *Economics, Interests, Politics* (in Czech), Prague, 1962.

27   More and more Soviet economists are coming to the opinion that transition to more detailed planning, based on the use of electronic machines, will be made possible by the increasing integration of activities within the different branches. This integration makes it possible to utilise mathematical methods of management, and electronic machines, *first of all* at the level of the production-units and branches, and only later at the level of the national economy as a whole. This does not, of course, rule out the use of mathematical methods and electronics even now at the level of national economic planning; but for the moment such use can only be very limited, must lead to successive repetition of processes, and cannot serve as the sole or even principal basis for present-day socialist planning. See on this subject the writings of J. Kornai and Th. Liptak, *Two-Level Planning*, a study in programming, prepared at the Calculation Centre of the Hungarian Academy of Sciences (roneoed document in English, Budapest, 1963).

28   "The subdivisions and organisation of distribution are determined by the subdivisions and organisation of production. Distribution is itself a product of production, not only in so far as the material goods are concerned, since only the results of production can be distributed: but also as regards its form, since the definite manner of participation in production determines the particular form of distribution, the form under which participation in distribution takes place." (Marx, *Introduction à une critique de l'économie politique*, p. 325: Eng. edn., p. 284.)

4:   On some concepts of the transitional economy

Nowadays there are a number of countries engaged in building socialism, and this constitutes an experiment on a huge scale that is of concern to a thousand million human beings directly, and indirectly to the whole of mankind.

Life itself has shown how complex are the problems posed by the building of a new world which must not merely put an end to the exploitation of man by man but also ensure man's increasing control over nature and social development. Thus, men are to be gradually freed from the constraints and limitations that have weighed upon them since human society began. In this way what the founders of scientific socialism called the "pre-history of mankind" will come to an end.

In face of the rich experience accumulated by the countries which have taken the road of building socialism and which are today in different stages of an economy of transition towards this new social mode of production, it is essential not to remain satisfied with repeating general formulae that were worked out before there had been any social experience of the transitional economy. This is necessary, too, when confronted with the distortions that Marxism has suffered under the influence of various tendencies in bourgeois thought (positivism, empiricism, and so on) or under that of dogmatism or idealism. The time has come when it is essential to make use of the method of dialectical materialism, in order to try and grasp the theoretical meaning of a number of practices connected with the building of socialism. It is essential, too, to undertake criticism of certain analyses that have been made of real and topical problems, using a method which, though allegedly inspired by dialectical materialism, is, in fact, remote from it.

(For practical reasons, the paper most frequently criticised in this discussion is Ernest Mandel's article called "The commodity categories in the transition period" [*Economica*, Havana, June 1964]. My purpose is not, of course, to dispute particularly with this writer more than with any other, but to try and define some essential theoretical and methodological positions.)

I Abstract and concrete

In his *Introduction to a Critique of Political Economy*, Marx contrasts two methods—one which proceeds from the concrete to the abstract, and the other, proceeding from the abstract to the concrete, which he describes as the only scientifically correct method.

"It seems," he writes, "to be the correct procedure to commence with the real and concrete aspect of conditions as they are. . . . Yet, on closer consideration, it proves to be wrong. . . . The [method which starts from general conceptions and proceeds to concrete ones] is manifestly the scientifically correct method. The concrete is concrete because it is a combination of many objects with different determinations, i.e., a unity of diverse elements. In our thought it therefore appears as a process of synthesis, as a result and not as a starting point. . . . [By the scientific method] the abstract definitions lead to the reproduction of the concrete object in the course of reasoning. . . . The method of advancing from the abstract to the concrete is but a way of thinking by which the concrete is grasped and is reproduced in our mind as a concrete." (*Op. cit.*, Editions Sociales edn., pp. 164–5: Eng. edn., pp. 292–4.)[1]

It is clear that Marx does not advocate that science should stop at the level of the most abstract categories, but that he calls upon scientific activity to think its way back to the concrete by way of synthesis of what he calls "the abstract definitions".[2]

II Marxist analysis and pre-scientific "analysis"

The fundamental and "specific" difference between Marxist analysis and pre-scientific (ideological) analysis is that the former recognises that the field to which it is applied is a "complex whole structured in dominance" (to use the expression of Louis Althusser, in his article on materialist dialectics in *La Pensée*, No. 110, August 1963, reproduced in *Pour Marx*, Edit. Maspero, 1965: Eng. edn., *For Marx*, Allen Lane, 1969) and that it therefore uses concepts which are linked together dialectically, their inter-relation expressing the relations and contradictions of the very field to which it is applied. This means that it does not proceed dogmatically and "abstractly", because the very concepts which it employs teach that the "*principal*" contradiction in a given *concrete* situation, and the principal aspect of any contradiction, may vary from one moment to another.

This is why one must always find the principal contradiction in each situation, and the principal aspect of each of the various contradictions (this is the problem of the "decisive link" or the "leading link"). It is clear that one cannot "grasp" this link "mechanically", that to do it requires a series of mental efforts, which eventually make possible a conceptual structuring that gives as faithful an expression of reality as can be achieved.[3]

Thus, depending on whether we take our examples from the sphere of politics or from that of economics, we shall see that in a given situation the principal contradiction may be between proletariat and bourgeoisie, or between peasantry and large-scale landowning, or between poor peasants and rich peasants, etc., or else, from the economic standpoint, between consumption and investment, industry and agriculture, the iron and steel industry and the chemical industry, etc.

These contradictions are never, of course, presented, so far as historical materialism is concerned, as *absolute* contradictions, but as being underlain by the unity of the contradiction. Also of course, these contradictions are based on those between the productive forces and the relations of production, but the latter do not exhaust the content of the contradictions: they are a specific and fundamental (which does not mean principal) degree of this reality, and possess driving power in relation to the other degrees, while the latter, in turn, react upon this fundamental contradiction (which means, for example, that contradictions in the superstructure may hinder or even block the development of the productive forces). The whole thus operates like a complex structured whole, always marked at any given moment by a principal contradiction.

These contradictions merge, at a certain moment, in a certain way, and this amalgamation gives rise to a new situation which is *qualitatively different from the preceding one.* In this new situation the principal contradiction is not the same as it was in the previous situation, and, in general, the hierarchy of contradictions and of their aspects has been profoundly modified. Such qualitative changes mean, when they take place in the socio-economic field, either that a new mode of production has been entered upon, or else a new stage of a given mode of production, or a new point has been reached in this stage. To say that the principal contradiction has been modified is also to say that the decisive link by which the situation can again be modified is different as compared with the previous situation.

Thus, depending on the nature of the principal contradiction and the principal aspect of the contradictions, the *line of practical action* will be different. By taking examples from the field of politics and economics we shall see that, depending on the situation, the principal link which has to be grasped in order to change this situation is constituted now by the grouping of the revolutionary forces around the proletariat, the dictatorship of the proletariat allied with the peasantry over the other social classes, or allied with the poor peasantry only, now by the priority of industry over agriculture taken as basis of development, with industry as the driving force, the relatively extensive use of market forces (N.E.P.) or rapid collectivisation, centralised planning or the use of economic levers, etc.

III The Specificity of Marxist dialectics

However, contradictions must not be studied in themselves (in the Hegelian manner); they need to be considered as forming part of "the very essence of things", as Lenin puts it.

This is where the specificity of the contradiction lies, in Marxist dialectics. It is this specificity that brings it about that, in dialectical materialism, every contradiction reflects the existence of a complex process and consti-tutes *one contradiction amid a series of others.* This is also why, in the totality of contradictions that makes up a structured whole, there is always one contradiction which is the principal one. As Mao Tse-tung says:

"In the process of development of a complex thing, many contradic-tions exist; among these, one is necessarily the principal contradiction. . . ." (Mao Tse-tung, *On contradictions,* p. 55: Eng. version from *Selected Works,* Vol. II, p. 35.)

From this there also follows the necessary distinction between the principal aspect and the secondary aspect of the contradiction, which is merely the reflexion "within each contradiction of the complexity of the process, that is, the existence within it of a plurality of contradictions, one of which is dominant . . ." (cf. Louis Althusser, *La Pensée,* August 1963, "Sur la dialectique matérialiste", p. 27).

Materialist dialectics is thus something very different from the simplifying abstraction, remote from the historical, the complex and the concrete, which Ernest Mandel offers us as "Marxist dialectics".[4] This kind of abstraction is not even at the level of idealist dialectics in its most finished form (the Hegelian form), but it starts, like idealist dialectics, from the basic presupposition of a simple contradictory unity which develops within itself by virtue of the negative element in it, so that the "concrete" totality that results from this development always brings us back to the original simplicity. It is especially important to stress that the desire to consider only "simple" categories, to refuse theory access to the concrete, leads precisely to the errors that it is sought to avoid.

Take, for example, the problem posed by the fact that the proletarian revolution has been victorious in a number of countries with relatively underdeveloped productive forces. Confronted with this situation, an attitude which does not correspond to that of dialectical materialism can lead, and does in fact lead, to two sorts of "explanation", neither of which has anything in common with Marxism, and which, furthermore, though mutually exclusive, are both sometimes accepted by those who decline to recognise the specificity of Marxist dialectics:

(a) The first "explanation" leads to declaring that, though the produc-tive forces of the under-developed countries were in themselves too weak to provide the source of the revolutionary movement, it was nevertheless the contradiction between productive forces and production-relations that was the source of the revolution that occurred in these countries, because what counts is not the "local" or "national" level of the productive forces but the world contradiction between productive forces and production-relations.

This way of allegedly "solving" the problem brings in, first of all, a purely idealistic relationship between what is internal and what is external, and, in addition, it reveals that those who offer this "explanation" have not understood that the contradiction between the level of development of the productive forces and the production-relations, although it is the fundamental contradiction, is *only one of the contradictions* in the complex situation of the country where the revolution has occurred, and is not necessarily, and even, *generally speaking, does not constitute the principal contradiction.* The latter may be found at quite a different level. It was constituted, for example, by the revolt of the Russian peasant soldiers against continuing the imperialist war. This war itself, of course, resulted from the contradiction, on the world scale, between the level of development of the productive forces and the production-relations; but this contradiction had attained its maximum sharpness only in the most highly developed countries.

This contradiction existed, too, though to a lesser extent, in the countries where the revolution occurred, and this was what made it possible for the revolution to assume a socialist character. However, the revolution took place in these countries not because the contradiction between productive forces and production-relations had reached maximum sharpness there, but because there was a principal contradiction (not identical in each country) which had become very acute, and because the revolutionaries of these countries were able to lay hold of this contradiction so as to effect a radical transformation. This transformation assumed a socialist character in so far as these revolutionaries did not confine themselves to acting upon the principal contradiction (guiding the masses in their struggles for peace, or for freedom, or for land) but undertook the task of resolving the fundamental contradiction of our age.

(b) The other "explanation" of the development of the revolution in countries where the productive forces have not yet reached a high level of development leads (and this is the idealist alternative) to a denial of any role to this contradiction between productive forces and production-relations, and explaining the revolutionary process by revolutionary consciousness alone, by the example set by the socialist countries, and so on.

We thus see how refusal to appreciate the complex and concrete character of Marxist analysis leads either to idealistic positions or to mechanistic ones. It is noteworthy that all the conceptions which depart from Marxism in this way finally end up in eclecticism.

Actually, if, as Mandel thinks, Marxism were incapable of analysing "real capitalism as it has developed historically . . . as it has developed concretely . . ." but only a "pure and abstract capitalism. . . ." (*art. cit.*, pp. 9–10), it would provide us merely with a "pure" and "simple" theory which would therefore be remote from concrete conditions, which are particular, historical, contingent and accidental. These conditions, while they are those of practice, would thus elude the grasp of theory. Henceforth, as the well-known expression has it, "the necessary would make itself felt through the accidental", and the latter would therefore have either to be ignored or else made the object only of short-sighted practice, of empiricism.

A conception like this can obviously provide no guidance for effective practice, since, if it is to be effective, theory must be capable of grasping the allegedly "accidental", that is, of conceiving reality as a complex, structured whole, involving a totality of contradictions which are never congealed once for all in an immutable hierarchy. This is what Lenin expresses when he says: "Concrete analysis of the concrete situation is the soul of Marxism." This is so because Marxism is not an "abstract" theory but a theory which leads to the concrete, and which therefore can be a guide for practice. Thanks to this, Marxist practice in the economic and social spheres can operate upon all the contradictions. It is able to do this because it enables us to grasp the links that exist between all the contradictions, and to ascertain what, at any given moment, is the *principal contradiction*, which is such because by acting upon it one can eventually act upon all the contradictions.

For Marxist analysis there is not, on the one hand, an abstract model functioning in the realm of ideas, and, on the other, a reality which comes more or less close to this model, and includes, besides the categories of the "model", some "accidental conditions", that is, some purely "external" factors. Marxism does not lead to such a superficial view of things. It considers every reality as a structured whole which has to be analysed as such, with its principal and secondary contradictions.

Lenin provides a precise *theoretical* explanation of the October Revolution by taking account of the totality of the conditions that existed at the time of that revolution, that is, the real, historical, concrete conditions. Only thus can one understand why the socialist revolution, dictated fundamentally by the contradiction between productive forces and production-relations, broke out, not in the countries where this contradiction had been brought to its maximum acuteness, but in those where a number of historical and concrete "conditions" came together. An explanation which resorts to taking account of these "conditions" can avoid eclecticism and empiricism only if these conditions are theoretically reintegrated in the overall conception of a structured complex whole. More precisely, these conditions have to be understood as they are, that is, as the conditions of existence of a complex whole, taken in its totality.

If, in the name of the "purity" and "simplicity" of theory, one leaves the conditions out of account, then one is left operating outside reality, which is always complex, historical, concrete and structured, and always includes principal and secondary contradictions, and contradictions whose "order of importance" changes with changing circumstances.

So long as one remains at this level of ideological abstraction, one can know only a "pure" capitalism, on the one hand, and a "pure" socialism on the other. On the political plane this can lead either to "ultra-leftism" (for instance, with the slogan, mechanically applied in all circumstances, of "class against class") or to opportunism, waiting indefinitely for real capitalism to become sufficiently "pure" for the coming of "pure" socialism to be inevitable.[5]

When what is on the agenda is building socialism, the "purest" conception of socialism is of only limited value, because history is never "pure", nor is it "straight and even as the Nevsky Prospekt" (which means, among other things, that the features which will characterise developed socialist society are not only not all necessarily to be observed in the society of transition, but that it may even happen that, during certain stages of the development of this transitional society, some features that one may expect to be possessed by the socialist society of the future will temporarily become blurred, and will not at all necessarily become increasingly clear-cut).

What matters, therefore, if theory is to be capable of throwing light on the way forward for the transitional society or the conditions for the building of socialism, is analysis of the concrete conditions of this transitional society or of this building of socialism, in a particular country. This analysis must obviously deal with the significant wholeness of the situation. Here again it is a question of analysing the totality of the contradictions, bringing out the principal contradiction and the secondary contradictions, and the principal and secondary aspects of the contradictions. Only thus can the specific character of a situation be brought out, with the specific character of the contradictions that are characteristic of it.

The specific character of the contradictions (in a given country at a given time) is only the reflexion of the conditions of existence of this country (the level of development of its productive forces, its culture, its traditions, its size, the level of consciousness existing at a particular moment) on the contradictions in general, and the principal contradiction in particular. This is precisely why socialism is not being built under the same conditions in Cuba, in the USSR, in China, and so on. Whoever refuses to take account *theoretically* of these "specificities" is not a Marxist. That is where one falls into empiricism and eclecticism, because one wants to *keep theory outside of history.*

Except from the point of view of ideology, practice and theory are never outside of history. What they have to deal with, in reality and in thought, is never a "pure" mode of production but always an *historically given social formation*, with all its specific contradictions, its principal and secondary contradictions, and so on. Marxism is the only theory that enables us to deal practically and theoretically with a reality like this (which is what Mandel refuses to do, not only theoretically but also practically).

With a living approach like this, of course, the contradictions and categories are no longer univocal; they do not have one fixed role and meaning, given once for all. At the same time, they are not "equivocal", for, while they are no longer determined once for all in their role and essence, "they show themselves to be determined by the structured complexity" which assigns them their role (cf. Louis Althusser, *art. cit.*, p. 37).

The problem of dialectical materialist analysis is precisely that of revealing why and how it is that successively dominant contradictions do not follow each other in an arbitrary way: and the problem of Marxist practice is to grasp what at each moment is the principal contradiction, and how by acting upon it (that is, by acting on what Lenin called the "decisive link") one can pass from a situation dominated by one contradiction to a situation dominated by another.

The generality from which the scientific approach starts is not itself the outcome of an abstracting process, but of complex social processes taking place at the level of technique and ideology. It is upon these abstractions that science works in order, gradually, to go forward to fresh abstractions, enriched by increasingly "concrete" *knowledge,* and thus forging scientific concepts (which will eventually become the negation of the ideological and technical concepts with which investigation began).

It is this process of enrichment (of progress towards the concrete) that is the essence of scientific thought and of the dialectical materialist approach. One must avoid substituting for this scientific and dialectical approach the simplifying procedures of deduction, that is, of mere formal logic.[6]

IV Dialectical synthesis and the factor of practice

Ernest Mandel would appear to be right when he says: "One must avoid *confusing* complex reality with its simplified reproduction in theoretical thought; that is, one must not close one's eyes to all the complexities of reality, always infinitely richer than theory, which by its very nature tends to simplify things."[7] This statement is true, however, only in relation to the most impoverished forms of theoretical thinking. Also, Mandel is at fault in not practising the precept he states, for he tries to deal with the complex reality of the transitional society by means of the simplest and most abstract economic categories of "pure" and fully developed socialist society.

What Mandel actually tries to do is to *deduce,* from the most abstract categories relating to socialist society, the more concrete economic categories that characterise this society, or the transitional societies, together with the practical laws that govern the working of these societies. By so doing, he fails to follow the road that leads from the most general abstractions to the concrete in thought. In order to traverse this road one needs to go outside the simple relationships of formal logic (deduction and reduction), and use the methods of dialectical synthesis.

It is in fact impossible to re-create the concrete by merely adding abstractions together. It has to be reproduced by means of dialectics, which is, indeed, the way in which one gains access to reality. And in order to reach reality in this way, one has to proceed by mediation, *by reconstituting in concepts the organic totality of a socio-economic formation,* something that can only be done by taking account of *all the factors* that make up this totality, including, of course, the factors of practice, *beginning with economic practice itself*: and this is true, also, when one is trying to construct the theory of socialist economy.[8]

In order to work out a "theory of socialist economy", Mandel does not hesitate, like Bukharin forty years earlier,[9] to operate with the most meagre of concepts, the only ones that could be worked out before there had been any *social practice* in the building of socialism. At the same time, he rejects as "impure", and unworthy of being accorded any theoretical value, the concepts which it has been possible to work out since then, as a result of social practice in the building of socialism.[10]

As often happens, the positivist approach, that is, the mechanical contrasting of a dead "reality" with an equally dead abstraction, becomes transformed into a kind of idealism which renounces all approach to reality through practice.

This attitude is very similar to that adopted by those opponents of Marx who, like Böhm-Bawerk and others, have tried to set Book I of *Capital* (the theory of value and the laws of price-formation in simple commodity economy) against Book III (the theory of price-formation in capitalist society), by saying that Marx denied in Book III what he had asserted in Book I. These opponents of Marx accused him of sliding down from the plane of abstract and theoretical analysis in Book I to the "practical" conceptions of Book III. According to them, all that appears in Book III is a pragmatic description of the actual practice of capitalists. This view ignores what is essential, namely, that Marx's scientific approach makes it possible to express the *theoretical foundations* of this *practice* (which is that of capitalism).

In the same way, the political economy of socialism cannot restrict itself (unless it is to remain sterile) to repeating the most general abstractions, or trying to deduce from these the whole of the political economy of socialism. It has to explain theoretically (that is, by bringing out its theoretical meaning) the practice of the countries which are actually building socialism[11] or taking their first steps along the road of transition to socialism.

Similarly, too, the theory of the proletarian revolution cannot restrict itself, after nearly a century of practice (from the Paris Commune to the Cuban revolution) to the mere general categories that are to be found in the writings of Marx and Engels previous to the Commune. This theory must be enriched by the experience of the Soviet revolution, that is, the practice of Leninism, and the practice of the other revolutions that have taken place; otherwise it is incapable of becoming a theory which is as rich as it needs to be, because incorporating all the lessons of experience.

Finally, refusal to take account of social practice in order to construct a living theory leads to dogmatism on the plane of thought and, in a way that seems paradoxical but is in fact strictly logical, to practicalism on the plane of action, that is, to the absence of any revolutionary theory—without which, as Lenin often emphasised, there can be no revolutionary action.

In the field of the building of socialism, a conception like this leads, *inter alia*, to treating as theoretically well-founded those practices which *formally* seem to express the most abstract categories.

Moreover, this methodological attitude gives rise to the illusion that it is possible to choose, among "possible" modes of practice (as one imagines these laid out for one's choice, in the field of abstractions), those that seem "morally" the best.

Unless enriched through social practice and experience (which practice also includes, of course, theoretical practice), abstract concepts seem to open on to a multitude of "possible" lines of action, so that practicalism links up with subjectivism and voluntarism.

V Theory and the Contradictions of Practice

For a Marxist, there can be no question of seeking to impoverish theory merely in order to make it more "intelligible". On the contrary, the problem is to enrich theory so as to make it an increasingly efficient guide to practice.

Marx's method, as we know, consists in starting from social practice and its results. In the economic field, Marx begins with the simplest, historically given relationships. Since every relationship has two aspects, which are both related and contradictory, Marx studies the contradictions within it and the way in which these have been actually resolved in social practice. Then he studies this resolution and the development of the relationships it implies, and thus the contradictions involved in these relationships, and so on. This method is that of dialectical materialism applied to social and historical reality. It therefore requires that analysis be made of the contradictions that have been bequeathed by history and have developed in the course of practice.

The political economy of socialism, or, more generally, the political economy of the societies which are building socialism, can be worked out only in this way, by seeking the contradictions that are characteristic of this economy or these societies, as of all living reality, and analysing how practice resolves these contradictions. When doing this, of course, one has to be careful not to put on the same plane the principal contradictions and the secondary ones, or forget that the fundamental contradiction of *a mode of production* must be situated in the sphere of production itself. Marx founded political economy as a science precisely by basing his analysis on the sphere of production: he showed that the phenomena which take place in the sphere of distribution are the corollary of those more fundamental phenomena that develop in the sphere of production.

The fundamental contradiction of the transition period (that is, of a period in which socialism has not yet been built because the level of development of the productive forces is not yet high enough) is that which contrasts an advanced form of appropriation (made necessary by the development of the productive forces on the world scale) with the low level of these productive forces locally.

Consequently, the essential problem in building socialism—in the economic sphere—is to overcome this contradiction by raising the local productive forces as quickly as possible to the level that corresponds to that of the forms of appropriation, while safeguarding these forms of appropriation from the dangers of degeneration which threaten them so long as they have not been filled by sufficiently developed productive forces. The struggle against the possible degeneration of the advanced forms of appropriation implies, of course, struggle against bourgeois ideology and the penetration of bourgeois standards of behaviour.[12] It also implies correct handling of the fundamental contradiction, that is, the development of the indispensable intermediate forms[13] between the social forms of appropriation and the not yet complete domination by society of all the aspects of production.[14]

"Ché" Guevara correctly criticises[15]—but mistakenly ascribes to me— a "mechanistic" conception of the law of conformity between the level of development of the productive forces and the character of the production-relations.

If, in Cuba as previously in China or in the Soviet Union, the socialist revolution has been victorious, this is not because the contradiction between the level of development of the productive forces and the character of the production-relations had reached maximum acuteness there, but because the *specific conditions* in which this contradiction developed made possible the victory of the workers over the forces of the possessing classes and of imperialism. Nevertheless, this specific situation and this victory do not alter the fact that in the countries where the proletarian revolution has been victorious up to now, the relatively low level of development of the productive forces makes a more or less prolonged *transition period* essential —a period marked precisely by the circumstance that the new property-relations and production-relations are "in advance" of the local level of development of the productive forces.

This is one of the specific problems of the building of socialism in the economically under-developed countries. The existence of this problem necessarily dooms to failure the attempts made by Mandel and others to deduce, from the general remarks made by Marx and Engels regarding the way a developed society works (one in which the level of development of the productive forces is in conformity with the new property-relations), the conditions in which the *transitional society* operates.[16]

The principal contradiction of a society, however, must not be confused with the fundamental contradiction of a mode of production, that is, with the contradiction between the production-relations and the level of development of the productive forces. The principal contradiction may be situated, at a particular moment (and this may even be frequently the case), in the superstructure—usually the political superstructure, but also in the ideological, religious, etc., superstructure. Only an understanding of the complex unity to which this principal contradiction belongs can enable one to drive it to the limit and thus explode the other contradictions as well (including the fundamental ones).

If the principal contradiction is not driven to the limit then, as a rule, only secondary restructurings will take place. These will bring about a change in the principal aspect of the principal contradiction (e.g., a change of regime or of political status), but not a change in the mode of production, or, more precisely, in the class nature of the state.

For example, the contradiction between national aspirations and imperialist repression constitutes the principal contradiction during the struggle of a colonial country for political independence. All the other contradictions concentrate (merge) in this principal contradiction. A Marxist party which does not grasp this fact (theoretically and practically) is incapable not merely of understanding the situation but also, and *ipso facto*, of directing the way it will develop. It is necessary also to grasp what the principal aspect of this contradiction is (e.g., which is the class that, at a given moment, is in the vanguard of this struggle). On this condition only is it possible to foresee how victory in this struggle (the merging process, the transition from contradiction to identity), accession to independence, will sharply change the status and the very structure of the contradictions, making another contradiction (e.g., peasants versus landowners, or working class versus bourgeoisie) the new principal contradiction that has to be grasped in order to lead the struggle (by keeping or winning leadership). With the capture of power, a new structure of contradictions emerges, and so on.

What, of course, follows from this is that, after a revolutionary transformation, the elements in the situation (a new situation) on which one has to act in order to go forward are no longer the same as before, and it is no longer the same attitudes, slogans and forms of consciousness that are decisive. It is from this that, in the absence of a *high degree of theoretical consciousness*, the difficulties of transition from the armed struggle to the stage of economic construction arise. Hence also the great dangers involved in appealing, in the construction phase, to the same qualities or attitudes as in previous phases. Thus, while in the phase of struggle for power what was characteristic of the revolutionary consciousness was the spirit of sacrifice and discipline, capacity for military organisation, and so on, other subjective elements will usually be decisive in the construction phase: sense of economic analysis, ability to grasp new social contradictions, spirit of technical organisation, and so on.

Accordingly, declarations about the importance in the struggle for socialism of "revolutionary consciousness" *in general* are void of any precise content (they are neither true nor false). All that can be decisive is a particular concrete manifestation of this "consciousness".

VI Science and ideology

In discussions about the role allegedly played by "consciousness", in the most general sense, as a quasi-autonomous force in the struggle for socialism, or in the building of socialism, reference is often made to the theses of the *Economic Manuscripts* of "the young Marx". This is done because of the "humanistic" character of these theses and the central position assigned in them to "man". Frequently quoted is the following passage from the *Economic and Philosophical Manuscripts of 1844*, in which Feuerbach's equation, "humanism means naturalism" is accepted:

"Communism as the *positive* abolition of private property, of human *self-alienation*, and thus the real *appropriation* of *human* nature through and for man. It is, therefore, the return of man himself as a *social*, i.e., really human, being, a complete and conscious return which assimilates all the wealth of previous development. Communism as a fully developed naturalism is humanism and as a fully developed humanism is naturalism. It is the *definitive* resolution of the antagonism between man and nature, and between man and man. It is the true solution of the conflict between existence and essence, between objectification and self-affirmation, between freedom and necessity, between individual and species. It is the solution of the riddle of history, and knows itself to be this solution."[17]

When this quotation is used, an essential fact is overlooked, namely, that later on, as Louis Althusser has quite rightly pointed out: "Marx based his entire conception of political economy on criticism of this presupposition (*homo oeconomicus*, and his legal or moral abstract form, 'the philosophers' Man') . . ." ("Contradiction and overdetermination", in *Pour Marx*, p. 109).

The fact that Marx, in 1844, still accepted the equation he had borrowed from Feuerbach shows the line that separates the consistent materialist positions taken up by Marx in his later writings from the humanistic positions he was still defending in the *Economic and Political Manuscripts*. It was in the latter, moreover, that Marx expressed himself thus regarding materialism:

"We see here how consistent naturalism, or humanism, is distinguished from both idealism and materialism, and at the same time constitutes their unifying truth."[18]

As E. Bottigelli rightly observes, at that time materialism was "still, for Marx, a point of view that had to be transcended in the name of a humanism of which, it must be said, he was never again to speak in the terms by which he defined it in the *Manuscripts*". Bottigelli adds also this sound observation: "In 1844, Marx's thought was still a long way from having reached its definitive form. The *Manuscripts* are evidences of the clarification-process of thinking that, on many points, is still seeking its way, rather than the expression of finished thought."[19]

Actually, the *Economic and Philosophical Manuscripts* contain, not yet entirely eliminated, Feuerbach's idea of an essence of humanity, regarded as a fact, or even a "truth" of humanity. It is therefore not accidental that these *Manuscripts* have given rise to controversies and polemics, and have encouraged some interpreters to find proof in them that Marx's thinking, at least in the *Manuscripts*, was fundamentally ethical.[20]

We know how Engels, in a letter to Lafargue dated 11th August 1884, refuted the view of those who wanted to make Marxism a system of ethics:

"Marx would protest against the economic 'political and social ideal'" which you attribute to him. When one is a 'man of science' one does not have an ideal; one works out scientific results, and when one is a party man to boot, one fights to put them into practice. But when one has an ideal, one cannot be a man of science, for one starts out with preconceptions."[21]

However, even if in some of the passages in the 1844 manuscripts Marx's positions seem still to be very close to Feuerbach's, Marx realised even this early that human nature cannot exist before history and cannot be defined once for all time. It was in this work that Marx wrote: "History is the true natural history of man."[22]

Man as producer, man producing himself, and not man conscious of himself, is Marx's point of departure. Accordingly, man's truth is in his becoming. Despite certain appearances, we no longer have here a purely intellectual approach, and are far beyond Hegel's "self-consciousness".

In short, referring to the humanism and the role of consciousness that we find in the terms used in the 1844 manuscripts means referring to Marx's thought as it was before Marx himself had taken his stand definitively on the platform of dialectical materialism. In these writings the concept of production-relations does not yet appear, nor that of the class struggle as the driving force of history.

Another point that must not be forgotten is that in the *Manuscripts* the concept of "alienation" (used in the context of the quotation previously given) is still one of the fundamental concepts. It was to lose this status later, for Marx would replace it by the concept of "praxis". It is doubtless not accidental that those who like to refer to the *Manuscripts* and the allegedly ethical positions taken up by Marx do not accord to praxis the place that it was to occupy later in the work of the author of *Capital*.

The foregoing reflexions on the significance of the passage quoted may seem pointlessly lengthy. However, I do not think so. This passage, and, more generally, the *Economic and Philosophical Manuscripts of 1844*, are not only the reference-point of a number of writers who want to be Marxist without being Leninist, but also a sort of line of demarcation within Marx's own work. It is certainly in this passage that Marx carried farthest his *philosophical* analysis, giving this word, as Louis Althusser rightly says, "the very meaning on which Marx was later to pass pitiless judgment".[23]

If the 1844 manuscripts represent the "unbounded theoretical triumph" of philosophy and the "radical dominance" of philosophy over economics, this was because at that time Marx still accepted bourgeois political economy at face value, that is, without questioning the content of its concepts and their systematic relationship.[24] Here everything is still expounded on the plane of "the abstraction of the economy",[25] which, as Althusser observes, gives authority also to the other "abstraction", that of philosophy.[26]

It is important to recognise these facts. They enable us to understand better the relations linking some of the references made to the 1844 manuscripts with certain intellectual and ideological approaches and attitudes of the present day. Thus, when one reads the *Manuscripts* it may seem that philosophy, i.e., "consciousness", can resolve the contradiction in political economy by thinking it out. Again, when one reads the *Manuscripts* it may seem that, while remaining faithful to Marx's spirit, one can draw conclusions from the "dialectics of concepts" alone, without needing to engage in analysing *praxis* or undertaking a dialectical synthesis on the basis of this analysis and the notions first worked out on this plane.

An approach operating on the terrain of the "dialectics of concepts" leads to the claim, for instance, that "the *essence* of socialism is planning", or that "the *essence* of planning is the budgetary system" which logically must lead (and has not failed to lead some, including Ernest Mandel) to the conclusion that it should be possible to work out in advance a political economy and even a philosophy and a morality for socialist society, in the belief that one can draw this philosophy, political economy and morality from concepts, instead of building them in a scientific way on the basis of social *praxis*.

It will be seen how decisive it is to appreciate the radical line of demarcation that separates the Marx of the *Manuscripts of 1844* from the Marx of *Capital*.

Depending on whether or not one recognises this line, one conceives of Marxism as a new philosophy, or a new morality, or one conceives it as a dialectical approach directed towards the *concrete* and towards *action*, and constantly enriching itself at the source of *social practice* (which includes political, economic and theoretical practice, i.e., scientific practice).

By taking the former standpoint one is led to suppose it possible to deduce from a few "primary truths", or a few "essences", a whole set of rules of behaviour, including a "morality", a system of economic organisation superior to any other, an economic policy which is rigid and valid for all circumstances, and so on. These are the typical positions of dogmatism.

If, however, one recognises that Marxism is not a philosophy but above all a theory of the development of reality, society, mankind, etc., one arrives at a quite different way of looking at the relations between theory and practice, consciousness and the world, idea and reality. Thenceforth, it is no longer a matter of measuring reality by an idea. The categories that Marxism itself worked out, and is still working out, are seen as the outcome of a process, an historical development, in which, to be sure, consciousness plays the final role, but a development which is above all that of social practice (and not of intellectual speculation).

A theory like this does not merely offer a way of interpreting the world, it opens the road to the domination of reality by practice. It opens the road to revolutionary transformation of the world, and makes it possible *to subject this new world to a new analysis just as living and revolutionary as that to which it subjected the old world.*

If consciousness is here only one of the factors in revolutionary transformations, this is because these are not only or even mainly transformations of consciousness, but transformations of social, political and economic reality. A certain moment of these transformations passes, of course, through people becoming aware of reality, whether by way of class consciousness or of theoretical consciousness, but the condition for the role played by consciousness to be *decisive* (and it is decisive) is that this role must *enter into the movement of objective forces*, since only in this way can it change the latter.

What living Marxism sets in movement are objective forces, economic and social forces, masses and organisations. What it overturns are class relations, and what it directs, after the taking of power, is the development of the productive forces. If that is what Marxism is, and the work of Marx and Lenin (and I speak, of course, not merely of their writings but of their whole historical achievement) proves that it is, then it is clearly something quite different from a philosophy of consciousness and essence.

(Published in *La Pensée*, No. 125, February 1966, pp. 3–20.)

NOTES TO CHAPTER 4

1   It may be useful to recall here what Hegel wrote in his *Logic*, and Lenin's comments on this. Hegel wrote:

" 'It is only a notion', is a thing commonly said; and not only the Idea, but sensuous, spatial and temporal palpable existence is opposed to the Notion, as something which is more excellent than it. And the abstract is counted of less worth than the concrete, because from the former so much of that kind of material has been omitted. To those who hold this, the process of abstraction means that for our subjective needs one or another characteristic is taken out of the concrete in such a manner that, while so many other properties and modifications of the object are omitted, these lose nothing in value and dignity. They are the real and are reckoned as counting in full, only they are left on the other side; and it is only the incapacity of understanding to absorb such riches that obliges it to rest content with meagre abstraction." (Vol. V, Part 2, "The subjective logic of the doctrine of the concept [or notion] in general": Eng. version from Hegel's *Science of Logic*, trans. Johnston and Struthers, London, 1929, Vol. II, pp. 221–2.)

In the preceding passage Hegel critically sums up the ideas of Kant, and Lenin notes on this subject:

"Essentially, Hegel is completely right as opposed to Kant. Thought proceeding from the concrete to the abstract—provided it is correct [N.B.] (and Kant, like all philosophers, speaks of correct thought)—does not get away *from* the truth but comes closer to it." (Lenin, *Cahiers philosophiques*, Editions Sociales, 1955, p. 142: Eng. version from *Collected Works*, Vol. 38, p. 171.)

2   It is thus wrong to claim, as Mandel does in the article quoted, that

categories never enable us completely to grasp reality. Actually this is true only of the most abstract categories, whereas a scientific method, that of dialectical materialism, must aim at working out categories which are more and more concrete, more and more capable of reproducing reality and thus of grasping it completely, so as to make it possible to change reality consciously.

We know that Lenin, in his work on "Left-wing Communism", showed that the root of the mistaken position of the "Left" Communists was, precisely, their inability to get beyond the level of the most abstract categories.

3   It will be observed that the margin existing here between conceptual structuring and real structuring is secondary as compared with the "abstract models" to which Mandel refers, for this margin can always be narrowed by means of an effort of conceptual structuring. It is only because this effort is not worth while, in terms of the extra effectiveness it could bring, that it is not undertaken.

4   Mandel's underestimation of the real and concrete, and of its complexity is shown first and foremost by his assertion that "science" and "dialectics" develop at the level of "simple" categories. This is indeed what happens so long as one remains at the level of *ideological* abstractions. *Scientific* categories, however, are never simple, but are always involved in a concrete living and complex whole.

5   This is the same ultra-leftism that is found in the formula criticised by Marx in his *Critique of the Gotha Programme*:

"The emancipation of labour must be the work of the working class, relatively to which all other classes are only one reactionary mass." (*Op. cit.*, Editions Sociales, p. 26: Eng. edn., p. 23.)

Marx set against this one-sided formula the phrase of the *Communist Manifesto*:

"Of all the classes that stand face to face with the bourgeoisie today, the proletariat alone is a really revolutionary class. The other classes decay and finally disappear in the face of modern industry; the proletariat is its special and essential product."

In his *Critique of the Gotha Programme* Marx makes an admirable distinction between the contradictions, when he shows us that the bourgeoisie can be regarded as a revolutionary class in relation to the feudalists and the middle classes (and so, he adds, feudalists and middle classes do not form a single "reactionary mass" along with the bourgeoisie). He shows too, as the *Manifesto* puts it that the middle classes are revolutionary "in view of their impending transfer into the proletariat". We thus have before us the principal contradiction, between proletariat and bourgeoisie, and the secondary contradiction, between middle classes and bourgeoisie.

6   Deduction, of course, has its role to play too in scientific thought, but it is a subordinate role, that of exploring a field which has already been defined and delimited.

7   *Ibid.*, p. 10.

8   Marx showed us, in *Capital,* how to proceed from internal relationships to the surface of things, from the constituent elements to the constituted reality, from the rate of surplus-value to the average rate of profit (which, from a superficial standpoint, looks like the non-dialectical negation of the rate of surplus-value).

9   Cf. Bukharin, *The Economy of the Transition Period.*

10   There is no question, of course, of accepting uncritically the many concepts which, here too, have arisen from non-scientific practice, both technical and social, and which may be ideological in content. The point is to start from these concepts, and the actual practice that they strive to express, in order to work out, using the method of dialectical materialism, new *scientific* concepts. Every explanation is not a justification: sliding from the one into the other is what happens when one falls into ideology, in contrast to science. Scientific analysis also requires that the contradictions of this practice be revealed.

11   In an article written in 1964 (*Cuba Socialista,* June 1964, p. 21), "Ché" Guevara blames me for concluding "pragmatically" from the fact that the commodity categories (and the corresponding juridical categories) *exist* in the socialist countries, that they are *necessary,* and starting from this basis, going forward analytically to a point where "theory and practice come into conflict". He adds that I am forgetting here that "the transition period is young, historically", and that inevitable mistakes of appreciation may have been made. He writes further: "Why suppose that what 'is' during the transition period necessarily 'has to be'? Why claim that the blows dealt by reality to certain bold measures are merely the result of boldness, and not also, or entirely, of technical mistakes in administration?"

The question is well put. There can indeed by no question of claiming that "everything that is real is rational" or necessary. However, there can be no question, either, of according privileged status, to the detriment of practice, to the most abstract theoretical models, or the most general prophecies, that preceded any actual experience of building socialism. The problem that confronts us today is not one of constructing out of our imaginations the political economy of socialism, or the transitional society (something that Marx and Engels, and Lenin too, refused to do), but one of analysing theoretically the essential features of economic practice in the different countries which are at different stages of transition towards socialism, or in building socialism.

In order to be scientific, this analysis must be critical. It must illuminate both what corresponds to the laws of development of a society advancing towards socialism, to the contradictions that are specific to this society and to the appropriate ways of mastering these contradictions, and also what constitutes a divergence from this. In order to do all this, it must analyse concretely the problems that have arisen, or are arising, in the various countries and at various times. The answers given to these problems must be analysed critically.

It is thus not a matter of justifying, or describing, but of producing new

knowledge. This new knowledge will form the theory of the transitional economy and the theory of socialist economy. It will help in solving new practical problems. The fact that the problems of the transitional economy or of the building of socialism are not only political but also economic means, of course, that they cannot be solved merely by means of an economic theory: while this is indispensable, theoretical knowledge must always be complemented by a concrete analytical effort to reveal the specific contradictions of each social formation, at the particular stage it has reached in its real development. This constant discovering of contradictions, both principal and secondary, and of the shifts undergone by these contradictions as the productive forces develop and social consciousness progresses, is the essence of revolutionary practice. This practice does not aim merely at showing or explaining, but at accomplishing what, without it, would not have existed.

12   This struggle is usually understood as being made necessary by the existence of "capitalist encirclement", which, however, is only a secondary aspect of the reality. The principal aspect is that the very contradiction between the advanced forms of property and the low local level of the productive forces constitutes the internal source from which bourgeois and petty-bourgeois tendencies arise, tendencies which have to be combated in order to safeguard the advanced forms of property and the actual class character of the state which defends this propery tagainst internal degeneration and external attack.

13   This is what is not seen by those who ignore social practice and the contradictions of this practice, and who therefore fail to develop theoretical analysis, so that they usually remain on the plane of moralising practicalism.

14   This point will be developed in the next article.

15   *Cuba Socialista*, June 1964, pp. 13 et seq.

16   Another methodological mistake which is unfortunately current is that of transposing to socialist society, or to the transitional economies, the conclusions of Marx's analysis of capitalist society. This "method" has frequently been used in discussions about problems of price policy.

17   French text from Emile Bottigelli's translation, Editions Sociales, Paris, 1962, p. 87: Eng. version from Marx, *Selected Writings*, ed. Bottomore, p. 155.

18   *Ibid.*, p. 136. (English version from *ibid.*, p. 206.)

19   Both quotations taken from Bottigelli's introduction to the Paris edn. of the *Manuscripts*, p. LXIX.

20   Bottigelli notes that among these interpreters are to be found both Social-Democrats like Landshut and Mayer, and also existentialists, Neo-Thomists, and theologians like E. Thier, Father Bigot, Father Calvez, etc.

21   *Correspondance Engels-Lafargue*, Paris, 1956, Vol. I, p. 235 (Eng. edn., I, p. 235).

22   *Manuscrits, op. cit.*, p. 138 (Eng. edn., p. 158).

23   Cf. "Chronique philosophique: Les Manuscrits de 1844 de Karl

F

Marx", by Louis Althusser, in *La Pensée*, February 1963, pp. 106–9: also in *Pour Marx*, pp. 153 et seq. (Quotation taken from p. 158.)

24   Which does not mean that he accepted all its conclusions.

25   This "abstraction of the economy" means, among other things, that the economy is understood *from outside*, as a group of categories detached from *praxis*.

26   "Chronique philosophique" (see note 23), p. 159.

5: Planning and production-relations

One of the characteristic features of certain writings, such as the article by Ernest Mandel which I have already quoted,[1] is that they deal with "economic categories" of an impoverished kind which, despite the terminology used, belong not to the economic categories of Marx's *Capital* but to those of economic ideology, or even, to employ E. Bottigelli's expression regarding the *Manuscripts of 1844*, to that "economic phenomenology" which is still to be found in the *Manuscripts*. To be convinced of this it is only necessary to see how alien to Marx's thought, as it developed *after* the *Manuscripts of 1844*, is the way in which Mandel deals with the categories of private ownership and social ownership.

For example, in his article he introduces the section dealing with "the form of ownership and the mode of production" with the following proposition: "Transition from private ownership of the means of production to collective ownership means transition from the anarchy of capitalist production to the objective possibility of socialist planning." (*Art. cit.*, p. 11.)

A formulation such as this is too vague and lacking in precision to help us take even one step forward in solving the problems under discussion. Rather does it drag us back, to the level of the general declarations of what Marx and Engels called "vulgar socialism", which lacks any definite scientific content.

Mandel's formulation tends to conceal what is the real controversy today, namely: what are the conditions under which "the objective possibility of socialist planning" can be transformed into actual socialist planning? By merely repeating that collective ownership makes socialist planning objectively possible one does not contribute in the slightest to solving the essential problem, which is how to prevent a specific type of anarchy of production (disproportion, inefficiency, decline in productivity, etc.) from developing on the basis of collective ownership—something that can happen and which it is important to prevent happening.

Here are some observations provoked by Mandel's formulation:

First of all, we note that it is a question here of "private ownership of the means of production" being wholly transformed into "collective ownership". This transformation thus appears to cover equally, and without any specific difference, *capitalist* property and the *private* property of the small individual producers. In the passage quoted the very concept of "capitalist property" as, first and foremost, *private ownership of social means of production* is not even employed, either here or further on, precisely because Mandel remains on the plane of the most general categories, those that Marx used before he wrote *Capital*.

In *Capital*, however, Marx emphasises that even the phase of *private capital* is only a *transient phase* of capitalism, since the latter itself abolishes private property in the strict sense of the word. Let us re-read at this point what Marx writes regarding joint-stock companies:

"The capital, which in itself rests on a social mode of production and presupposes a social concentration of means of production and labour-power, is here directly endowed with the form of social capital (capital of directly associated individuals) as distinct from private capital, and its undertakings assume the form of social undertakings as distinct from private undertakings. It is the abolition of capital as private property within the framework of capitalist production itself."[2]

Still discussing the significance of the formation of joint-stock companies, Marx further observes that in these companies even the labour of management is henceforth separated from ownership of the means of production. He writes:

"In stock companies the function (of management) is divorced from ownership of means of production and surplus labour. This result of the ultimate development of capitalist production is a necessary transition phase towards the reconversion of capital into the property of producers, though no longer as the private property of the individual producers, but rather as the property of associated producers, as outright social property. On the other hand, the stock company is a transition toward the conversion of all functions in the reproduction process which still remain linked with capitalist property, into mere functions of associated producers, into social functions."[3]

In this analysis as in many others, Marx does not confine himself to talking about "private ownership" in general, but takes account of the nature of the productive forces which are subjected either to private ownership, or to capitalist private ownership, or to capitalist ownership of social enterprises, and he highlights the decisive importance of the changes that take place in the level of development of the productive forces and in the character of the production-relations. As a result of these changes, indeed, the same juridical concept of "private ownership" covers a succession of economic realities which differ profoundly, since they range from simple commodity production to state monopoly capitalism, with, in between, capitalist private production, capitalist social production and monopoly capitalism.[4]

If we neglect all these analyses made by Marx, so instructive not only in their conclusions but also in the *method* used, we are unable to understand: (a) how a new social order is prepared for inside capitalist society itself; (b) what the specific contradictions are at the different stages of capitalism; (c) what specific contradictions characterise the economies within which socialism is built.

Let us return, however, once more to the passages where Marx writes about joint-stock companies. He adds:

"This is the abolition of the capitalist mode of production within the capitalist mode of production itself, and hence a self-dissolving contradiction, which *prima facie* represents a mere phase of transition to a new form of production. It manifests itself as such a contradiction in its effects. . . . It is private property without the control of private property."[5]

And he goes on:

"The capitalist stock companies, as much as the co-operative factories, should be considered as transitional forms from the capitalist mode of production to the associated one, with the only distinction that the antagonism is resolved negatively in the one and positively in the other."[6]

These analyses are highly significant. Not only do they prove that Marx was not at all content, as some allege, to study "pure and abstract" capitalism, they show that he strove, on the contrary, to study capitalism theoretically in its development and its successive phases.

The practical and political bearing of these analyses is equally clear. We need only recall that, in his criticism of the Erfurt Programme, Engels used the same categories as those offered by Marx in Book III of *Capital*; as, for example, when he wrote, criticising Paragraph Four of the document that Kautsky had sent him:

"Paragraph 4. 'The absence of planning which is rooted in the very nature of capitalist private production'—this requires serious improvement. I am acquainted with capitalist production as a social mode, as an economic phase, and capitalist *private* production as a phenomenon occurring in one form or another within that phase. What is indeed capitalist private production? Production by the individual entrepreneur; however, this is becoming more and more an exception. Capitalist production by *joint-stock companies* is no longer *private* production, but production for the joint account of many. Not only *private production* but also *lack of planning* disappear when we proceed from joint-stock companies to trusts which control and monopolize whole branches of industry. Delete the word 'private' and, at a pinch, the sentence may pass."[7]

Here we see, in passing, how Mandel's general formulation about the "anarchy" of capitalist production, while correct as to fundamentals, is at the same time inadequate.

We know that Lenin, after quoting, in *The State and Revolution*, Engels's phrase about "the end of planlessness", immediately adds:

"Here we have what is most essential in the theoretical appraisal of the latest phase of capitalism, i.e., imperialism, namely, that capitalism becomes monopoly *capitalism*."[8]

Though the anarchy of capitalist production is not abolished (but is rather carried to extremes) either by the development of monopoly capitalism or even by the appearance of state monopoly capitalism and capitalist programming, it is none the less true that the content and the very form of this anarchy are profoundly modified[9] (to the advantage of the monopolies) and that the attempts at planning and programming which are features of present-day capitalism constitute proof of the existence within it of the material conditions for another social order, the socialist order.

As Lenin said:

". . . state-monopoly capitalism is a complete *material* preparation for socialism, the threshold of socialism, a rung on the ladder of history between which and the rung called socialism *there are no intermediate rungs.*"[10]

If, in considering the problems of transition from capitalism to socialism, it is not enough to confine oneself to general formulas about "private ownership", this applies even more to "collective ownership".

As we have seen, Marx uses the term "collective ownership" to designate alike collective ownership by the shareholders of joint-stock companies, workers' production co-operatives, and state ownership of the means of production.

Marx and Engels were never satisfied with analysing economic problems on the basis of "juridical categories". Their analyses show, on the contrary that it is not the "juridical form" of ownership that determines the mode of production, but the concrete social relations. Thus, depending on the class nature of the state, "state ownership" may be merely "capitalism pushed to an extreme", as Engels puts it in *Anti-Dühring* or, on the contrary, it may mean "seizure of the means of production in the name of society".

In order that "collective ownership" may mean "the objective possibility of socialist planning", it must be ownership by the proletarian state. But even this state ownership is not yet *social* ownership (that is, ownership by society *as a whole*). It is so far only seizure of the means of production by the proletarian state "in the name of society", as Engels puts it, and this then becomes social ownership only in proportion as the state withers away.[11] While state intervention in social relations becomes progressively unnecessary in one sphere after another, parallel with this process commodity production declines and withers away, and what remains of anarchy in social production is replaced by ever more conscious and systematic organisation. Seizure of the means of production by the proletarian state may take the form of a single act, but taking possession of the means of production *by society*, the withering away of the state, the ending of commodity production, constitute, on the contrary, an historical process (conditioned by state ownership) which necessarily extends over a long period, this period being itself divided into successive phases.

Just as Mandel has failed to distinguish, in the passage quoted, between simple commodity production, capitalist private production, capitalist social production, monopoly capitalism, and state monopoly capitalism, so also he fails to distinguish between the transitional society, socialist society and communist society (and their various stages). Thus, all the problems are dealt with as though they could be settled on the basis of the simple antimony between "private ownership" and "collective ownership", as if socialist society were *from the start* a developed socialist society, in complete control of the productive forces. The fact that this is not so, and cannot be so, is at the heart of the socialist world's present problems.

To sum up what has been said so far and to tackle another question closely linked with the foregoing, we can say that what is primarily decisive about establishing ownership by the proletarian state of the principal means of production is *not* that it makes immediately possible the introduction of real socialist planning, since it makes this possible only as something *for the future*.[12] What is immediately achieved by proletarian state ownership is the abolition of the economic and political power of the bourgeoisie and—what is decisive for the future—the transformation of the class structure of society and the class nature of the state.

The fundamental fact is the radical transformation of social relations. All the rest—planning, social control over production—is, at the start, still only an abstract possibility, the progressive transformation of which into reality constitutes the condition for the consolidation and flowering of the new social order.

I Possibility and reality

We see how dangerous it can be to identify *possibility* with *reality*. The whole problem of building socialism is precisely that of creating the conditions that will ensure that what exists as a *possibility* (on the basis of the expropriation of capitalist ownership and the development of collective ownership) may become a *reality*.

In order to ensure this transition from the potential to the real, however, one has to begin by asking certain questions.

Is the fundamental characteristic of socialism, or of an economy in which socialism is being built, that it is subjected to a plan, or develops according to a plan; or is it that this economy is subordinated to social needs and develops according to the requirements of these needs (of which the plan must be an expression, as adequate as possible in the given economic, social and political conditions)?

Is it enough for the proletarian state to work out a plan, lay down targets and decide on priorities, for this plan to correspond to the objective possibilities, the requirements of maximum saving of labour, the requirements of proportionality, and, as in the previous question, the social needs themselves?

Further, is it enough that priorities have been decided by the plan for real economic development to conform to them?

One has only to ask these questions, and to be only a little aware of the objective reality, to appreciate that the answer must be in the negative, that is, to admit that what is "possible", from the standpoint of a mistakenly abstract conception, is not necessarily real.

It has to be accepted, then, that the true problem, the one that it is important to answer and from which follows the solution to all the others,[13] consists in establishing the conditions which, at each stage and in conformity with concrete conditions, make it possible for the economy to be genuinely planned, and for the plan to correspond, so far as it can at the given stage, to the requirements of social development, social needs, proportionality, efficiency, and so on.

If we fail to examine these problems and remain content with manipulating abstract categories which we mistake for reality, we remain in the realm of bad philosophy, do not get on to the plane of concrete problems, and remain incapable of providing even the beginning of an answer to these problems.

Let us take an example. After recognising that socialist planning presupposes effective capacity on the part of society to account for and allot the productive forces in an efficient way, Mandel asks:

"In a country like Cuba, is it possible to 'account for and allot efficiently', that is, to plan the machinery, the raw materials and the work-force in the several thousand industrial enterprises in the country? The answer is, of course, yes. No doubt this is being done, at first, in an imperfect, partial, inadequate way; but the trouble here is not the level of development of the productive forces but weaknesses in organisation and lack of experience, and these can and must be gradually corrected through the gaining of experience and the formation of adequate cadres, through control and creative initiative on the part of the masses, etc. Any other conclusion would, indeed, put a question mark over all socialist progress in an under-developed country." (*Art. cit.*, p. 13.)[14]

In its general form, the proposition at the beginning of this passage means nothing at all, for the real question is to know *under what conditions* it is possible to "plan", with what delays, through what forms of organisation, given what relations between production-units, to what degree of efficiency.

At the end of the passage quoted, Mandel gives the impression that he is outlining the beginnings of an answer when he writes: "This is being done, at first, in an imperfect, partial, inadequate way; but the trouble here is not the degree of development of the productive forces, but weaknesses in organisation and lack of experience, etc." Here, too, we see the author avoiding reality and falling into the eclecticism (which ends in explaining everything by "circumstances") of which he is so ready to accuse others. This "fall" of his results from the fact that, for him, the categories are "pure" and "abstract" notions (abstract in the bad sense of the word) and that consequently it is necessary to make a leap in order to get from these "pure and abstract" concepts to the analysing of concrete reality.

Thus, in the foregoing passage, we see that the notion of "level of development of the productive forces" has been emptied of all concrete content, since it does not include the lack of experience and inadequate training of the cadres, the weaknesses of organisation, etc. Yet all these enter into the level of development of the productive forces and define the higher or lower level of development of these forces.

In fact, it is only by taking into consideration the level of development of the productive forces that we are able to understand that the same juridical form (proletarian state ownership) can cover different concrete production-relations and determine a very varying degree of efficiency in accounting for goods and allotting them. This is why the forms and the degree of efficiency of planning are closely linked with the level of development of the productive forces—whence the possibility or impossibility, depending on this level, that commodity relations will cease to apply between the production-units that form part of the nationalised sector under the dictatorship of the proletariat.

II Nationalisation, socialisation and the transitional economy

The problems just mentioned are so important, both for Cuba and for all the countries which have taken or will take the road of building socialism, that it is essential to look more closely at the way in which Lenin presents them, especially in his work called *"Left-wing" childishness and petty-bourgeois mentality*, a work which is quite fundamental in this connexion.

Let us first re-read the various passages in this work where Lenin distinguishes, and even contrasts, nationalisation and confiscation, on the one hand, and socialisation, on the other.

"One may or may not be determined on the question of nationalisation or confiscation, but the whole point is that even the greatest possible 'determination' is not enough to pass *from* nationalisation and confiscation *to* socialisation. The misfortune of our 'Lefts' is that by their naive, childish combination of the words 'most determined policy of socialisation' they reveal their utter failure to understand the crux of the question, the crux of the 'present' situation. The misfortune of our 'Lefts' is that they have missed the very essence of the 'present situation', the transition from confiscation (the carrying out of which requires above all determination in a politician) to socialisation (the carrying out of which requires a *different* quality in the revolutionary).

"Yesterday, the main task of the moment was, as determinedly as possible, to nationalise, confiscate, beat down and crush the bourgeoisie, and put down sabotage. Today, only a blind man could fail to see that we have nationalised, confiscated, beaten down and put down more than we have had time to *count*. The difference between socialisation and simple confiscation is that confiscation can be carried out by 'determination' alone, without the ability to calculate and distribute properly, *whereas socialisation cannot be brought about without this ability*."[15]

It is clear that Lenin is here contrasting the juridical act of nationalisation (or confiscation) with socialisation, that is, with control by society or, "in its name", by the state,[16] over what has been nationalised or confiscated.

The distinction made is thus a distinction between a juridical category and a social reality: though large-scale industry has been nationalised it has not been effectively socialised, that is to say, managed in an efficient way on behalf of society. In this passage, indeed, what Lenin is concerned about is not the direction to be given to the petty-bourgeois or simple commodity sectors of the economy but the way to manage modern large-scale industry. This is why he envisages at that time what he calls "state capitalism" under Soviet power. This state capitalism, in the actual situation that Soviet Russia was in at that time, was expressed in the fact that the Soviet state was willing to entrust the "management" of the most important enterprises to what Lenin called "cultured capitalists", not in their capacity as capitalists but as specialist technicians or organisers, and to pay them high salaries for this service.

It was thus a matter, concretely (in the form, and at the level which were possible at that moment), of ensuring the socialisation of the large-scale enterprises by creating the conditions necessary for efficient management under the control of the proletarian state. What Lenin was concerned to do was temporarily to entrust the "management", that is, certain executive functions (under the control of "workers' commissars or workers' committees who watch the manager's every step, who learn from his management experience and who not only have the right to appeal against his orders, but can secure his removal through the organs of Soviet power"), of "the *largest* types of enterprises, which actually supply products to tens of millions of people", to "cultured capitalists".[17]

For Lenin, nationalising the largest enterprises did not, therefore, constitute a sort of magical formula which would ensure "automatically" a regular and harmonious growth of production, the adaptation of the latter to social needs, and so on. For that it was, though a necessary condition, not a sufficient one. What was further needed was to ensure, under concrete conditions, the effective socialisation of the social means of production, which implies, among other things, efficient accounting, allocation and management, under social control.

The problem is obviously not one of knowing whether modern large-scale industry is "ripe" for nationalisation, since it is. The problem is to determine the precise conditions in which nationalisation will lead to real socialisation. Clearly, the formula of "state capitalism" under Soviet power solved this problem only very partially, imperfectly and temporarily, and did this under the very special conditions of the beginning of the first proletarian revolution. Very soon it was necessary to find other forms, equally transient, through which the management of the state enterprises and the overall direction of the economy could be better and better subjected to effective control by society.

These are the concrete and precise questions that have to be asked and answered in order to ensure the building of socialism. These are the problems of the economy of transition to socialism.

What is involved is not just nationalisation, not just statisation, it is the wielding by the state power, through measures adapted to the objective political, economic and social conditions of the country, of effective and efficient control over the production and distribution of goods. As Lenin rightly says in the same passage:

"Those who fail to understand this are committing an unpardonable mistake in economics. Either they do not know the facts of life, do not see what actually exists and are unable to look the truth in the face, or they confine themselves to abstractly comparing 'capitalism' with 'socialism' and fail to study *the concrete forms and stages of the transition*[18] that is taking place in our country. . . . It was not without reason that the teachers of socialism spoke of *a whole period of transition*[18] from capitalism to socialism and emphasised the 'prolonged birth-pangs' of the new society. And this new society is again an abstraction which can come into being only by passing through a series of varied, imperfect concrete attempts to create this or that socialist state."[19]

These are, indeed, the concrete problems of the transition from capitalism to socialism which are posed *for an entire historical period* and which have to be solved *in each country under specific conditions*.

Up to now, many fundamental problems of the economy in transition towards socialism have been connected with the fact that the revolution has not taken place in countries where the productive forces were most highly developed but, on the contrary, in countries where the productive forces were relatively less developed. This means, to use Lenin's formula, that these countries are *politically advanced* but *economically backward*.

Two further observations regarding this valuable work of Lenin's.

Strongly emphasising the character of the Soviet economy of the time as an economy of *transition* from capitalism to socialism, Lenin points out that the fact that the Soviet Republic calls itself a *Socialist* Soviet Republic does not imply "that the new economic system is recognised as a socialist order",[20] but rather "the determination of Soviet power to achieve the transition to socialism".[21]

It is clear that at the present time the Cuban economy, for example, is not yet a socialist economy but an *economy in transition* from capitalism to socialism. Thus, all deductions and "recipes" formulated on the basis of an abstract conception of "socialism" are without any practical bearing for this economy.

To suppose that decisions to expropriate or nationalise settle everything and ensure the coming to birth of a new mode of production is truly to fall into "juridical illusionism".

In all the writings in which he dealt with problems of organising the Soviet economy, Lenin emphasises the transient nature of that economy as it was at that time, and expresses his concern to see a *concrete adjustment of the forms of organisation to the level of development of the productive forces*.[22]

This means that it is necessary to determine, in each concrete case, the specific forms to be given to the new production-relations and to the organisation of production.

In order to ensure the effectiveness of the management of the economy, these specific forms must be adapted to the level and the specific features of the development of the productive forces of each country, and also to all the characteristics—historical, political (including the level of class-consciousness) and cultural—of the given country and even of the different branches of its economy.[23] Thus it is not by accident or by mistake that the agrarian reform in Cuba has specific features that mark it off from the agrarian reforms carried out in other socialist countries.

If the concrete forms of managing the economy could be deduced from abstract categories, there would be only a single "model" for the transition to socialism, a single model for agrarian reform, etc. The experience of the socialist countries themselves, especially that of Cuba, shows that this is not so. What exists is only "a series of varied, imperfect concrete attempts",[24] at creating a new social order.

III The withering–away of the commodity categories

The passages in Mandel's writings which deal with the survival and withering away of the commodity categories in the sphere of the distribution of consumer goods do not call for any particular comment. It is otherwise, however, when he criticises the idea that the means of production still retain today the character of commodities inside the socialist sector, even in the economically most advanced countries, such as the Soviet Union. Here we find the old Bukharinist claim (from the time when Bukharin was an "ultra-left") that at bottom there is only "transfer of a product from one factory to another within a single great state trust".

In order to develop discussion on this important subject let us take some of the arguments formulated by Mandel in the article already quoted. One of his arguments is that in the sphere of production of means of production in a planned economy, the labour expended is always and in all circumstances socially necessary labour.

To "prove" this claim he says that it is only when the "possibility of overproduction" exists that labour-time can be wasted. Well, now, he goes on, though it is certainly possible that some consumer goods produced by socialist industry may remain unsold, it is inconceivable that the same thing could happen to means of production. He writes:

"Can there be 'overproduction of the means of production' in the socialist sector? Obviously not. If 'by bad luck' the production of means of production exceeds the plan figures or runs ahead of the plan's technological forecasts, there is nothing to stop socialist industry from using this surplus in order to go forward to a more advanced stage of expanded reproduction, either at once or in the future. Consequently, the means of socialist production, being never 'unsaleable', cannot contain 'socially unnecessary' labour. They crystallise social labour immediately and automatically, and have no need of the medium of exchange in order to do this. They are therefore not commodities" (*Art. cit.*, p. 24.)

The superficiality of this "proof" is obvious. In the concrete reality of the transitional economy, or even in the entire first stage of the socialist economy, there may and do exist many reasons why, in practice, the means of production supplied by the socialist sector and intended for the same sector may prove to be ultimately unsaleable, or unsaleable for a more or less lengthy period, or of mediocre utility. This can happen because of short-comings in the quality of production, disproportion in the production of different means of production, and so on. When this happens, on a socially significant scale (and it does happen, and not only in Cuba), it means that the level of social forecasting of the needs of the production sphere and of the technical and technological conditions of production is still low. Yet it is only a sufficiently high level and quality of forecasting of social needs that can determine in advance that the labour expended in producing means of production will be socially necessary. So long as this level of social forecasting is unattainable (and this is a programme that is very much more than a mere matter of planning technique), it is still mainly the case that means of production are *sold*, and sold at prices roughly corresponding to their *value*, within the framework of production-programmes that conform to the central plan, which shows the socially-necessary character of the labour expended in their production and the investments committed in order to make this possible.

Here we come again upon another fundamental point, related to the notion of "socially necessary labour": it is not enough for a product to be "sold" for the labour expended to produce it to be *wholly* socially necessary. For that, the total amount of social labour expended on producing the given article must correspond to the *social utility* of this article. This is what Marx says in his letter to Kugelmann of 11th July 1868. Mandel refers to this letter, but without drawing the conclusion to which it leads us, namely, that one of the fundamental problems is to determine, in a socially satisfactory way, how to distribute society's labour among the various branches of production, which implies distribution carried out proportionally to the respective needs that exist for the various products.

At the present time this cannot be completely accomplished by the plan mechanism alone in any of the socialist countries.

To a very large extent, still, the distribution of social labour among the different branches of production, and the adaptation of this distribution to the relative importance of the various needs, and to social utility, can be effected only through mechanisms which are similar to those of the market but which operate in subordination to the plan's targets and social purposes. As the economy becomes more and more complex, the tendency is increasingly for direct links to be established between the production-units, and, when these units are not technically and economically integrated, to the concluding of contracts which lay down in concrete terms the quantity and quality of the various goods that have to be supplied by one enterprise to another.

Actually, in a socialist economy, even in the countries with the highest-developed productive forces, the distribution of means of production among the factories takes place only *partly* through the plan. In a very large number of cases, the plan allocates *not* particular use-values (i.e., definite means of production), but financial resources.[25] These financial resources are for more or less *general* use. The *concrete* provision of material goods, of means of production, is accomplished often, and even more and more frequently as the economy grows more complex, by way of buying and selling transactions. It is thus necessary at present for millions of economically elementary decisions to be taken, relating to millions of means of production. These decisions, and the operations of production and distribution that follow from them, are *regulated* by means of money—in accordance, of course, with the volume of credit assigned by the planning organs. If this is so, the reason is that, in a very large number of cases, *economic calculation* ("business accounting") cannot yet be fully effective at any level higher than that of the production-units.[26]

These are facts, and facts that do not result from mistakes or deviations from an abstract model of the socialist economy. They result from present-day objective necessities. One may think, of course (I think so myself) that these necessities are destined to disappear in the fairly near future, and this will alter the conditions in which the planned economy operates, but for the moment these necessities exist. To try to ignore them can lead only to squandering the labour expended by the producers and reducing the *effective* domination of the economy by the planning authorities. While giving oneself the illusion of planning "more closely" one would merely be planning less well.

When we go deeper into these problems we come again upon the question of the conditions necessary for the commodity categories to wither away. This withering-away is not, in my opinion, linked with increasing centralisation, but rather with ever closer integration of the different production-units, that is, with the development of closer and closer organic ties between these production-units. One of the consequences of a development like this, itself bound up with the automation of production and management, will be the assigning in advance of an increasing number of means of production to their ultimate users, and this on the basis of rigorous forecasting. This will form one of the objective foundations for the withering away of the role of money within the socialist sector. But this is not yet the situation today.

If we are unable to recognise the specific features of the present situation, if we try to apply forms of organisation and forms of circulation of the means of production that do not correspond to the level of development attained by the productive forces, we shall achieve only a great deal of wastage and a very serious state of inefficiency in the economic system.

To refuse to recognise that there are objective reasons why the commodity categories still exist inside the production sector, or to try and "exorcise" this reality in the name of an abstract and "pure" image of socialist society, is to promote the wasting of resources and hold back the development of the socialist economy, and so to delay the coming of the moment when the commodity categories will disappear because the time for this to happen will really have arrived.

IV The prospects of technico-economic integration

It is noteworthy that the conceptions we have just been criticising are at variance not only with the actual situation in the socialist economies, or the economies in transition to socialism, but also with the real tendencies which, at the present stage in the development of their productive forces, are characteristic of the recent evolution of these economies.

In fact, the very growth in the volume of production, with the increasing diversification of products, and of the technological channels by which the different products can be obtained, are everywhere accompanied today by a more and more obvious need to recognise the existence of the commodity categories within the socialist sector. This need is especially imperative when it is sought to cut down as much as possible the expenditure of necessary labour for obtaining a social product adapted to social needs.

At the present stage of development of the productive forces of the socialist countries it is possible to see clearly that detailed production-programmes for enterprises supplying consumer goods cannot be worked out from above but must result from the orders received by these enterprises.[27] From this standpoint, the current plan for the production of consumer goods, worked out at the national level, must ultimately take very full account of the needs expressed by the consumers, in so far as this is physically possible (given the resources available), and while respecting the requirements of coherence between the plans and, above all, of *social priorities*.[28] If the needs expressed by the consumers are not taken into account, what results is that the labour contributed is wasted.

In the second place, some of the need for raw materials or semi-finished goods on the part of the enterprises supplying consumer goods cannot be determined centrally, and this has to be done by way of direct agreements between the enterprises supplying consumer goods and those which provide them with raw materials or semi-finished goods. Actually, in the present state of things, this is how it is possible for qualitative and quantitative adjustment to take place effectively between the needs of one group and what the others supply.

Finally, once the plan has laid down, centrally, the targets for investment, the allocation of investments by production-categories, the essential conditions for their location, and the main types of equipment to be produced as a result of these investments, the concrete putting into effect of most of the programmes of production and investment, resulting from the central plan, which have to be carried out by the enterprises is also based on the presupposition that it is the latter who are to settle between themselves the volume, quality and delivery-dates of supplies, so as to ensure that the plan is realised under the conditions most advantageous to society.

In the conditions of today, the increasing complexity and diversity of production, the multiplication of the number of enterprises, and so on, make ever more difficult, and even impossible in practice, adequately detailed central forecasting of the different kinds of production and their allocation. It is this impossibility of sufficiently precise central forecasting of needs for different categories of products that makes it necessary to establish direct links between production-units, a system of orders, purchases and sales, and so the temporary extension of the sphere of commodity activities inside the socialist sector itself.

This extension takes place, however, only in so far as the growing complexity and diversity of production are not yet balanced by adequate progress in the technical and economic integration of the different production-units (which thus continue to be economic subjects).

The significance of this integration process is the following: within a large integrated group (and the practical forms of integration may vary), changes that the volume and structure of production undergo at one end have an impact which is precise (i.e. *calculable*) on what has to be supplied by the other members of the group. Thenceforth it is possible to make calculations in advance and calculations of optima (as experience has shown), and it is no longer necessary to use, between the different members of these groups, the procedure of contracts, orders, purchases and sales. In proportion as integrated technico-economic groups like this develop, it will really be possible for the commodity categories to disappear.

To consider the purely technical aspects of the integration process would be to go too far outside my subject. Let it suffice to say that this integration does not necessarily imply the formation of physically amalgamated "production-units". It may be assumed that what will play the decisive role in this connexion will be standardisation of products, increasing interdependence of branches of production, automation and the development of methods of managing production-units by electronic groups, with telecommunication links between these electronic groups.

Whatever may be the technical process whereby production-units become integrated (and so cease to be "economic subjects"), it will be seen that the prospect before us makes it foreseeable that from a certain moment onward the plan will have to concern itself only with relations between a relatively limited number of large integrated economic groups. Thereafter, forecasting on the social scale will become increasingly precise and strict. At that moment the commodity categories will be able to vanish for good.

This prospect must lead us to make a careful distinction between *administrative* centralised planning, which was, for particular historical reasons, the form taken by the first Five-Year Plans of the Soviet Union (not so much because of the low level of development of the productive forces as because of the exceptional investment effort that had to be made at that time), and *technico-economic* centralised planning, which, in my view, will be the form characteristic of a fully developed planned economy.

V Prices and calculations in labour–time

The foregoing discussion can be continued on another level.

It is a fact that in none of the socialist economies, or the economies in which socialism is being built, are economic calculations made in terms of labour-time. Everywhere these calculations are made in prices, and this is true both for consumer goods and for means of production, for goods passing from the socialist sector into the other sectors of the economy and for goods circulating within the socialist sector. We have to consider the underlying significance of this fact.[29]

The only possible explanation, from a Marxist standpoint, is that the labour-time actually expended on producing means of production is not yet, under present-day conditions, wholly and "automatically", *socially necessary* labour-time, i.e., labour-time proportionate to the social utility of the different products. This is one reason, among others, why it is unavoidable not merely to reckon and calculate in terms of *prices* but also to make *payments* on the basis of prices which are not and cannot be strictly and always proportionate to the labour-time actually expended.[30]

The prices used in the socialist economies of today thus may, and indeed must, diverge from values, because there may have been devoted to the production of a given product (whether an article of consumption or a means of production) more social labour or less than was justified by the social need for this product. In turn, this possible divergence between the time actually expended and the time socially necessary may result either from the objective impossibility of measuring beforehand the social need for a product (this is thus not merely a matter of occasional mistakes), or from the impossibility of determining in advance the amount of labour per unit necessary for the production of a particular category of products, taking into account the qualities and the specific features these must have in order to be able to satisfy social needs.

Similarly, divergences between prices and values may be made necessary if it is desired to ensure optimum use of existing plant, within the framework of a plan the final targets of which have been laid down, while the economic subjects in the production sphere are allowed decision-making powers corresponding to their degree of effective control over the production processes.

In so far as a sufficiently detailed and exact forecast of, on the one hand, needs, and, on the other, the means of labour necessary in order to satisfy these needs, together with the conditions for optimum use of these means, is not yet possible, calculation in terms of "prices" (differing more or less from values) is therefore necessary.

What follows from this is that calculation of prices and calculation of costs are two different things. Accordingly, the economic and social basis for the survival of the commodity categories lies in the fact that at the present time the interdependence of the different productive activities is neither strictly predetermined nor always capable of exact predetermination, and that, consequently, the different production-units or economic subjects are obliged to behave as "relatively independent producers".

Between these "producers" (which are working groups), mediation has to be provided, and this cannot at present be done by the plan alone. The socialist market has therefore to play a part in fulfilling this task. Within it, the different economic subjects, whose basic production targets are laid down by the plan, are both decision-making centres and units for specific calculations.

VI Ownership and subordination

The foregoing amounts to saying that the economy does not yet function as a single unit for the appropriation of nature, or as a single working group. In other words, in the socialist societies of today each production-unit, or each economic subject, still constitutes a relatively autonomous centre for the appropriation of nature.

This economic situation finds juridical expression in the fact that each production-unit "owns" its means of production and its products. This "ownership" obviously has nothing in common with what Roman law means by ownership, or with capitalist ownership, since it is "ownership" subordinated to the wider ownership of its enterprises by the proletarian state. In practice, the pre-eminence of State ownership means not merely that the enterprise is currently subordinate to the plan but also that the state is able, should this be socially advantageous, to abolish a particular enterprise, or to transfer part of its means of production to another enterprise. The continuity of expanded reproduction obviously requires that operations like these (transfer or abolition) should take place only in exceptional cases.

These are some of the facts revealed by analysis of present-day concrete situations. Failure to recognise these facts, either in the name of an administrative conception of planning or in that of "theoretical" views which which reflect the absence of any concrete analysis[31] of the conditions for building socialism, and of any exact notion of the transitional phases through which the economy of a country building socialism has to pass,[32] leads to attempts to establish relations between production-units which do not correspond to objective requirements.

Attempts of this kind can entail disastrous consequences in the actual working of the economy, and this for many reasons. They set up a system of imagined relations, or an "explicit model" which does not correspond to the real relations. The latter form, so to speak, an "underlying" model, behind the "explicit" one, but since this is not without influence on the actual working of the economy, the result is a "real model" which has its own laws of operation, laws which are partly masked by the "explicit model", so that the "transparency" of the economy is much reduced.[33]

On the practical plane, this leads to a generalising of irresponsibility and waste, and makes true economic calculation difficult or even impossible—and likewise, therefore, real social control. In extreme cases, the effect is to make planning itself to some extent illusory.

It is simplistic to suppose that recognising the existence of a certain form of subordinate "ownership" by economic subjects of their means of production (or, if the expression is preferred, a certain right of use and disposal of these means of production) must involve "negating" ownership by the state. In reality, as has been stressed, these economic subjects are themselves *subordinate* subjects so long as the economic plan and state ownership play a fundamental role in all major decisions.

The fact that the different economic subjects of the production sphere are subordinate subjects is shown in the way that the state plan lays down the conditions for forming accumulation funds and consumption funds. The total amounts of these funds, and the main ways in which they are to be used, are not determined by the laws of the market but by society's will. Investment funds are assigned (allocation of investments between branches in accordance with the long-term aims of development, choice of principal production techniques, main decisions about location, etc.) in conformity with socially determined targets. There must, of course, be coherence between the socially made choices, both at the level of investments committed and at that of aims to be attained. It is the fundamental task of planning to work out such coherence in advance, together with the socially optimum use of resources, in order thus to ensure the achievement of society's purposes. In this way an economy develops which is subject no longer to the laws of profit, but to social priorities and aims.

The formation, at the level of society, of the accumulation fund means that, through proletarian state ownership, whatever is not "labour for oneself" takes the form of "labour for society", and is no longer labour for an exploiter.

Depending on the extent of social control which it is actually possible to exercise over production and expanded reproduction, that is, depending on the stage of development reached by the transitional society, or the socialist society, planning can play a great variety of roles.[34] It is not, in the main, by the degree and forms of planning that the "extent to which socialism has been achieved" is to be judged. Indeed, the "essence of socialism" (if one wants to use this expression) is not planning but *the ending of exploitation of man by man*. The latter, in turn, presupposes not only the juridical form of state ownership but also, and *above all*, a specific content of state power and specific conditions in which it is exercised (role of the party, etc.). These are concrete questions which require that the problems be studied in their totality, taking account of the inter-relation between the economic, social and political facts of the situation.

(Article published in *La Pensée*, No. 126, April 1966, pp. 57–76.)

NOTES TO CHAPTER 5

1 *Economica* (Havana), June 1964. Cf. *supra*, Ch. 4, note 1.

2 Ch. 27 of Book III of *Capital* (p. 477 of the Moscow German-language edn. of 1933; p. 102 of Vol. VII of the Editions Sociales edn.). (Eng. version from *Capital*, Vol. III, FLPH edn., p. 427.)

3 *Das Kapital*, Book III, p. 478 (pp. 102–3 of Vol. VII of the Editions Sociales edn.). (Eng. version from *ibid.*, p. 428.)

4 It will here be seen how, when analysing real social relations, Marxism goes far beyond narrowly juridical categories, and this, among other things, enables it to grasp concretely the extreme diversity of the social relations that can be covered by the general and abstract category of "collective ownership" or "state ownership".

5 *Das Kapital*, III, pp. 479–80 (p. 106 of Vol. VII of Editions Sociales edn.). (Eng. version from *ibid.*, p. 429.)

6 *Das Kapital*, III, p. 482 (p. 106 of Vol. VII of Editions Sociales edn.). (Eng. version, *ibid.*, p. 431.)

7 *Critique du Programme de Gotha et d'Erfurt*, Paris, Editions Sociales, 1950, pp. 81–2. (End. edn., p. 54.)

8 *State and Revolution*, in Vol. 25 of Lenin's *Oeuvres complètes*, 1962 edn., p. 478. (Eng. version from *Collected Works*, 4th edn., Vol. 25, p. 442.)

9 Thus, to the cyclical retardation of the development of the productive forces, or even the cyclical setback or destruction of these forces, is now added the systematic directing of an ever greater proportion of the accumulation fund towards non-productive ends (armaments, etc.), that is, an attempt to sterilise permanently an increasing proportion of the productive forces.

10 Lenin, "The Impending Catastrophe and How to Combat it", in *Oeuvres complètes*, Vol. 25, edn. of 1962, p. 390. (Eng. edn., *Collected Works*, 4th edn., Vol. 25, p. 359.)

11 State and society show the unity of a contradiction. It is from this very contradiction that there follows the contradiction (and the unity) of state ownership and social ownership.

12 Is it necessary to recall that ten years passed between the proclamation of Soviet power and the First Five-Year Plan? Do we have to recall that this plan answered only very partially the requirements for socialist planning, and this not because of reasons connected with "planning technique" but because of profound social and economic reasons connected especially with the degree to which the productive forces were really socialised?

13 Cf. Bettelheim, "Formes et méthodes de la planification socialiste et niveau de développement des forces productives", *La Pensée*, February 1964 (*supra*, Ch. 3) and "Les cadres socio-économiques et l'organisation de la planification sociale", *Problèmes de Planification*, Cahiers No. 5, Centre

d'Etude de Planification Socialiste, Ecole Pratique des Hautes Etudes (Vi^e
Section), 1965 (*infra*, Ch. 5).

14 We will ignore the last phrase, with its polemical content, which could
be turned against the writer himself by retorting that, if he asks this question it is perhaps because he is one of those who think that if reality does
not conform strictly and immediately to the picture they have of the
socialist economy, then one must doubt whether socialism is possible in
countries that do not conform to their *a priori* view of things.

15 Lenin, *Oeuvres complètes*, Vol. 27, pp. 348–9. (Eng. edn., pp. 333–4.)

16 Cf. the quotation from Engels, *supra*, p. 165.

17 Vol. 27, pp. 360 and 365. (Eng. edn., pp. 345 and 349.)

18 My emphasis, C.B.

19 *Ibid.*, p. 356. (Eng. edn., pp. 340–1.)

20 *Ibid.*, p. 350. (Eng. edn., p. 335.)

21 *Ibid.*, p. 350. (Eng. edn., p. 335.)

22 A particularly interesting passage is this one, taken from a resolution
adopted at the Ninth Congress of the Bolshevik Party (in 1920), a document
drawn up under Lenin's direct inspiration:

"The way in which industry is organised at present is transient. The
workers' state has nationalised the capitalist trusts, making various
enterprises in the same industries join these trusts, and uniting, in
trusts conceived according to the pattern of these capitalist trusts,
industrial enterprises which had not been trustified under capitalism.
Industry has been formed into a series of mighty vertical organisations, economically isolated from each other and linked together only at
the top, by the Supreme Council of the National Economy.

"Whereas under the capitalist regime each trustified enterprise could
obtain raw materials, labour, etc., in nearby markets, these same enterprises have today to receive everything they need through the orders of
the central organs of the unified economy. With the huge size of the
country, however, and owing to the extreme instability and uncertainty
of the principal factors of production, the disorganised state of transport . . . the as yet highly inexact procedures and methods of economic
statistics, the centralising methods that have resulted from the first
period of expropriating bourgeois industry, and which have inevitably
led to the dissociation of the enterprises (in the towns, provinces, dis-
tricts and regions), have given rise to monstrous forms of 'red tape'
which are doing irreparable harm to our economy." Quoted from Lenin,
Oeuvres complètes, Vol. XXV of the edn. of 1930, p. 621.

23 The need for these adaptations (and of great creative initiative in
conceiving them) must not be confused with some strict "proportionality"
or other that allegedly has to be maintained between economic forces and
political ones, or between economic forces and forms of organisation.
Such strict "proportionality" cannot exist, under the conditions of a
transitional economy marked by internal unevenness of development. As
Lenin says:

"Such an argument can be advanced only by a 'man in a muffler' who forgets that there will always be such a 'discrepancy', that it always exists in the development of nature as well as in the development of society, that only by a series of attempts—each of which, taken by itself, will be one-sided and will suffer from certain inconsistencies—will complete socialism be created by the revolutionary co-operation of the proletarians of *all* countries." (*Oeuvres complètes*, Vol. 27, p. 361. Eng. edn., pp. 345–6.)

24 *Ibid.*, p. 356. (Eng. edn., p. 341.)

25 Hence the important role played by the "financial plan".

26 It is not possible to undertake here an examination of the *conditions* and *limits* of the *social* effectiveness of this elementary (or "basic") economic calculation. I say something about it in No. 5, already mentioned of *Problèmes de Planification*. (See Ch. 2 of this book.)

27 Most often, these orders will reach the producing enterprises through state trading organisations which are themselves in contact with the consumers. This is the mechanism perfected in China and which at the present time makes it possible for the detailed production-programmes of the enterprises supplying consumer goods to be brought up to date every quarter (see *La construction du socialisme en Chine*, by Ch. Bettelheim, J. Charrière, and H. Marchisio, Paris, Maspero, 1965).

28 At this level, respect for social priorities can be ensured to some extent by using the retail price mechanism.

29 Quite obviously, it is no answer to the questions that this brings up to say that there is nothing here but the retention of the "external forms" of commodity transactions, on the grounds that, when what are involved are means of production that do not leave the socialist sector, they are not "real" commodities. The appearance or disappearance of an economic category (here the 'category' called a 'commodity') cannot be decided by juridical property forms but only by the objective conditions under which the economic system itself functions. It is no answer, because the connexion is overlooked between the existence of prices, together with sales and purchases, and the non-existence (and present impossibility) of reckoning in terms of labour-time.

30 This brings up the problem of prices and what they signify in the socialist economies of today—a problem too enormous to be tackled here. Let me merely recall that prices play an extremely complex role in a socialist economy. They express both value and social utility. They provide the basis for centralised calculations and also for decentralised ones (at the level of the production-units or economic subjects, for whom prices serve as information in a condensed form). They are one of the foundations of the circulation of money among the enterprises, and so on.

To the extent that prices not only reflect the present market situation and the individual forecasts of economic agents, but also take account of both value and social utility, they serve as the basis for the functioning of a *socially controlled* market. So long as such a market is still needed, the planning of prices is, alongside the planning of investments and incomes, the most effective means of social control of the development of production on the basis of state ownership. (On the relation between value and price, see Maurice Godelier's contribution to No. 3 of *Problèmes de Planification* (École Pratique des Hautes Études).

31   Very often the absence of concrete analysis results from facile identification of "administrative planning" (through which, it seems, countries are more or less obliged to pass immediately following a thorough change in the mode of production) with the economic planning which is characteristic of the further development of a society on the road to socialism.

32   This proposition does not mean that in all countries the transitional phases must necessarily bear the same features. This is a complex question on which I have no time to dwell here.

33   The terms "explicit model", "underlying model" and "real model" are used in a theoretical analysis by Isy Joshua, as yet unpublished.

34   It will be seen that all this brings up the problem of the distinction and the relations between a planned economy and a market economy. Simplistic contrasting of these two types of economy can be relevant only at a level of abstraction which has nothing to do with any practical reality. The real problem is that of the *class* character of a given society and the *dominant features* of a concrete economy. Besides, the relations between the market forces and the forces of the plan are obviously bound to change in the course of time, with the very development of the productive forces and all the changes that accompany this growth, on the planes of organisation, of consciousness, etc.

6: The problem of prices in the socialist countries of Europe (Some reflexions on a recent debate)[1]

For about ten years now the problem of prices has been extensively discussed in the socialist countries. This problem is one of decisive theoretical and practical importance for the further development of the socialist economy: a coherent price-system in conformity with the requirements for the building of socialism is an indispensable tool both for good day-to-day management of enterprises and for satisfactory economic planning.

A system of prices like this is, of course, needed from the very beginning of the process of transition to socialism, but the need for it makes itself felt still more acutely as the economy becomes more complex and inter-relations are multiplied between the different branches and centres of production. Only at a still higher level of the productive forces will conditions exist for the value form to disappear, and, with it, the role of prices.[2]

In the present period, prices still have an indispensable role to play, but they can play it only if they are not fixed "arbitrarily", that is, provided that they express the social conditions of production and the requirements for changing the economic and social structures.

For many years, most decisions relating to prices in the socialist countries of Europe have been taken on a day-to-day basis. Generally speaking, these decisions did not reflect any overall theoretical conception.[3]

In the same way, for a long time the economists of the socialist countries mostly confined themselves to describing current practice, trying to justify it and analysing certain of its consequences, in order, sometimes, to suggest changes on one point or another, usually some point of detail.

The recent debate has therefore presented, in the breadth of its subject-matter, a striking contrast with past habits. Nevertheless, the results of this discussion still remain very limited.

When we try to consider the debate as a whole, we are struck by the absence of any firm and uniform statement of the problems at issue. This has contributed to no small extent to rendering the debate unfruitful. On the theoretical plane it would not be exaggerating to say that the discussion has failed to result in any decisive step forward; this does not mean that there were not a certain number of important contributions, thanks to which the nature of the questions raised is today clearer than it was before.

This being so, it is not surprising that the impact of the discussion on the practical measures that it had become urgent to take was relatively limited, although some of the decisions adopted during recent years, in certain socialist countries of Europe, have been inspired by theses that were put forward in the course of the theoretical discussion. It should be observed that the mutual contradictoriness of these theses has found expression in the lack of uniformity of the measures adopted in the various countries.[4]

The (on the whole) unsatisfactory character of the debate about prices, from the theoretical standpoint, explains too why price-reform in the Soviet Union (especially reform of industrial wholesale prices) has been put off from one year to the next, though it was announced so far back as 1960. There are, of course, practical reasons, too, that account for these postponements, but the latter have now resulted in such substantial disadvantages for the Soviet economy that a price-reform must be carried through on 1st July 1967.[5] It is to affect, in the first place, wholesale prices in heavy industry. (Cf. Sitnin, No. 57, p. 45.)

If the debate can be described as comparatively sterile, this is because, at the theoretical level, it has not noticeably advanced the analysis of the problem, as is shown by the reappearance again and again, during the period concerned, of the same themes and the same arguments, a sign of the circular nature of the discussion.

Very recently, however, the discussion escaped from this circularity, but only in so far as it moved on to fresh ground and confronted fresh problems. This shift in the subject-matter of the discussion (which had at first been centred mainly on the problem of prices and later mainly on problems of the management of enterprises and of planning the economy), when the questions previously under consideration had been answered only very partially and inadequately, confirms that the way the theoretical problems were presented was unsatisfactory, something I shall have more to say about later.

While it is important to consider the content of the discussion and the main themes tackled, which is what I propose to do here, it does not appear to me to be useful to go over the history of the debate itself, owing to the restricted nature of its outcome.

On the other hand, it does seem necessary to recall what has been, and still largely continues to be, the price-system in the Soviet Union, that is, in the country where the discussion began and whose price-policy has, in the past, inspired to a very great extent the decisions taken in this same sphere in the other socialist countries of Europe. A quick look at this price system will enable us to understand better what were the most

immediate concerns of those who took part in the discussion, and the
limits which these concerns imposed on the scope of the problems discussed, from which follows the need for more precise formulations.

I The price–system in the Soviet Union at the beginning of the 1950s

The price-system prevailing in the USSR at the beginning of the 1950s
was a real product of history, being, in a sense, derived from the price-
system left behind by the N.E.P. The latter was, broadly speaking, a
system of market prices which had already been partly modified by regulation based on political and social considerations, and above all, by the
dominant role played in industry by the state sector.[6]

At the start of the Five-Year Plans, those prices which had not already
been regulated were brought under regulation, which meant that from
then onward all industrial prices were transformed into *"administered"* or
"regulated" prices,[7] fixed by the relevant state organs.[8]

Transactions between state enterprises had to take place on the basis
of these prices. Wages also being regulated (taking account, to start with,
of their historically determined level), the state enterprises operated within
a framework of "regulated costs".

As time went by, the price-system that was the "legacy" of the N.E.P.
naturally underwent modifications, which, though considerable, were
usually partial in character, and never called in question the "historical
basis" of the prices concerned. Thus, when new products were manufactured (and millions of new products have appeared between 1927 and the
present time), their prices were determined by taking as basis their cost
of production—this being itself determined by historically given prices—
at the time when they began to be manufactured (or the cost of production
expected when manufacture had been extended to a sufficiently large
scale), plus a certain "profit-margin". The entry of new products into the
production cycle of a particular group of users gave rise, also, to revision
of their selling prices. However, the price-system was never really recast so as to take into account the specific requirements of a planned
economy.[9]

Thus, although, in the end, prices taken individually have become
increasingly different from what they were in 1927 (owing to technical
changes and changes in wage-levels), the *structure of the price-system* has
continued to be deeply marked by its origins.

True, with the passage of time this structure has also become marked
by a number of decisions which were relatively independent of the changes
that have come about in production-processes and costs of production.
Some of these decisions were mainly inspired by financial necessities,
while others aimed at using prices as tools of "economic calculation"
("business accounting").

As regards financial necessities, these led to changes, big and small,
in the profit-margins added to the costs of production of the various

products, and also to changes in the rates of the taxes (this meant, mainly, the turnover tax) embodied in the prices paid by users.

Consequently, the ratios between costs of production and selling or buying prices varied a great deal from one period to another. They were also very different as between one product and another.

Generally speaking, the variation in ratios between selling prices and costs of production was not the result of applying coherent principles to differing situations, but rather of decisions taken in different directions in response to the varying requirements of different periods, or, quite simply, of the greater or lesser convenience of using one particular product rather than another as a source of financial receipts.

This situation greatly reduced the possibility of using prices as a tool of economic calculation. In general, therefore, they were used for this purpose only in an accessory way. Prices were considered above all as a means of accounting for the receipts and expenditure of enterprises, that is, of checking on their operations from the financial point of view. In principle, investment decisions and production plans were not supposed to be much affected by the financial results of the working of individual enterprises or branches of the economy. The drawing up of plans was to be based, above all, on determining a number of targets regarded as being strategically important for the general development of the national economy and the satisfaction of the people's needs. Adjustments between targets were thus effected, during the drawing up of the plan, essentially by way of using technical coefficients and material balances.

In fact, it was never possible to be confined exclusively to these principles. In practice, a certain number of decisions, especially regarding the use of a particular raw material or the introduction of a particular technique, were determined or influenced by considerations of price, or of "efficiency" measured by price, despite the very slight economic significance of the prices concerned.

On the other hand, it was generally agreed, even before the reform of the management of Soviet enterprises decided on in September 1965, that the quality of the management of enterprises could be estimated by observing their costs of production. Within the framework of *khozraschet* (the autonomy of enterprises in respect of accounting), which has existed since the N.E.P., *one* of the criteria for evaluating the quality of management has always been the progress of the profits made by each enterprise, and the latter's achievement of a certain planned level of profitability; if it was a loss that was planned, as was the case with many enterprises, and even whole branches of production, the *reduction of losses* was one of the criteria for estimating the quality of management.

Thus, in practice, a large number of decisions, some important and others only affecting matters of detail, but amounting together to something very substantial, were taken on the basis of calculations made in terms of prices.

The consequences of this situation have always had a very big bearing both on the making of technological choices and on day-to-day production operations. It was, indeed, practically inevitable that those responsible for preparing technical projects, or for managing enterprises, should prefer to take decisions that "seemed" more advantageous because they could make it possible to reduce costs of production or permit a "saving" of investments, even though the "advantages" or "savings" calculated like this were, more often than not, merely the result of a certain way of fixing prices and were thus far from necessarily meaning real economic advantages for the national economy.

The tendency to use prices as a means of "economic calculation" has always been regarded as self-evidently justified. This is why the prices of a large number of machines were deliberately fixed at a relatively low level in order to "encourage" their use. Similarly, complicated procedures (often necessitating recourse to subsidies) were introduced in order to encourage both the production and the use of certain products.

In fact, the use of prices as a tool of economic calculation and a way of evaluating whether enterprises were managed well or badly was felt as an objective necessity which came increasingly into contradiction with the price-structure itself, owing to the complexity and even incoherence of this structure.

II The initial concerns of the participants in the debate about prices

The state of the price-system in the Soviet Union about ten years ago, and the similar state of the price-systems in the other socialist countries of Europe, was thus one of the reasons why the debate on prices began. The purpose of this discussion was to make possible a coherent revision of the price-system.

At the start, one of the main concerns of nearly all of those who took part in the debate was to try and simplify the price-structure, by making the formation of prices and their subsequent evolution subject to a few simple rules. It was fairly generally agreed that the simplicity and universality of the rules applied in the formation of prices ought to make the latter comparable, and so "economically significant". It was further agreed that such prices ought to ensure the *profitability* of nearly every enterprise. The problem was seen in almost the same terms in the Soviet Union and in most of the other socialist countries of Europe, in particular in Hungary, where they were primarily concerned to put an end to what was called the "dismemberment of the price system" (Csikos-Nagy, No. 17, p. 256). Some economists (such as Novozhilov, see Nos. 54 and 55) did not accept this "simplifying" point of view, for they were convinced of the complexity of the social cost of production which prices ought to measure, and of the need, if this measurement was to be accomplished, of employing mathematical methods. However, the trend of thought represented by these economists, though important theoretically, has remained a minority trend both in the Soviet Union and in the other socialist countries. This is doubtless due to the fact that the theoretical and practical problems raised by the proposals of these economists are very big ones, which call for further research, involving collaboration with mathematicians.[10]

In any case, in relation to the central line of the debate, the conceptions of those economists who advocate the use of mathematical methods for the establishment of a price-system occupy a position apart. I shall return to this point later.

While the formulae suggested for price-fixing were varied, they were none the less nearly all inspired by two concerns which were added to the aims already mentioned, of simplicity, universality and making profitability general.

One of these concerns was to eliminate "subjectivism" in the fixing of prices—a concern which, in principle, goes back a long way. Its necessity was declared already by Stalin in his work on *Economic Problems of Socialism in the USSR* (No. 58).

The other concern, which is undoubtedly the most fundamental, is to reconstruct the price-system so that it can function as an instrument of *economic calculation*, that is, a means of *guiding* certain decisions. This is bound up, as has been said, with a practice that employs calculations in price-terms to estimate the "advantages" or "disadvantages" of a particular decision—a practice which, moreover, is unavoidable.

The content of this second concern is given very general expression in formulae such as this: "Prices should reflect the socially necessary labour inputs, that is to say, social costs" (Csikos-Nagy, No. 17, p. 255). Or: "The most important principle of price-formation under socialism consists in ensuring that the prices of commodities correspond to the socially necessary expenditure of labour in producing them" (Tsagolov, No. 61, p. 405).[11]

III The main proposals

Agreement between the writers stops as soon as the ground of their initial concerns is left behind and they go forward to offer proposals. They are, indeed, divided by very great differences of opinion when it comes to defining how to "measure value", lay down practical "rules" for price-fixing, and allow for "exceptions" to these "rules".

To say something at once about the last-mentioned point, it is observable that the exceptions most generally allowed, to the rules proposed, correspond to social and political considerations. These considerations may lead to certain products being sold relatively cheaply, because they are regarded as "cultural", or there may be others the cost of which is relatively high but which it is desired to keep, or cause to be, in widespread use (new means of production, for instance). The exceptions to the rules that are proposed are related also to the fact that quality is taken into account in fixing prices, and, again, following a practice already mentioned, to desire either to "encourage" certain lines of production by paying high prices to the enterprises that supply them or, on the contrary, "restricting demand" for scarce goods (Tsagolov, No. 61, p. 405).

The great number of "exceptions" may cause one to ask whether they are not perhaps manifestations of some law overlooked by the proposed rules, but the question has rarely been put in this way, except by economists who take a different line from that of composing "rules" accompanied by more or less numerous exceptions; that is, mainly by the mathematical economists.

As has been said, it is not only on the nature of the exceptions to be allowed to the price-fixing rules that the writers differ, but also on the rules themselves, in other words on the way in which socially necessary expenditure should be calculated.

Close examination of the proposed rules would probably show that there are several dozen of them. In Hungary, for instance, where the debate has been especially lively, the National Prices Office has registered 32 different price-systems (or "models") (Csikos Nagy, No. 17, p. 255), merely for the purpose of carrying out calculations with a view to choosing the "best" system.

Actually, despite their very great diversity, most of the proposals correspond to three basic conceptions, and combinations of these three. We will first examine the three basic conceptions, and then some others which deserve special attention.

1 *Prices based on "value"*

One conception is aimed at providing a price-system "based on value", referring to Book I of *Capital*. In practice, this conception is interpreted as implying that to the *money costs* of the various kinds of production must be added a *"net income"* proportionate to the expenditure on wages required for these kinds of production. One of the first upholders of this conception was the Soviet economist Strumilin (No. 59, pp. 503–80). Though practice has always been remote from anything corresponding, even very roughly, to this point of view, it has almost always been accepted officially that prices are (or ought to be) "based on value", while at the same time the need has been allowed for many "exceptions".

This point of view is the one expressed in the Political Economy Textbook of the USSR Academy of Sciences. Among the exceptions regarded as justifiable the Textbook mentions the "fixing below value of the prices of means of production" (USSR Academy of Sciences, No. 1, p. 524). "Fixing below value" is meant in the sense of prices lower than the price that would be fixed if one were to follow strictly the conception of prices "based on value".

Tsagolov's *Course of Political Economy* (No. 61), published in 1963, also takes this line, as we have seen. He allows more or less the same exceptions to the "value" rule as those allowed by the Textbook.

The calculations that have been made in order to compare the various prices (if they had been fixed in this way) with the actual prices are, of course, very complicated. It is, indeed, not sufficient to carry out separate calculations for each product, adding to present money expenditure the total of actual wages multiplied by a coefficient equal to the average ratio of the net overall income (on the social scale) to the total wages of the workers in the production sector (or the industrial sector). If this were the procedure followed it would leave entirely out of account the fact that the money expenditure of all the branches would itself be altered by the changes that the alteration in the price structure would bring about in the prices charged by their own suppliers.

The problem can be solved only by *calculating all the price-changes at the same time*, something that calls for the use of tables of inter-industrial relations. However, it is out of the question, with the means of calculation available up to now, to work on the millions of actual prices. The calculations that have been attempted have been based on the average prices of the different branches of production. There is no point in emphasising here the technical problems to which such calculations give rise and the necessarily limited significance of the results obtained, owing to the fact that they relate only to the "average prices" of the branches.

At the same time, it is not without interest to illustrate the implications of proposals of this kind by referring to the results of calculations carried out in Hungary, where they have shown special interest in this question.

To make these calculations, the national economy has been assumed to be divided into 56 production sectors, which have then been grouped into seven branches. Calculations have shown that, as compared with actual prices, "prices based on value" would be 10·5 per cent lower in industry, 49 per cent higher in agriculture, 18 per cent higher in transport, and so on (Ganczer, No. 24). This reveals how far the actual price-system is from being founded on the "rules" that would be imposed by the conception of prices "based on value". According to calculations that have been made, the same is true of other socialist countries, including the Soviet Union.

2 Prices based on "own costs"

A second conception has inspired proposals that aim at reconstructing the price-system by "normalising" it, that is, by applying in as systematic and uniform a way as possible the rules of price-fixing which had been adopted in practice more or less spontaneously.

This second conception is often referred to as that of prices "based on average value". The point of this expression seems to be above all to conceal what the conception really amounts to, namely, a conception that has nothing at all to do with "price based on value". It is sometimes described, with more meaning, as the conception of prices equivalent to "own costs".

Concretely, the procedure adopted is this: in order to work out what ought to be the selling price, one adds *to the cost of production, in money terms*, of each product a "net income" obtained by multiplying this cost of production by a certain "standard of profitability".

To a large extent this is in fact how prices were for a long time actually determined, in the Soviet Union and in most of the other socialist countries,[12] though, as we shall see, this procedure is now being departed from to an increasing extent.

Through this practice, each time a new product appears and is produced in sufficiently large quantities to warrant its being given a regulated price, the latter is actually fixed by reckoning the cost of production plus a certain standard of profitability. This is what happens with the *selling prices* of industrial enterprises; the prices actually paid by the buyers may be higher, as a result of various taxes being added to the price.

Further, with regard to actual practice, two more important observations need to be made:

(1) The cost of production which serves as base for calculation is not necessarily the actual cost of production, but is usually an "official cost of production", i.e., the cost of production as "confirmed" by some administrative service. This official cost of production is usually, though not always, the *average* cost of production, as estimated at a certain moment, and it may therefore differ widely from the "actual cost of production" of a particular enterprise.

The problem whether one ought to take as basis for calculation the *average* cost of production for the given branch, or the *maximum* cost of production (cost of production of an additional unit-product, or of an enterprise which operates *at the highest cost*, but is nevertheless essential if needs are to be covered) is increasingly discussed. With a few exceptions, especially relating to the prices of the products of the extractive industries, practice continues to favour taking the *average* cost of production as basis for calculation, and this is also the view of many economists.

Nevertheless, a strong current of opinion has appeared which favours the adoption of the *maximum* figure, especially among those economists whose attitude to the system of "own costs" is a critical one.

(2) The "profitability margin" is generally very variable as between different products.

However, despite the lack of coherence between the different practical procedures, that is, the extreme variety of standards of profitability and of conditions under which costs of production are calculated, not to speak of the incidence of a number of taxes, calculations show that, by choosing an adequate uniform profitability-standard it would be possible to arrive, using this procedure, at a price-system that, on the average, diverged relatively little from the actual price-system.

Taking the example of Hungary again, we see that there, on the basis of calculations similar to those mentioned above, the prices obtained by applying a uniform standard of profitability (itself calculated so that the average level of retail prices was the same as the actual level) would be, in the case of industrial prices, only 0·4 per cent higher than the actual prices. On the other hand, prices calculated in this way would be 27·9 per cent higher than actual prices in agriculture and 14·4 per cent higher than in transport (Ganczer, No. 24, p. 74). The size of these divergences, where agriculture is concerned, is due to the fact that agricultural prices are fixed in a special way, that is, they are not worked out by adding a "profitability-standard" to a cost of production.

The writers who supported the system of "own costs" were mainly in favour of the procedures in force when the debate opened. What they criticised in these procedures was largely the very wide diversity of "standards of profitability" which were applied to different products. For them, "true prices" required that a uniform standard be applied to all of them.

From this point of view, one of the main criticisms made of the "traditional practices" was the "fixing below value" of the prices of means of production, as compared with what these prices would be if a single standard of profitability were applied.

At first, criticism of the traditional practices, in so far as this aimed not at rejecting but merely at "rationalising" them, was on the whole successful. Thus, to an increasing extent, in the Soviet Union the "standards of profitability" applied to the costs of production of the various products were brought closer together, though not reduced to uniformity. For example, in heavy industry, the margin of profitability, which was only 2·6 per cent in 1940, rose to 13 per cent in 1960 (Tsagolov, No. 61, p. 509).

During the same period, the share of net income in the prices of consumer goods was reduced, though it remains, on the whole, higher than in the prices of means of production. Nevertheless, it is no longer possible to speak of the Soviet Union's having an only slightly profitable heavy industry alongside a highly profitable light industry. Indeed, as a result especially of the policy adopted regarding agricultural prices, a number of branches of light industry are working at a loss (the meat industry) or at the minimum level of profitability (fish and dairying industries).

In general, despite the "rectifications" to which the Soviet price-system has been subjected in recent years, it continues to lack much coherence and to present a number of weaknesses. V. Sitnin, Chairman of the Prices Committee (attached to the Gosplan organisation), has analysed some of these weaknesses in an article in which he also lists the chief features of the reform of industrial wholesale prices now in progress (No. 57).

One of Sitnin's criticisms of the present price-system in the Soviet Union is that, in many cases, selling prices do not even cover costs of production. Another of his criticisms relates to the very wide variations in the "rates of profit" that present-day prices produce. Thus, the coal industry works at a planned *rate of loss* of 16 per cent of the value of its production-funds (accounts of 1964), while the precision instruments industry works at a rate of profit of 50 per cent. The writer shows that even bigger variations can be found between the rates of profit realised on the different products produced by one and the same enterprise, some being produced at a loss and others at rates of profit of 200 or 300 per cent or even more, without there being any justification for this disparity (No. 57, pp. 37-8).

The lack of coherence in the present price-system in the Soviet Union

G

makes it very difficult to "rationalise": to do this, except within rather narrow limits, must in fact entail considerable disturbance in the structure of prices. This is no doubt one of the practical reasons why it has been necessary to wait so long for the reform the of price-system, announced as far back as 1960, to take shape in reality.

The present situation involves disadvantages which are all the more numerous because, since 1965, an increasing number of Soviet enterprises have gone over to a new method of management, which includes evaluating their activity on the basis of profitability.

In other socialist countries in Europe, price-reform has gone further than in the Soviet Union, and has culminated, in most cases, in abandonment of the system of "own costs". The latter nevertheless continues to be applied, at least partly in Poland, in the G.D.R. and in Romania. Even in these countries, however, they are moving farther and farther away from a "pure system" of "own costs", because this system is being combined with others (mainly by including in the price a "rate of profit" calculated in proportion to the investments tied up in the various lines of production).

So as not to have to go back over the system of "own costs", let me say straight away that its chief justification is that it is extremely simple to operate: at any moment the actual or standardised cost of production of a type of product can be worked out by taking the actual money expenditure as one's basis, without having to concern oneself about what this expenditure means or about what is represented by the value of the funds invested.[13]

It is undoubtedly on account of its comparative simplicity that this "procedure" for calculating prices has remained in force for such a long time and continues to be favoured by many practical men. At the same time it must be observed that no serious theoretical argument can be adduced to justify it. A. Emmanuel is right when, comparing the different price-systems, he writes, regarding the system of "own costs":

"This is the most irrational and absurd system that could be, as regards both its internal implications and its effect in the sphere of foreign exchange. It raises the price of the products of those branches where the coefficient of raw material is high (these are not at all the same as those with a high organic composition, but indeed are generally industries with a low organic composition, such as the light-industry branches), while it lowers the prices of the branches with a low coefficient of raw material, which are generally the ones with a high organic composition, such as the heavy-industry branches." (A. Emmanuel, No. 20, p. 5.)

The lack of theoretical consistency in the system of own costs explains why it is that the writers who have analysed the mathematical structures of the main price-systems (especially so as to bring out the economic implications of a change from one system to another) have, as a rule, not thought it worth while to analyse the structure of the system of "own costs" (Brody, No. 15).

3 *Prices based on "prices of production"*

The last of the three main types of proposal mentioned is often described as a system of "price-of-production"-type prices, because most of the economists who advocate calculating prices in a way that can take account not only of the *individual cost* of each product but also of as large a part as possible of its quantifiable *social cost* have sought to refer to the concept of "price of production", as this worked out in Book III of *Capital*. The proposals put forward by these economists have, however, provided only very limited answers to the problems which preoccupied them, and most of the criticisms directed against these proposals are justified. This, however, should not make us lose sight of the decisive importance of the problems of taking into account the actual social costs of different kinds of product.

Within the limits of this article it is not possible to analyse these problems in detail. To do so would take us too far from our study of the discussion on prices (one of the shortcomings of which was, indeed, that it did not tackle these problems, or did so only to a very limited extent). The essence of the matter, however, can be put like this: as a general rule, unless a simultaneous calculation of costs is made, reduction to the minimum of *individual* costs of different products fails to ensure the reduction to the minimum of their *total social cost*, for by reducing the individual cost of some products one causes an increase in the individual cost of others—at least, after a certain stage has been reached in the socialisation of the productive forces.

On the basis of private ownership of the means of production, the negative effects, from the angle of the *total social cost* of production, of a particular technique or procedure are a matter of indifference to the capitalists, since the objective laws of the capitalist mode of production cause the decisions taken by the agents of this mode of production to be dominated by their striving for maximum individual profits.

In an economy dominated by social ownership of the means of production, and aiming not at individual profit but at maximum satisfaction of social needs, indifference to social costs is unacceptable, and this is what gives rise to a series of proposals intended, in principle, to make it possible to estimate these costs, which are never seen *directly* by the agents of production themselves.

In what may seem a paradoxical fashion, most of these proposals appear to try to "restore" the prices of production which are characteristic of the capitalist mode of production. Up to a point, this paradox is only an apparent one: price of production represents, in fact, an elementary (or "primitive") way of taking account of certain social costs, those which the very working of capitalism *indirectly* obliged the agents of this mode of production to reckon with. As Novozhilov correctly observes (No. 54, p. 215), it is only by analysing the working of a mode of production which is marked by a *higher* level of socialisation of production that one can grasp that this is the actual function of "price of production". However, while recognising this, it is also necessary to recognise the *capitalist limitations* of this price, and what, therefore, the specific changes are that must be made to it in order that it may become something different, a real social price that can effectively be used for certain economic calculations that have to be made under the conditions of transition from capitalism to socialism.

There can be no question of developing here all the implications of the proposals mentioned; that would mean going off on to another subject. I will therefore confine myself to a few points only:

a) One aspect of indirect social costs is this: when production funds are invested for a certain purpose, this usually increases the costs of production for other branches where these funds might otherwise have been invested—since the more that is invested in one direction, in order to reduce costs of production there, the less can be invested in other spheres, where costs are therefore relatively and indirectly increased. This connexion between costs means that *minimisation of the cost of social production* as a whole can be achieved only in so far as the reduction of some costs does not entail an increase of others. The application of an average rate of profit to the investments made in various kinds of production, and the formation on this basis of a price of production, makes it possible to measure, in an elementary way, this aspect of the indirect social costs of every investment in production.

b) This capitalist measurement of resultant indirect social costs cannot be transferred, just as it stands, to a socialist economy or to transitional economies.

Without going into a detailed study of the changes that must be made in this price[14] (some of them still need to be worked out theoretically), it can be said that the chief aspects of these changes are as follows:

(1) The socialist economy, as it evolves towards socialism, has not and cannot have any "average rate of profit" (which itself results from the law of value being applied both to the products of labour and to labour-power itself); what it has and must have is a *minimum rate of labour-saving*. This rate can be calculated only as part of a plan: it is not given ready-made by the "economic system", but has to be worked out on the basis of political and social decisions;

(2) Measurements of social costs cannot be confined to applying a simple "mathematical rule", for the size of the indirect social cost of a particular line of production depends on the total structure of production within which this particular production takes place. Now, whereas under capitalism this total structure of production is dominated by the laws of expanded reproduction of capital, under socialism, or under social formations transitional between capitalism and socialism, this structure is dominated by the plan, in which society's estimation of its own needs is expressed. Only on the basis of the plan itself, therefore, can social costs be estimated. I shall come back to this point later.

Unfortunately, most of the economists who have sought to bring out the social costs of production (with the exception, to some extent, of Novozhilov), have failed to show all the inadequacies of "price of production" as such. This is why what ought to have been an adumbration of a way to reckon up social costs of production appears usually as a mere "application" of a system of "prices of production".

After this parenthesis, the aim of which was to show the nature of the problems raised by the conceptions here mentioned, and the inadequate treatment given to these problems, we can return to describing the main features of the proposals that have been put forward.

In general, according to these proposals, the price of every product should be calculated by adding to its cost of production[15] a net income proportionate to the investment made in producing this product.

The way of calculating prices thus proposed seems, formally speaking, to consist in applying a "rate of profit" to the investments committed to the various kinds of production, and this is why, as has been shown, this system of prices is described as a "price-of-production" system.

Depending on the particular economist, the investments to which the "rate of profit", or of "profitability", is to be applied are either the entire investment committed to the given line of production (i.e., both fixed funds and circulating funds), or only the fixed funds.

When it comes to the conditions for determining "rates of profitability", the proposals are again very diverse, owing to the empirical or eclectic character of these proposals. It has been proposed that rates differentiated by sectors be applied (cf. Nemchinov, No. 51), or else a uniform rate determined by the ratio between the total amount of investment laid down by the plan and the amount already invested, or one determined by the ratio between planned accumulation and planned consumption, or, again, a minimum rate worked out on the basis of calculations from plan variants, and so on.

In recent years, an increasing number of economists in the Soviet Union and the European socialist countries have come out in favour of conceptions of this sort. In the Soviet Union, one may particularly mention, as supporters of this system, Z. Atlas (Nos. 4, 5 and 6), I. Malyshev, and V. Sobol (No. 42), V. D. Belkin (No. 11), E. Kats and A. Rozhansky (No. 29), and also, though with considerable qualifications, Novozhilov (Nos. 54 and 55) and Nemchinov (Nos. 51, 52 and 53).

Contrary to what is widely supposed outside the socialist countries, this conception is not necessarily bound up with the writers' ideas in favour of extensive decentralisation, making planning "more flexible", providing material incentives, or using "profit" as the chief index to the activity of enterprises.

Liberman, for example (Nos. 38 and 39), has advocated over a period of several years his views aimed at enabling the profit criterion and material incentives to play a greater role, but without declaring himself either for a substantial change in the price-system generally or, in particular, for introducing a system of the "price-of-production" type. Even when, in 1962, Liberman spoke in favour of a conception of "profitability" which would be defined by the ratio between profit and amount of investment in production, he does not seem to have advocated a recasting of the price-system along the lines of "prices of production". Moreover, when the "price-of-production" idea is advocated in its strict form, it is seen to include *in* the "price of production" a "charge for investments" which does not benefit the enterprise but *is paid into the exchequer*. Consequently, far from being favourable to an increase in the profits recorded by each production-unit, this proposal tends, in principle, to reduce these profits.

Conversely, we observe that most of the supporters of a price-system of the price-of-production type have also declared at the same time for a high degree of centralisation. This is so, in particular, in the case of Nemchinov (cf. No. 51, pp. 40–2) and Novozhilov,[16] who are both far from advocating a "pure price of production" but are rather in favour of certain procedures that come close to the reckoning-up of social costs.

It is also important to emphasise that most of those in favour of this more or less pure price-of-production system have taken up their position not on the basis of theoretical arguments, such as those aiming at bringing out the indirect social costs of different products, but rather by bringing forward arguments of a "practical" order.

Thus, one of the arguments most frequently advanced by supporters of this kind of price is that it enables the central planning organs to exercise better control over the use made of production funds by the enterprises.

In the same way, it is often said that, if these proposals were adopted, this would make it possible to reduce the investments required by the enterprises. It is, indeed, commonly the case that the enterprises' invest-ments greatly exceed their real needs. In this way the managers try to create "reserves" of production-capacity. This practice, which is bound up with the difficulties the enterprises often experience in obtaining machinery or spare parts at the moments when they need them (owing to defects in the working of the system of technical supply), results, in fact, in a considerable waste of fixed funds. Thus, in 1962, a census and some samplings carried out by the USSR Central Statistical Office showed that about half the stock of machine tools was not being used (on the basis of two-shift working, taken as the norm). This stock represented, accord-ing to the investigation, a total value of one thousand million roubles. The same investigation revealed that there was about six thousand million roubles' worth of plant which had not been installed. This amount corres-ponds to approximately half of the annual investment in new plant (F. Khachaturov and D. Lvov, No. 30).

In any case, there is nothing to be gained for our present purpose by listing the various arguments that have been put forward for or against this conception of the price-system. To do so would be to enter into the details of the discussion itself.

It is to the point, however, to note that the price-system that has been introduced in the Soviet Union during 1967 is inspired by the system of prices of production, although it involves substantial divergences from what the logic of this system would demand. The following figures illustrate this point.

For heavy industry as a whole, the rate of profitability foreseen (this rate is measured in relation to the production funds) is about 15 per cent *on the average*, which entails an increase in the wholesale prices of industrial products by 11–12 per cent (V. Sitnin, No. 57, No. 41). This rate of 15 per cent compares with a previous rate of about 10 per cent (A. Komin, No. 31, p. 13).[17] For a variety of reasons, however, this average actually results from the use of different rates of profitability for different branches: 7·5 per cent in the coal industry (hitherto working at a loss), 15 per cent in the metallurgy of ferrous metals (where previously it was 8 per cent) and non-ferrous metals alike, and in the extraction of oil and gas, a little less than 15 per cent in machine-building, about 15 per cent in the chemical industry (hitherto 20 per cent, on average), 20 per cent in the timber industry (hitherto 8 per cent), and 10 per cent in electric power production. In light industry it would appear that rates of profitability are to vary, if the proposals of the State Committee on Prices are accepted, between 30 and 35 per cent.

As will be seen, although formally prices are to be constructed as "prices of production" (cost of production plus rate of profitability on production funds), in reality the adoption of rates of profitability that differ widely between the branches means that the actual price-structure is far from that which would be given by a price-of-production-type system.

The reasons for these divergences are essentially practical ones. A quick look at a few of them will reveal some of the difficulties involved in going over from one price-system to another, and also the implications of the present price-reform in the USSR.

We must observe, first of all, that to have adopted a uniform profitability rate for all branches would have meant raising certain prices which it seemed necessary to keep stable (retail prices, and prices of certain goods intended for agricultural use). Secondly, account had to be taken, at one and the same time, of this consideration and of the problems posed by the mutual substitutability of certain products, the prices of which it was thought necessary to keep linked. The most typical case is that of "fuel and power" products. Here, the application of a uniform rate of 15 per cent would have meant that a ton of coal would have cost four times as much as its caloric equivalent in oil and twenty times as much as its equivalent in natural gas. On the other hand, equalising the prices of caloric equivalents, with a profitability of zero for the coal-mining industry, would have given profitability-rates (in relation to production funds) of 41 per cent to oil-extraction, 108 per cent to oil-refining and 250 per cent to the natural gas industry (Komin, No. 31, p. 15): the average profitability of the fuel and power branch would thus have been 36·8 per cent. The solution adopted took account of these problems, but resulted in a large number of coal-mines continuing to work at a loss.

This illumines another problem, connected with the considerable un-evenness of the costs of production of the different production-units within one and the same branch of production. When this exceeds a certain level, some of the production-units are working at a loss (if the cost of production that serves as basis for the calculation of selling prices is the average cost) while others record extremely high profits. In the case of the fuel and power industry, these difficulties were partly eliminated by using different accounting prices for the different coal-mines, and by taking as basis the costs of production of the least favourably situated oil and gas wells, the rest being obliged to pay a differential rent (Sitnin, No. 57, p. 43).

Finally, it must be pointed out that the unequal intensity of investment in different kinds of production, combined with the unequal speed of rotation of these investment funds, also presents a number of problems. Thus, in oil-extraction, the ratio of production funds to annual current production expenses is 7 to 1, whereas it is 1 to 7 in the clothing industry. This means that a profitability-rate of 15 per cent applied to these two industries produces a standard of profitability (ratio of profit to cost of production) of 100 per cent in the former and 2 per cent in the latter. With a standard so low as 2 per cent, more than half of the production units in the clothing industry would be working at a loss. The situation being similar in many light industries, it has appeared necessary in such cases to bring the standards of profitability up to 6–8 per cent, which means a considerable increase in the profitability-rates of the funds invested in these industries. It is obvious that this type of difficulty results from taking the average cost of production as basis when calculating the selling price.

To sum up, we see that the reform of wholesale prices carried out in Soviet industry is far from having resulted in simplifying the conditions for fixing prices by unifying the rules for doing this. Consequently the price-system expresses only very imperfectly the difference in social costs between different products. This may have only limited disadvantages for the economic calculations carried out at the level of the planning organs, since the latter possess other sources of information about costs. But it may have unfavourable consequences as regards the decisions that enterprises have to take on the basis of prices; and the reform of the management of enterprises is making the latter take prices as their guide when adopting a large number of decisions and in trying to increase their profits. It is important to observe that, while profitability-rates serve to determine selling prices, the receipts that result from the application of these rates are by no means all paid into the exchequer (which would follow logically from the adoption of a system of prices of production)— on the contrary, they mostly appear in the form of profits of the enter-prises. Only a relatively small proportion of these profits has to be paid into the exchequer, in the form of a tax proportionate to the amount of the production fund. This tax should come to about 6 per cent in most industries.

The difficulties involved in the price-reform, especially in combination with the reform in the management of enterprises, are widely acknowledged by Soviet economists. They consider that the present reforms are only the starting-point of a long process of change in the system of prices, of management and of planning.

As has been mentioned earlier, besides the three basic systems of price-formation that I have just described, some other systems were also proposed. A few words must be said about some of these proposals, especially about those that aim to "base" the internal price-structure on the prices that prevail on the world market, and those that combine various features of the systems previously examined.

4 Prices based on world prices

The supporters of a system of internal prices "based" on world market prices seem to have been especially numerous in Hungary, doubtless because relations with the capitalist world market play an important role for this country. According to those who put forward the most systematic proposals of this kind, it is not only the prices of exports and imports that should be fixed on the basis of world market prices but also those of all other goods, since world prices represent, it is said, "the expression in money of labour that is socially necessary on the international scale" (cf. Tarnovsky, No. 60). This is a highly controversial argument at a time when world prices are increasingly influenced by international monopolies and oligopolies and by the strategy of the principal capitalist states.

S. Ganczer (No. 24, p. 69), after setting forth the thesis of the supporters of a price-system based on world market prices, adds that in his view this thesis is unacceptable because it is necessary that "in every country the price-system must, in the first place, reflect the prevailing conditions of production". He correctly notes, moreover, that it is very difficult to determine what world market prices actually are.

Altogether, the proposals aimed at "basing" internal prices on those of the world market have had only a limited influence on practical policy. This influence has shown itself, however, on the one hand at the level of exchanges between the socialist countries of Europe, for whom the Council of Mutual Economic Aid (Comecon) has decided that the prices used should, in principle, be the same as those prevailing on the capitalist world market in recent years;[18] and, on the other, within some of the member-countries of Comecon measures have been adopted which aim at taking account of world prices. Thus, in Bulgaria, it is proposed to establish a close link between the formation of internal prices and prices in foreign trade, and to establish a direct relationship between the receipts of enterprises and their "utility" from the standpoint of exports. In Hungary, the accounts maintained between industrial enterprises and foreign trade organisations must be kept in such a way that the producing enterprises receive world market prices for their products. Somewhat similar measures are being prepared in Poland and Czechoslovakia (Tarnovsky, No. 60).

In spite of these measures, the principal prices in the European socialist countries are essentially formed on the basis of one of the three price-systems described earlier, or of a combination of these.

IV Combinations of price–systems and "two–channel prices"

The reasons given in favour of these "combinations" are, in general, essentially practical ones.

Against the use of prices based principally or entirely "on value" it is argued that such prices do not make possible evaluation of the cost to society of the considerable investments that certain techniques necessitate.

In opposition, however, to the use of a "pure price of production", it is sometimes pointed out—using certain calculations which have been made—that if it is sought to ensure that investments and other collective expenditure are covered by means of a "net income" the amount of which would be added to the cost of production of the different products, in proportion to the funds invested in their production, then the result will be "excessive restraint" on the introduction of equipment making possible savings in living labour and, consequently, maintenance of a demand for labour-power that will exceed what is available. This argument has been developed, in particular, by Andras Brody (No. 15, p. 65).

What is really concealed behind this argument is a different one, concerning the relation between the conditions for expanded reproduction of labour-power and the conditions for expanded reproduction of production funds. For those, like Brody, who make use of this argument, only the needs of financing the second kind of reproduction can justify the addition to costs of production of a profitability rate to the amount needed for this purpose. Whatever is needed for expanded reproduction of labour-power Brody considers to be a socially allocated fraction of the workers' consumption fund, and therefore he sees it as forming the equivalent of a "wage", from the standpoint of expanded reproduction.

As will be seen, these arguments aim above all at building a price-system that enables expenditure on investment and on collective consumption to be covered, while the problems presented by the measurement of the social costs of various kinds of production are treated as being of only secondary interest.

However that may be, it is on the basis of a set of practical considerations like those mentioned above that a number of more or less complex price-systems have been worked out, including the one which has been called the "two-channel price-system". What is meant by this is a system under which the price of each product is made up by adding together the following elements:

(1) The wages actually paid to the workers who make the product under consideration:

(2) A certain percentage of this amount, regarded as corresponding to the "social wage":

(3) Expenditure on the purchase of products which enter into the manufacture of the product under consideration.

(4) Depreciation of the production funds invested in the given line of production:

(5) A charge for the tying-up of the production funds, calculated by applying a profitability-rate to the value of the production funds in question:

The employment of a system like this necessitates determining:

a) The percentage of the "social wage",

b) The profitability rate to be applied to the production funds.

It is clear that, in order to maintain a certain price-level, it will be necessary, if one of these percentages is varied, to vary the other one in the opposite direction.

When it comes to deciding what rates to use, many different proposals are put forward, owing to the essentially empirical nature of such proposals. Thus, in Hungary, where this system has been studied especially thoroughly, proposals have been made:

a) To apply a charge of 10 per cent to the funds invested (which amounts to saying that, on the basis of a stable ratio between production funds and products, the national product should increase by 10 per cent per year) and to estimate the "social wage" *either* (as one of the proposals has it) as equivalent to 25–30 per cent of wages paid in cash (Brody, No. 15, p. 65), this equivalent being paid into the exchequer by the enterprise, in the form of a tax assessed on the wages it actually pays, *or* (according to another proposal), by calculating what the rate of the wages-tax should be in such a way that the product of this tax covers the difference between what is produced by the 10 per cent charge on the funds tied up and the total amount of the net product needed for financing investments and other collective expenditure (Ganczer, No. 24, p. 69):

b) To evaluate the "social wage" as the equivalent of 35 per cent of wages paid in cash (still in the form of taxes paid by the enterprises to the exchequer), the balance of the net product needed for the planned growth of the economy and the financing of collective consumer expenditure being then related to the value of the funds invested, so as to show the profitability rate to be applied to the production funds invested in the various forms of production.

As will be seen, all these proposals are quite empirical. In the case of Hungary, too, they have tried, by way of a large number of calculations (the dimensions of which obviously necessitate using electronic machines, since changes in some prices indirectly affect all other prices), to determine the most "adequate" percentages, that is, those that best "correspond" to the structure of the economy, in the sense that they make possible a "reasonable" use of its production capacities, a socially acceptable and practicable level of employment, and, therefore, the pattern of development which it is desired to achieve.

Under Hungarian conditions, where the two-channel system has been *adopted to some extent,* they have sought a method of price-formation which includes the following features (I am referring here not to proposals but to actual decisions which, in principle, are to come into force completely in 1968): in order to work out the selling price of an industrial product, one adds to its cost of production the equivalent of 25 per cent of the wages actually paid for producing it (10 per cent representing a contribution to social security and 15 per cent a "tax" on wages payable by the enterprises) and a charge for the funds invested, equivalent to 5 per cent of their value. Apparently, this profitability rate is to be raised later on to 10 per cent.

For certain goods, which it has seemed necessary to sell at a higher price than could be obtained in this way (for example, so as to restrict demand for them) and which would therefore bring the enterprises producing them a very high income (described as a "rent"), a production tax has been introduced.

All these expenses and charges are included in the "cost" of producing the goods, so that there is no question here of a source of profits for the enterprise, unlike the reform of industrial wholesale prices in the USSR. The various taxes mentioned are to make up 50 per cent of the net income realised through the sale of industrial products. A 20 per cent addition to net income is to be provided by a turnover tax, levied at varying rates for different goods (the receipts from this tax are, of course, also destined for the exchequer), and a 30 per cent addition to net income as "profit" of industrial enterprises. The conditions under which these two fractions of the net income are determined can be varied, so that prices are thus "disengaged" from strict proportionality to "costs", all the more so because the profit margin for the enterprises is only "indicative"; actual prices can vary around this norm, so as to adapt to the conditions of the "market" (Csikos-Nagy, No. 17, p. 263). This is a point to which I shall come back later.

This outline shows that, despite the efforts made to simplify the price-system, unify rules for calculation, and bring prices closer to "real social costs", they are still a long way from achieving these aims. This is so regardless of the price-system adopted, whether one based essentially on the idea of "own costs" or one using the ideas of the "price-of-production" type or the "two-channel price".

V Some questions raised by concrete price-fixing

The foregoing outline shows that *concrete price-fixing* constantly gives rise to problems which, in the light of "price-systems" built according to various "models", appear as "special problems" requiring to be dealt with by special rules or, more precisely, calling for "exceptions" to be made to the rule, or to the principal rules.

Without spending a lot of time on this question, a few words must be said about it, because it brings out some of the weaknesses in the approaches to the price problem which have been looked at, weaknesses which confirm the view that no theoretically satisfactory solutions have been found for the problems that it was hoped to solve when the discussion on prices began.

When we leave the world of price "models" to go over to the concrete fixing of prices, or to the planning of prices, a great number of questions arise to which the "models" provide no answer. Here are some of them:

(1) What is to be done if, at the price dictated by the model, the quantities of an article that can be produced do not correspond to the demand, being either too great or too small? Should the price be altered, upward or downward? Should the production-plan be changed? Should differential prices be introduced? If the trouble takes the form of a shortage, should rationing and administrative distribution be resorted to? These questions, which are all connected with the problem of the scope to be allowed to the law of value, have received every possible answer, depending on "circumstances".

(2) How is it to be ensured that enterprises buy new products which they ought to buy because it is thought that they will be of greater benefit to the national economy than those formerly used, though their cost of production is still high (either because the relevant production-technique has not yet been mastered, or because their production is, at the start, only on a small scale)? Should they be sold below the "normal price", thus "penalising" the enterprises that produce them—the very ones that are making innovations? Or should these enterprises, while still having to sell at a loss, be subsidised? Or should the subsidy be paid to the purchasing enterprises? Or should certain enterprises be obliged to buy the new products at the high price? Here, too, all possible answers have been given and, depending on circumstances, put into practice.

(3) How should one proceed when, within one and the same branch of production, different enterprises have very different costs of production? Should the average cost in the branch be taken as "basis" for price-fixing? If so, should the enterprises which, on this basis, do not cover their costs, be subsidised? Or should they be shut down, or modernised? Or should the fixing of a uniform price not be attempted, and prices used instead which correspond to the "individual values of the goods"? If this is done, how will it be possible to compare the working of enterprises which obtain their supplies at different prices? Should differential taxes be introduced? And so on. Here, too, almost every possible solution has been proposed and applied.

(4) How should one proceed when the "same" article varies a great deal in quality? Should quality be taken into account in price-fixing? If this is done, does it not amount to violating the law of value, according to which the price of an article is to be determined by the labour-time socially necessary to produce it, and not by its use-value?[19] And if not, how to ensure that those who buy goods of poorer quality are not "penalised", or even that they do not refuse to buy them at all? Should purchasers be

assigned a single supplier? Should subsidies be paid? Here, too, almost every imaginable solution has been proposed and put into practice.[20]

Practice certainly has to answer these questions, and many others, as best it can. Once it has answered them, however, we find ourselves confronted with a system of actual prices that no longer has much in common with the initial "model".

This, in itself, may not seem a very serious matter. After all, it will be said, if the "model" cannot provide an answer to concrete problems, then it is inadequate, and it matters little if actual prices have little in common with it.

Unfortunately, this is not a tenable attitude, because, ultimately, the initial preoccupations are still there, and are justified. It really is necessary that the socialist economy should have a "significant" price-system. This price-system must be sufficiently "transparent" for what *looks* advantageous, on the basis of a price-calculation, to be really so, not only for whoever makes the calculation but also for the national economy. The price-system ought not be surrendered to subjectivism: prices should express "social costs".

But how is this to be achieved? The discussion on prices has thrown little light on the subject, though this was its purpose, and negative consequences too serious to be ignored are bound to follow.

VI Some consequences of the discussion about prices

The fact that the discussion has done little to illumine the questions that were put forward when it began has had negative consequences in the field of economic practice itself, that is, in particular, at the level of day-to-day economic decisions. Indeed, if the problem of prices has come up, and has held the attention of the economists and the leaders of the socialist countries of Europe for so long, this is obviously not due to purely "theoretical" reasons, but because, as I recalled at the beginning of this article, the problem was presenting itself in an acute form.

Not only was this happening, it is still happening, and often even more acutely, because the old price-system has "aged" still further, so that the prices constituting it tend to correspond still less to present-day conditions of production.[21] True, over the last ten years many changes have been made in prices, but it is by no means certain that the readjustments decided on since the discussion began, and the reforms undertaken, have always had a favourable effect, enabling the price-structure to give better expression to the structure of actual social costs.

As we have seen, the "general rules" which have guided the various reforms are extremely empirical and their theoretical basis is therefore not strong. This explains why the discussion on prices is still going on, and why a more thorough theoretical analysis is still being sought. It explains, too, why nearly every one of the European socialist countries has "its own formula" for building a price-system.

The divergences between the price-structure and the cost-structure have often increased because, for a number of "practical reasons" (the chief of which I have mentioned), the "rules" adopted have not been applied uniformly. As a result, the coherence aimed at in the price-system has remained unrealised.

This state of affairs must, of course, have an unfavourable impact on the efficient working of the economic system, especially at a time when, owing to the reforms adopted in respect of the management of enterprises, the latter have been given a greater degree of autonomy and are thereby called on to take a greatly increased number of decisions, in the sphere of investment amongst others, and to do this using the price-system as their guide, since this determines the relative profitability of a particular choice, in money terms. Thus, the national economy is much more sensitive than before to the weaknesses in the price-system.

Even when, as a result of revisions, the price-systems have been "rejuvenated" and some of their incoherences eliminated, the aim originally sought is still a long way off. The discussion aimed, indeed, at more than a mere "updating" of prices. And something more is certainly needed: the very progress of the productive forces is multiplying to an extraordinary degree the number of technical and economic choices that have to be made. Furthermore, it is increasing to an unprecedented extent the direct and indirect consequences of the possible choices. Whereas formerly the limited number of technical possibilities, and also the urgency of the problems, *imposed* solutions (that is, in practice they left no room for any choice), today things are very different. When setting up any large-scale project, one can now choose between a large number of possibilities, and call upon the participation of hundreds of enterprises, supplying equipment and machinery, in place of the one or two enterprises of earlier times.[22] This is precisely why it is essential to have calculating devices that can give significant information. Without them there is no certainty of making the right choice, which means not that the projects will fail to be carried out, but that they will cost the national economy much more than if meaningful calculations had been made. The waste that can result from this state of affairs holds back the growth of the national income and slows down the rise in the standard of living.

Not only that, but imperfect prices and, in general, a false notion of "costs", can systematically foster a wastage of resources that cannot be observed while it is happening, and the consequences of which do not make themselves felt until they have assumed alarming proportions.

Thus, to some extent, the old price-systems and the conceptions underlying them tended essentially to favour savings in the living labour *directly* necessary for *each* kind of production,[23] while neglecting to save past labour,[24] and failed to bring out the economic advantages resulting from rapid rotation of production funds as well as full use of them.

This bias in the preoccupations and the whole conception behind the price-system becomes a growing source of waste as the technical equipment of labour increases, that is, as the amount of fixed funds invested per worker becomes larger. The inadequacy of the price-system has certainly contributed its share to the slowing down, over the last ten years, in the economic growth of the most industrialised of the European socialist countries[25] (though this is not the only factor, since it is an extremely complex phenomenon, which cannot be dealt with in this article).

In any case, whatever role may have been played by other factors,[26] there can be no doubt that the limited character of the results of the discussion on prices has had negative effects on the working of the economy, since the more complex the latter becomes the greater is its need of meaningful and exact measuring devices.

However, the relative sterility of the discussion on prices is tending also to have negative consequences on the plane of theory itself, or ideology. This point calls for detailed consideration, owing, especially, to the effect that the evolution of general theoretical conceptions can have not only on price policy but also on other aspects of the economy's working. This brings us back to the actual problematic of the discussion.

VII The Problematic of the Discussion on Prices

As emphasised at the beginning of this article, one of the reasons why the discussion on prices has led only to mutually contradictory proposals and rather unsatisfactory results (which are generally admitted to be such) is that the problems to be examined were badly defined in the first place. This weakness meant that the real questions, the decisive ones, were not presented clearly.

Often, indeed, the questions raised, especially those addressed to *Capital*, were to some extent false questions to which no meaningful answers could be given. This is why, in the most recent period, when the balance-sheet of the discussion was drawn up and its relative fruitlessness was acknowledged, the temptation arose to abandon the ground on which the discussion first began and move to another, which it was hoped would prove more fertile. However, such a movement could be made in several different directions.

It could be agreed that the questions to be put to *Capital* are different from those which have been put so far, that is, that what is needed is a change in the theoretical problematic of the discussion, which implies a criticism of the previous approach. Or it could be decided that *Capital*, and Marx generally, can provide no answers to "new problems" and that a turn must therefore be made towards the innumerable technical ideologies available, considering that what is most necessary is to equip oneself with "efficient economic tools".

There are some indications that the latter line is no imaginary danger. Let us take, for example, the article by Csikos-Nagy which I have already mentioned. Here two series of symptomatic propositions are to be found:

a) After recalling how the discussion on prices began, the author writes: "Is the price debate today still characterised by the same features? No, that is far from being the case. The price system is no longer criticised today on the grounds that prices 'arbitrarily' deviate from the value or the production price. *The criticism is aimed mainly at the rigidity of the prices, at the administrative character of the price system.* The main objection is *that we are applying an essentially 'market phenomenon' in an administrative manner.*" (Csikos-Nagy, No. 17, p. 256: author's own emphasis.)

What the discussion is being blamed for here is that it tried to answer the following question: "How should we fix prices, that is, how should we plan them?" The question that it now seems more correct to ask is: "How can we stop fixing prices by administrative methods and allow the market mechanisms to have free play?"

b) At the theoretical level, the relative sterility of the discussion, and the consequent tendency to give a bigger place to the market mechanisms, direct "the attention of Marxist economists to the results achieved by their non-Marxist colleagues" (Csikos-Nagy, No. 17, p. 259), and the author adds: "Value is the crucial question of the price problem. This is the initial thesis of socialist price-theory. But must this thesis not be subjected to revision? Are the representatives of the school of marginal utility not right in rejecting the category of value, or in substituting for labour-value the concept of marginal utility? This question can and must be answered on a very practical basis. If all elements and all aspects of price phenomena can be determined with the short-term rules of the market, every reference to value is really only just a sort of ideological way of presenting the problem that can be discarded. But if practice convinces us that the essential problems of price phenomena remain unanswered in case the input principle is set aside, the starting-point of the socialist price theory can be taken for verified." (Csikos-Nagy, No. 17, p. 259.)

Csikos-Nagy himself considers that the labour theory of value provides a satisfactory "answer" and, therefore, that "nothing justifies that the socialist price theory should be reconstructed on new foundations" (Csikos-Nagy, No. 17, p. 265). This type of consideration tends, however, to remain essentially "academic" in so far as no system of concepts is produced, on the basis of the theory of value, that can be employed in working out a way to plan prices, which in turn can be integrated in the overall planning of the economy: this is so in so far as greater "efficacity" is allowed to market prices than to planned prices, which is the position that Csikos-Nagy and some other economists of the socialist countries are moving towards.

In some of these countries the role actually accorded to market prices by economic practice is getting bigger. We have seen that this is the case in Hungary, in connexion with the current reform in the system of direction and management. In this country the enterprises are now to have the right to vary their prices fairly widely, in accordance with the level of supply and demand. This is so in Czechoslovakia, too, where decisions taken in recent years have caused the prices of many products no longer to be centrally planned (Kosta, No. 27, p. 146).

In the Soviet Union the question has not been settled in this way.

The discussion goes on, and points of view favourable to the setting up of market prices are advocated alongside others that take the opposite line. During 1966 a small number of Soviet economists took up a firm position in favour of competition and market prices, declaring that prices fixed on a central basis are detrimental to the good working of the economy. This position was defended, for example, by Lisichkin, in *Novyi Mir*, and, especially, by B. Rakitsky (No. 56). It was opposed by a number of other writers, such as Kronrod (No. 36) and A. Bachurin, Vice-President of Gosplan (No. 8).

The fact that the validity of the labour theory of value should have been raised in the way it has been in the passage quoted above from Csikos-Nagy, where he asks whether the socialist theory of prices ought not perhaps to be reconstructed on new foundations, using the conceptions of marginal utility, shows just how inadequate the initial problematic was, and to what extent this is still true of the present problematic also.

The question whether a scientific theory is valid cannot, of course, be settled by direct reference to the problems and difficulties of day-to-day practice, not even the practice of planning organs. The criteria for the validity of a scientific theory are necessarily those of theoretical practice, and cannot be those of technical practice. It is no more possible to judge *directly* the scientific validity of the labour theory of value through some difficulty encountered in economic *technique* than it is possible to judge, for example, the validity of some theory about the elementary structure of matter through the difficulties experienced in using it *technically*, or to judge the validity of geometrical theorems by taking measurements of real objects.

Transition from the level of scientific theory to that of technical practice demands differential production, on the basis of *theoretical* concepts, of the *technical* concepts required by real practice. What is spoken of colloquially as the "testing" of a scientific theory, meaning the *technical realisation* of its theoretical concepts, and thus their use in practice, presupposes that these theoretical concepts have been "realised", both in *concepts* corresponding to the peculiarities of the real setting and in *technical* concepts which make it possible to lay down operative procedures (measurement, calculation, etc.) and determine the limits of their validity.[27]

This does not mean that without this twofold "realisation", achieved in detail, theoretical concepts are of no use, if not in providing a foundation, in the strict sense, for effective economic practice, then at least in giving it orientation. Effective economic practice can indeed be worked out by bringing together shrewd empirical work and general theoretical concepts which serve as "guides" for the direction it should take. Practice like this, though, however effective it may be at certain times, is unaware of the reasons for its success, and therefore of the limits (in space and time) of its effectiveness, so that, once these unknown limits are crossed, it experiences inevitable setbacks. In any case, such practice can neither confirm nor disprove the theoretical conceptions behind it.

Thus, only an adequate differentiated working of the theoretical concepts into empirical concepts and technical concepts can ensure the *unity* of theory and practice. This unity requires, first and foremost, full development of the content of the scientific concepts on the theoretical plane. The discussion on prices has not contributed to such a development in the field of price theory, and this is why it has proved relatively sterile. Hence, also, something which is at least equally serious, the doubt thrown upon the scientific validity of some fundamental theoretical concepts of Marxism, and the tendency to present in a non-dialectical way the problem of the possible relations between Marxist and non-Marxist theories about prices.

As regards these non-Marxist theories, the problem is not, as was suggested in some of the proposals put forward during the price discussion, one of accepting them or rejecting them *en bloc*, or of borrowing some of their conclusions. The problem is one of critically analysing these theories, in the scientific sense, that is, revealing what the presumptions behind them are, the implicit structures to which the concepts they use actually belong, and, on this basis, appreciating the significance of their various conclusions.

In this way the apologetical nature of these theories can be revealed, that is, their lack of scientific basis in so far as they claim to explain the working of the capitalist mode of production, while at the same time recognising the appositeness of some particular approach which they may make. It is precisely this local and limited appositeness that conceals the non-scientific character of the ideological system to which the particular approach belongs.

At the level of analysis of the part played by prices in the day-to-day working of the economy, of the influence of a certain price-system when used as a means of economic calculation, it is scientifically justified to examine to what extent and within what limits the non-Marxist theories have arrived, on some point or other, at certain conclusions which, reinterpreted by Marxism, can be helpful, at the technical level, in formulating a price policy. A considerable field lies open there for critical analysis, but this field can be made fertile only if it be worked upon with the aid of a solidly grounded theoretical problematic. It is Marxism that provides this theoretical problematic—always provided that we do not seek in *Capital* a source of directly usable "recipes", but take it as a structure of scientific concepts on the basis of which we can work out the technical concepts needed for economic practice and, in particular, for the economic practice of the social formations in transition between capitalism and socialism.

The preliminary condition for any scientific interpretation, or any useful employment, of a proposition put forward by a non-Marxist theory is that the ideological and apologetical basis of the theory be clearly revealed, together with the *limits* within which the proposition is valid, limits which will be determined by the conceptual field within which it is formulated. One cannot but be struck by the tendency of some Marxists to accept certain propositions from non-Marxist theory without observing these pre-liminaries.[28]

In this way the fact that the system of concepts on which these proposi-tions are based is not a scientific system is lost sight of. This system is made up of a group of hypotheses which place at the centre of economic analysis the consumer who is a prey to "needs" which are independent of all production-relations. "Maximising" the satisfaction of these "needs" is regarded as the criterion of "economic rationality". A system of con-cepts like this cannot explain the way any mode of production works, but this does not prevent some of the propositions it puts forward from possessing a certain validity on the practical level. The limits of this validity are, however, extremely narrow, as has been shown during the last ten years even by economists whose ideological positions have nothing in common with Marxism, like T. C. Koopmans (No. 32), William J. Baumol (No. 10), G. C. Archibald (No. 3), E. J. Mishan (No. 49) and many others.[29]

If some have tried to find in *Capital* "rules" or "formulae" for fixing prices, "rules" that can be compared to others borrowed from some system of economic thought, this is because they have been tempted to see *Capital* as a "theory of prices" on the same plane as non-Marxist conceptions, and capable of being "judged" merely from the standpoint of day-to-day economic practice. When this view is taken, sight is lost of the fact that the price-theory of *Capital* is inseparably bound up with the total structure of Marxist thought—that Marxism, as a philosophy, is a theory of the relation between theoretical practice and other levels of practice; that, as a science of history, it is a theory of modes of production, their structures, the laws of their formation, development and dissolution, and, among other things, a theory of social classes and class struggles. It is within this theoretical structure that the Marxist theory of value and prices has its place and significance, not amid the theoretical vacuum of pragmatism.

This, too, is why it is impossible to put the question of the validity of the Marxist theory of value and prices by standing on the level of narrowly conceived "economic practice". The question asked in this way is not pertinent. At this level, indeed, which is not that of science, that is, of proof and explanation, it is easy to show the "equivalence" between the "practical" conclusions that can be drawn from a certain pragmatic or empirical interpretation of the Marxist theory of prices and the con-clusions that can be drawn from a number of other theories that are sufficiently coherent.

Andras Brody, for example, analysing the conditions of simple reproduc-tion, has shown that it is possible to draw from Leontief's table of matrix relations the conclusion that prices "based on labour-value" form an adequate tool of economic calculation, because they ensure the perpetua-tion of the system under the best technical conditions (Brody, No. 15, pp. 58–60). But he also shows that in a matrix structure like this it is possible to construct a price-system by treating any commodity whatsoever as the "source of value". This system will have the same "practical properties" as one based on labour-value, because the resulting price vector will always be the same, up to a multiplicative factor (so that the structure of prices will be the same).

Brody then analyses in the same way the conditions for expanded reproduction, and shows that the "price of production" plays here the same role as value. He shows, too, that, in order to calculate these prices of production, one can base oneself on "expenditure of labour" or on any other material expenditure, and always arrive at the same price-structure (Brody, No. 15, p. 63). Similarly, when revealing the formal conditions for the formation of a rate of profit, he shows that the rate of profit that corresponds to Marx's definition is equivalent to the equilibrium rate of growth in Von Neumann's sense (Brody, No. 15, p. 64). From this he concludes that, at the level of *practical consequences*, the equations can be interpreted with equal validity in terms of labour-value, in marginalist terms or in terms of programming theory.

The radical differences separating Marx's theoretical conceptions from "price theories" do not show themselves at the level of "practical calculation" of prices, that is, at the level of the use of some "formula" or other, but at that of *explanation*, that is, at the level of science:

(1) First, what Marx's analysis *explains* are the very reasons for the *existence* of the value form, and so of prices, that is, the reasons why, in certain social formations, products are simply products, whereas in others they become *commodities*, endowed with that supra-sensible quality, their price. Marx explains this by the existence of *particular relations* among the producers and between them and their products. It is these relations that show through the value form and endow labour with the "social quality" of being a "producer of value", which it ceases to be when the same production-relations are not present, because prices themselves then disappear. It is in this quite precise sense that labour *involved in a certain structure of social relations* is the source of value.

(2) Next, Marx's analysis is the only one that provides an *explanation* of the historical, economic and social movement as a whole, which determines the appearance of the "transformed forms" of value and the connexion between the price-structure and the production-relations. It does this on the basis of an analysis of the specific character of the commodity called labour-power; this is one of the poles of the basic class-relations of capitalist society, which explains why changes in its price, or in the length of the working day, are the subject of intense social struggles, the outcome of which determines changes in the price-system and a particular form of progress of the productive forces.

(3) Finally, Marx's analysis in its fully developed form explains how prices are formed under the capitalist mode of production and constitutes the necessary starting-point for building a theory of prices under conditions of transition between capitalism and socialism.[30]

Thus, Marxism provides both a theory of value and prices and a coherent theory of social formations, of their specific natures and the laws by which they function and change. Any non-Marxist "price-theory", however, provides at best only one of the possible *descriptions* of the momentary inter-relations between prices, given certain "hypotheses". As for the "explanations" that non-Marxist theories are said to provide, they relate not to real social relations but to psychological categories ("man at the mercy of his needs"), or else technical ones, which dangle in an ideological void, that is, which cannot be fitted into any analysis of the actual movement of history. Indeed, these theories help rather to hide the nature of the movement of history—when they do not simply deny that there is any movement at all, by referring to a "general economy" existing outside of history, outside of time.

Let us now, however, leave this problem, and consider the inadequacies in the problematic which have helped to prevent the discussion on prices from producing useful results and which have given rise to the formulations we have just been studying.

VIII The theory of value and the planning of prices

Though the weaknesses in the problematic of the discussion present several aspects which affect each other, it seems correct to say that the most important of these aspects is the generally *empirical* nature of the problematic adopted. Nobody has sought in *Capital* the starting point for an explanation and a theory (which is still not fully constructed), but instead they have looked for practical answers to practical questions. In this way, they have usually taken the fundamental concepts of *Capital* not as theoretical concepts which refer to theoretical matters but as empirical concepts referring to empirically measurable matters. Consequently, nobody has tried, on the basis of *Capital*, that is, above all, on the basis of its method and its theoretical concepts, to work out the scientific concepts needed in order fully to conceive and to master the problems of the transition from capitalism to socialism.

1 *Value and socially necessary labour-time*

Those who have tried to find directly in *Capital* "rules" and "procedures" for price-fixing in transitional economies have therefore been putting questions to Marx's work to which it could not give a direct answer, the subject-matter of that book being quite different.

Since one of their aims was to construct a price-system that would make it possible to carry out calculations whereby the social cost of production could be minimised, they first put the following question: *how can one measure this social cost?* In most cases, they thought they found in *Capital* the following answer: *by calculating the "value" of production.*

This led to their second question: *how are we to carry out this calculation?* And here, again, they thought they found the following answer in

Capital; *by counting the number of hours actually expended on producing the various goods.*

After that, as we know, they thought they could multiply this number of hours by the wages actually paid, plus a certain "net income" calculated in some more or less complex way—the method chosen itself being "justified" by some interpretation of Marx's analyses of the working of capitalist economy.

In any case, it seemed to those who read *Capital* in this way important above all to find the axes around which prices oscillate, that is, the *regulating magnitudes* of the reproduction process under capitalism (value, price of production or other magnitudes of the same kind). These *axes* were seen as indicating the price-level representing social costs, whereas other price-levels were seen as expressing accidental deviations or faulty adjustments, all of them being "distortions" which the socialist economy would have to and would be able to eliminate, its prices being planned and not abandoned to the fluctuations of the market.

The inadequacy of this problematic, and its empirical nature, are clearly revealed when we examine what sort of fundamental concepts are actually worked out in *Capital*, with special reference to the concepts we have just been discussing.

Let us take, first, the concept of "socially necessary labour-time". Whereas the empiricist problematic that seeks in *Capital direct answers* to questions of economic technique assumes identity between socially necessary labour-time and empirically recorded labour-time, a reading of the book that avoids the empiricist illusion enables one to *see* that, on the contrary, these two ideas refer to *radically different matters*.

The concept of socially necessary labour-time is infinitely more complex than that of empirically recorded labour-time, because it refers to quantities produced in comparison with social needs. The latter expression, in turn, indicates not an empirical or ideological concept, like that of "human needs", but a theoretical concept that has a precise meaning in the structure of *Capital*, and the equivalent of which needs to be worked out for the theory of transition from capitalism to socialism.

It is obvious that one cannot indulge in the illusion of "freeing", the concept of socially necessary labour-time from its theoretical status except by refusing to "concern oneself" with the aggregate quantities that could be produced, so as not to "concern oneself" with anything but the average cost of a product in terms of labour.

This approach does not take us far, either theoretically or practically. In particular, if the problem which it is sought to deal with is that of prices that represent *social cost*, it is quite impossible to think this problem out by taking each cost *separately*. The problem cannot be studied except in terms of the connexion between the different branches of production, and, therefore, without taking into account the quantities produced or to be produced, and the totality of social needs.

Moreover, when what is wanted is to carry out calculations regarding the *future*, reference to *present average cost* in labour is quite meaningless, since the *future* cost of every product will depend on the means of production that will be used *in the years to come*. These means cannot be chosen within the framework of a plan unless one can determine in some other way what ought to be the labour-time socially necessary for each type of product, so as to endeavour to devote to its production precisely this amount, no more and no less. Here we leave the field within which calculation in prices can still have some significance, to enter one where estimates of labour-time on the scale of society are needed, together with application of the principle of economy in labour.

Attempts to "reduce", through tricks of calculation (that is, without first working out adequate theoretical concepts), the labour-time empirically expended on different kinds of production to the "socially necessary labour-time" are completely useless. This is even truer of attempts in which labour-time actually expended is calculated as though it were identical with socially necessary labour-time. Such calculations can never tell what it is desired they should tell, namely, e.g., how to use the investment funds available, in which branches to invest them, or whether it is socially preferable to effect a saving of labour in one branch of production rather than another.

All these questions can only be answered by using a concept of "socially necessary labour-time" treated in a suitable manner (that is, with a content *specific to the social formation in question*) and by working out, on this basis, the necessary empirical concepts which, themselves, have to be employed in a concrete way.

Given the misunderstandings that an empiricist reading of *Capital* has brought into the discussion on prices, precisely in connexion with the basic concepts of socially necessary labour-time and value, it will be useful to go back over certain theoretical positions which are often met with in the discussion on prices in the economies in transition between capitalism and socialism.

We know that, following a well-established empiricist interpretation of the problem, analyses are currently being expounded according to which it is the labour-time *actually* expended to produce a product that determines the "magnitude of the value" of the latter in a "mechanical sense", that is, in much the same sense as the amount of water in a container can be worked out by multiplying the time during which a tap has been left running to fill the container by the number of litres poured out per minute.

Interpretations of this kind conceal, of course, what they really are, the contradictions to which they lead, by means of considerations regarding the variation in "individual productivity" between the workers participating in production, or considerations regarding the "quality" of the different kinds of labour. So long, however, as only such considerations as these are taken into account, that is, so long as only the *technical* features of labour are considered, it is impossible to escape from a mechanistic interpretation of how value is determined by labour-time; in other words, to see the radical difference between Marx, on the one hand, and Smith and Ricardo, on the other. Those who take this approach see in Marx just a scholar who merely "perfected" the theory of value and prices (especially by his analyses of wages as the value of labour-power and his theory of price of production) and not a scholar who put the theory of value on *a quite different foundation* from his alleged "predecessors".

In other words, this interpretation (which underlies the "measurement of value" by labour-time empirically recorded or actually expended, and the price-systems which are *directly connected* with this measurement) ignores one of Marx's essential contributions to economic science, namely, that the apparent "property" that labour possesses to create "value" is not a "natural" property but a social one. This means, among other things:

a) That it is always necessary to distinguish between labour's productive character in the technical sense and in the *economic* sense.

In the first sense, what is meant is the character of *concrete* labour which produces use-values. This productivity is measured in technical terms, that is, in the form of a ratio between a quantity of hours of labour actually expended and the physical quantity of products obtained thereby. In the economic sense, however, what is meant is the character of labour as *abstract* producer of exchange-value. In this sense, the productive or non-productive character of labour is determined by the nature of the *social relations*. Thus, under the capitalist mode of production, only labour that participates in the production of surplus value is "productive" labour.

b) That it is the *structure of a labour-process* which itself forms part of a certain social structure that determines whether or not the labour involved in it is productive. Thus, from the moment when, in large-scale capitalist industry, a "collective labourer" confronts the means of production, it is not the nature of the task performed by each member of this "collective labourer" that determines whether his labour is productive or non-productive, but the productive character of the "collective labourer".[31] This is another aspect of the determination of the productive or non-productive character of labour by the *structure* to which the labour belongs.

c) That what produces "value" is not "labour in general" and that, consequently, this "production" is not the result of a "transitive causality" but of a "structural causality".

d) That the magnitude of the value "produced" by an hour of labour is itself determined by the *totality of the social relations* (and not merely by the production-relations): this is, indeed, what is meant by the term "social needs".

e) That, finally, the "reduction" of the labour-time actually expended to the *socially necessary labour-time* has to be mediated through *the whole of the social structure and all its authorities*, something that is obviously true, whatever the social structure, even if it does not give rise to commodity production.

This is why it is necessary to be always on guard against a certain anthropological line of talk which hails "human labour, creator of value and sole producer of wealth".[32] This is a way of speaking which, when not naively empiricist, usually represents an attempt to hide the fact (and here I shall borrow the actual language of anthropology) that labour which produces value is always "alienated" labour, subordinated to its own products and, eventually, exploited, for commodity production is always pregnant with capitalist production-relations. Far from symbolising man's mastery of his own products, "labour as producer of value" symbolises the subjection of man to his own products. A social formation's advance towards socialism gradually puts an end to this subjection and thus ensures that labour ceases to be value-producing labour—something that requires a high level of socialisation of production and a thoroughgoing transformation of production-relations.

The relative sterility of the discussion on prices, value, the social cost of production, and so on, shows some of the negative consequences that can result from an empiricist reading of *Capital* and from the anthropological language that reinforces it.

2 *Price and value*

The same empiricist problematic leads to regarding as *empirically ascertainable* magnitudes not only socially necessary labour-time but also value, price of production, average rate of profit, etc., and so to attempts at *directly "measuring"* these magnitudes, in order to use the results in "constructing" price-systems. All of which cannot, of course, lead anyone anywhere.[33]

It is only logical that giving empirical status to theoretical concepts has prevented full advantage from being got from what Marx says in *Capital* about the category of price, although what he has to say on this subject is decisive in relation to the questions at issue in the discussion on prices.

If too little attention has been given to some of the analyses that Marx devotes to empirical categories like prices, this is due to the very nature of the initial approach: if socially necessary labour-time and value are regarded as "empirical matters" that are "masked" by prices (or hidden in them), then it is these matters that are regarded as exclusively important; prices are then relegated to the status of "appearances", that is, "inessentials", for when concepts are taken for reality it is hard to grasp that what is called "appearance" is reality (*Wirklichkeit*) itself.

Now, Marx's approach is not one of seeking and "discovering", "behind prices", an ultimate "reality" which is more "fundamental" and alone "decisive". It is quite different: he did not "discover" but *worked out* theoretical concepts, or, more precisely, the theoretical structure thanks to which the *existence* of prices and their *magnitude* are explained. These concepts: abstract labour, socially necessary labour-time, value, etc., thus form a theoretical structure the various terms of which condition one another. It is therefore impossible to isolate any of these elements *empirically*. The fundamental concepts, such as those of socially necessary labour-time, value, price of production, etc., are the nodal points of this structure. What they describe are both production-relations and "regulating magnitudes", the sizes of which, not directly measurable, are determined by the totality of social relations.

The status of these "regulating magnitudes" in price theory is similar to that of "centres of gravity" in the physics of solids. A centre of gravity does not exist as an empirically ascertainable "reality". It is a *geometric position* determined by a structure and manifesting itself only by its effects. This does not mean that we have to know all its effects concretely in order to determine where the centre of gravity is. On the contrary, as we have known since Archimedes, it is enough to know the structure to be able to determine its centre of gravity and how the latter operates.

So far as our problem is concerned, since we lack concrete prices already formed spontaneously (the relation of which to the regulating magnitudes could be sought, provided we constructed the concept of the latter), it is quite useless to try and measure empirically the equivalent of the socially necessary labour, value, prices of production, and so on, by proceeding directly to measure physical magnitudes.

What is needed, before anything else is attempted, in the social formations which are in transition between capitalism and socialism, is, when no spontaneously formed price-system exists, to work out theoretical concepts that enable one to think out how to regulate expanded reproduction and the transformation of social relations, together with the laws making it possible to secure the utmost saving of social labour. These theoretical concepts and knowledge of these laws will enable us to build a price-system corresponding to the requirements of the development of this social formation and to the political aims being pursued (in so far as a price-system like this can exist at all).

If this path is not taken, the risk arises, sooner or later, of being tempted to declare for the "re-establishment of market prices",[34] that is, of the objective structure thanks to which it is no longer either necessary or possible to subordinate the development of the social formation to definite political purposes, since this development is ensured spontaneously by the very structure that makes possible the "re-establishment of market prices".

However, re-establishment of market prices is logically only the first step towards introducing "regulating magnitudes" which operate spontaneously. In fact, these prices will not produce the effects expected unless there are real markets available, not merely for consumer goods but also for means of production, production funds and labour-power. Hence the successive stages passed through by the Yugoslav "experiment", the very logic of which has led to the re-establishment of all these markets, and so of the production-relations which their existence presupposes.[35] The irony of history has brought it about that these production-relations are now obstructing the development of the productive forces to an increasing extent, so that the undertaking is not even getting the results that some people thought it would. Its ultimate end can only be a combination of monopolistic structures with state capitalism.[36]

To avoid becoming drawn into an adventure of this sort, the only path forward is that of working out, *for the transitional economies*, the equivalent of the concepts by which Marx described the "regulating magnitudes" of capitalism and revealed their connexions and functioning. What is needed is to work out concepts that, in the structure of these modes of production or social formations, will occupy *the same place* as the corresponding concepts in *Capital*. Some of them may even bear the same name, in so far as they can be differentially worked out on the basis of the concepts given in *Capital*. This obviously cannot happen with *all* the concepts in *Capital*, since some of them refer to production-relations which are specific to the capitalist mode of production and the real relations they describe therefore no longer exist under the new mode of production. In the latter they are replaced by others which, while fulfilling similar functions, do this in a radically new way.

This is, finally, the theoretical task which an empiricist problematic prevents us from seeing, though the need for it is *shown* by *Capital* itself, as soon as one stops looking in that book for what is not and cannot be there, and instead looks for what should be and is there; not, however, in the empirical form of objects merely needing to be discovered, but in that of concepts, which are theoretical means of production that have to be set to work.

Though the theoretical matrix of the concepts needed for cognition of the laws of the transitional economies is to be found in *Capital*, this does not mean that it is easy to work out these concepts. The task is a huge one, since what is involved is working out the theory of a new mode of production. Nevertheless, as soon as one starts reading *Capital* in a theoretical and not an empiricist way it becomes clear that the road ahead lies open.

This is particularly true because of what Marx tells us about prices. Thus, so early as Chapter 3 of Book I, he writes:

"The price-form, however, is not only compatible with the possibility of a quantitative incongruity between magnitude of value and price, i.e., between the former and its expression in money, but it may also conceal a qualitative inconsistency, so much so that, although money is nothing but the value-form of commodities, price ceases altogether to express value. . . . Hence an object may have a price without having value. The price in that case is imaginary, like certain quantities in mathematics. On the other hand, the imaginary price-form may sometimes conceal either a direct or an indirect real value-relation; for instance, the price of uncultivated land, which is without value, because no human labour has been incorporated in it." (Marx, No. 45, p. 112; Eng. version from *Capital*, I, p. 75.)

Here we find (as also, of course, in many other passages in *Capital*),[37] essential pointers for working out, on the basis of the theory of value, a price theory which, given differential handling, is applicable to all the various modes of production in which commodity production goes on. To expand this point would be to take us too far from our subject. It is worth stressing, however, that the propositions I have quoted reveal the need, if the working of any commodity mode of production is to be understood, to grasp not only the specific general laws that determine the *average magnitude* of prices, that is, the "magnitudes which are regulative" in the last instance (value, price of production and other transformed forms of value), but also the specific laws that determine the correspondence or non-correspondence between prices and these regulating magnitudes.

When we want to understand the fundamental tendencies of a commodity mode of production, knowing the laws that determine the *divergences* between price and magnitude of value, or any other regulating magnitude, and the laws that determine how "imaginary prices" are formed, is doubtless not so essential as knowing the laws that determine the average magnitude of prices. This is why Marx did not specially expand the remarks he formulated on various occasions regarding the laws that govern the divergences between price and value, or the forming of "imaginary prices". Thus, to an insufficiently attentive reader of *Capital*, price-fluctuations appear to be merely effects of the fluctuations of "supply" and "demand". Moreover, the day-to-day movement of prices is of only secondary interest for understanding the general laws of development of a social formation.

The order of importance of these problems changes when the task before us is both to understand how formations in transition between capitalism and socialism actually function, and to *concretely work out a price-policy*. It now becomes absolutely essential to know all the laws that govern the structure of prices and determine the objective properties of this structure. It is now of the highest importance to grasp the *limits* within which prices may *vary* without ceasing to fulfil their function, and also the *effects of these variations* on production-relations and the development of the productive forces.

In other words, while knowledge of the laws determining the average prices of the various commodities is sufficient for analysing the overall movement of a mode of production, this knowledge becomes inadequate when the task is to work out a concrete price-policy, that is, to fix prices in accordance both with a structure and a conjuncture (which is *not* any longer that of the "market", but is whatever corresponds to the social and political priorities of each period), so as to plan them.

In these circumstances the fact that it is not enough to know the laws that determine average prices makes itself felt in a number of ways. Thus, if a price policy is worked out on the basis of a knowledge of these laws alone, the concrete decisions taken, in so far as they are going to be effective, often appear to contradict these laws. The concrete prices then almost all seem to be "exceptions" to the laws. The latter then cease to look like what they are, but seem mere "rules" (since laws do not allow of exceptions, whereas rules call for them, in so far as the exceptions "prove" the rules).

One of the weaknesses of the discussion on prices is, as we have seen, that it has been above all concerned with the "regulating magnitudes" which determine prices on the average, that is, in the last instance, and has treated as "secondary" the laws governing the *divergences* between prices and regulating magnitudes. Once again, then, when a price-policy has to be worked out, that is, when concrete prices have to be planned, it is essential to know the laws that determine these divergences, their possible limits, and the objective properties of price structures which are marked by particular divergences between prices and regulating magnitudes.

What are needed at each moment for the planning and management of the economy are not "average" prices but concrete ones, whether real or "imaginary", and which, if they are real prices, must diverge under objectively determined conditions from certain regulating magnitudes. If the laws governing these divergences and their effects[38] have not been grasped, one is easily induced to fix only "average" prices and leave the market to "fix" the divergences from the average.

We thus see that the problem of planned variations of prices, and of the value-limits of these variations, now becomes an essential one. The concrete questions that arise usually concern the *limits* to variations. The problems that have to be solved at the level of planning and management usually arise in a form that calls for invocation of the limits in relation to which a particular kind of production, or a particular technique, begins or ceases to be worth while. Here we have to do with extremal problems or, more precisely, of interconnected extrema, which can therefore not be solved by means of mere average magnitudes. In particular, when the management of an economy is subordinated not to the law of profit but to the principle of saving labour, what have to be determined are the conditions under which calculations in price terms can make it possible to ensure the maximum saving of social labour in attaining targets which have been decided on for political and social reasons.

From all these points of view the pointers given in the passage from Marx quoted above are very important. Without going deeply into this matter, it is enough to mention that the proposition about "the imaginary price-form" which "may sometimes conceal" relations which are "real" though "indirect" contains in germ what price-theory needs in order to solve the problem of prices for means of production which are available in adequate quantity, and that of the prices for machines which have been used and are no longer being manufactured.

More generally, what we have here in germ is what has been partly rediscovered, following a different route, by the mathematical economists who have shown the need to include in prices what they call "costs of reverse linkage" (Novozhilov, No. 54), that is, the losses that the economy suffers from the use of a product in a particular activity, when this use alters the conditions in which other branches or activities function, for example, by increasing their costs of production. This is a point to which I shall have to come back in my conclusion.

This shows how necessary it is to take account of all Marx's propositions regarding prices, throughout *Capital*. Yet these propositions have often been regarded as being of secondary importance as compared with the analyses devoted to value and prices of production.

If attention is paid in this way, giving these propositions all the theoretical importance due to them, we see that everything vanishes which, because *Capital* has been read in an empiricist spirit, has led, in the discussion on prices, to the construction of "rules" that consist almost entirely of exceptions. This is so because, if we proceed in this way, we shall read *Capital* more carefully, and stop mixing up concepts with empirical matters, and as a result of this reading we shall obtain concepts that will enable us to work out the law of these alleged "irregularities", which are thus seen to be irregularities no longer, but the effect of the law itself.

IX The specificity of the price problem in the economy of transition

It is, of course, one thing to possess the concepts needed to construct a price theory in social formations in transition between capitalism and socialism, and quite another actually to construct this theory, without ever losing sight of the fact that the price-structure is dictated by *all the authorities of the social formation*.

Now, the action of all the authorities of the social formation upon prices involves consequences that go very much deeper in economies in transition between capitalism and socialism than in the capitalist mode of production, especially in the competitive stage of the latter. At this stage, indeed, the capitalist mode of production is marked by a dual form of conformity between the real-appropriation relations and the formal-appropriation relations: there is both conformity between the process of extraction of surplus-value and the process of appropriation of surplus-value, and conformity between ownership of the means of production and direction of the labour-process. This dual correspondence entails, as we know, relative autonomy of the economic instance,[39] and this implies that the other instances of the social formation act only indirectly and in a hidden way upon the economic one. Under these conditions, prices themselves seem to be entirely determined by conditions peculiar to the economic instance.

This can no longer happen in social formations in transition between capitalism and socialism: first, because, as social formations in transition, they are marked by specific forms of non-correspondence between the different social relations, including, of course, at the level of the production-structures,[40] which implies that the development of these social formations towards socialism necessitates domination of the economic instance by the political one; secondly, because socialism itself has to subject the productive forces to domination by the associated producers, which rules out spontaneity in the working of the economic level.

As regards, more particularly, the forms of non-correspondence which are specific to present-day economies of transition, a decisive role is played by non-correspondence between the social character of ownership and the mode of real appropriation which is not yet directly and wholly social. This contradiction, or this non-correspondence, shows itself through the existence of distinct economic subjects that *possess* means of production of which the State is the *owner*. This possession is based on the capacity the economic subjects have to operate efficiently the means of production under their control. In the industrial sector these economic subjects are usually state enterprises.

At the theoretical level, this objective situation in which *ownership* and *possession* are separate cannot be thought out in all its consequences without two related groups of concepts: on the one hand, concepts which account for the role played by state ownership as an element in the production-relations, and so for the planned character of the transitional economies, and thereby also for the already highly socialised character of their productive forces; and, on the other, concepts which account for the still "commodity" character of these economies, including concepts relating to the value form and its transformed versions, especially prices. These concepts, however, must be specific ones, that is, they must apply to the social formation of the transitional economy and therefore must *differ* from those which apply to the capitalist economy.

Here, too, we see that the concepts accounting for the commodity character of the transitional economy cannot be found "ready-made" in *Capital*. They have to be worked out differentially on the basis of that book. This is possible because *Capital* contains the theoretical matrix of these concepts.

The kind of differentiation that thus has to be carried out is determined by the already planned character of the economy. Therefore the content of this differentiation has to be found, in part, by analysing the categories of economic planning and economic calculation on the social scale. This requires that these categories be reduced to an adequate conceptual content. In doing this the necessary instruments will at the same time be obtained for transforming the actual practices with which these categories are connected.

Finally, the type of complexity which is specific to social formations in transition between capitalism and socialism requires that two sets of concepts be worked out: one which corresponds to the already highly socialised character of the economy, due to the change in production-relations, and another which corresponds to the still commodity character of this same economy, due to the not yet fully social character of the productive forces.

The first set of concepts operates in the field of planning. It relates together not exchange-values and abstract labour, but use-values: its fundamental category is that of *concrete labour*.

The concepts that make up this set correspond to the categories of planning. Once fully developed, they should make it possible to think out the conditions for *non-monetary* economic calculation, a *"direct"* kind of economic accounting which does not employ a price-system and which enables the labour-time socially necessary for different kinds of production to be determined directly.[41]

In so far as the field of this calculation is a highly complex social field, it is a radically new one. Relating together concrete forms of labour and use-values, it directly concerns what Marx called "real wealth", that which for capitalism is secondary.[42]

The second set of concepts corresponds to the still commodity character of the transitional economy. This set of concepts should make it possible to build a price-system by means of which complementary economic calculations can be undertaken—indirect calculations, in money terms, and subordinate in significance, corresponding to the day-to-day management of the economy.

It is this second set of concepts that, operating in the field constituted by a price-system, is bound up with the categories of value and abstract labour. This is where the discussion on prices has, or ought to have, its centre.

The working-out of these two sets of concepts is made necessary by the specific type of non-correspondence between some of the social relations in social formations which are in transition between capitalism and socialism. It is not complete until the way the two sets of concepts are linked together has also been specified, and thus their unity established. Given this condition, it becomes fully possible to think out the way the transitional economy works, and so to dominate it.

The unity and duality of the conceptual system needed in order to dominate in thought, and later in reality, the social formations in transition between capitalism and socialism thus results from the particular form of non-correspondence between property-relations and relations of real appropriation, because it is this non-correspondence that is the source of the particular complexity of these social formations in transition.

Thus, a specific form of duality of production-relations is behind the duality of the types of economic calculation (direct economic calculation, in use-values and concrete labour-time, and indirect economic calculation, in money, prices and abstract labour).

The problem of prices and of their role in the planned economies of today cannot usefully be dealt with unless account is taken of this duality, since the latter is the expression of non-correspondence existing at the level of the production-structures.

What makes it indispensable to work out theoretical concepts that will enable us to explain and dominate the operation of the transitional economies is that, without them, there is constant danger of being drawn into grave practical errors, both in respect of the planning of production (which is then often guided by prices that have no economic meaning)[43] and in respect of price-policy and (what can be even more serious) the place to

H

be given to calculation in price terms and to the action of the latter in the planning and management of the economy with the aim of building socialism.

Mistakes made in these last-mentioned fields, if combined with the effect of other social and political factors, may in fact lead to the withering away of the planned economy and the resurgence of an entirely commodity economy.

If there is such a danger, this is precisely because the social formations now in transition between capitalism and socialism are not yet fully constituted socialist economies but only transitional ones. It is because, being transitional economies, they still have a real mode of appropriation which is not completely social, that the value form exists and is actually a way in which "commodity relations manifest themselves". These relations are always likely to develop and escape from social control, if the contradiction between the mode of ownership and the mode of appropriation is not correctly dealt with.

Certain earlier formulations[44] which saw in calculation in prices and the value form not the expression of real production-relations but only a convenient method of calculation have contributed to underestimation of the risk of a resurgence of increasingly autonomous commodity relations, even in dealings between state enterprises.

It is especially worthy of emphasis that, in a situation of non-correspondence between the two fundamental relations in the economic field, "the connexion between the two relations no longer takes the form of reciprocal limitation, but becomes *the transformation of one of them by the other's effects*" (Balibar, No. 9, p. 318).

The transformation of one relation by the effects of the other may, indeed, mean either that the productive forces are gradually raised to the level of the production-relations, or that the opposite process takes place, namely, that the production-relations adapt themselves to the level of development of the productive forces. The first of these solutions is obviously the only one that corresponds to the needs of building socialism but it cannot take place without systematic intervention from levels other than the economic, namely, the political and ideological levels.

Quite concretely, intervention from the political level demands real economic planning and not mere "guidance" of the economy. Restricting oneself to the latter would mean ensuring the gradual predominance of commodity categories, that is, of the production-relations that these categories contain and necessarily develop through expanded reproduction of their own conditions of operation.

The need for intervention in the economic level from the political and ideological levels is a general characteristic of all periods of transition, but it is especially imperative in connexion with transition from capitalism to socialism, since the end-result of this transition is intended to be permanent subjection of the development of the economy to the other instances of the social formation, so that the pseudo-independence of the economic level, as expressed through self-regulation by the law of value, disappears from the historical scene.

Here I must mention the harmful effects not only of an empiricist tradition but also of a certain theoretical tradition which claims to establish a direct and reversible relationship between the evolution of the various levels of a social formation. This tradition tends to reduce the whole of social development to the development of the productive forces, the changes at the other levels being regarded as merely "expressions" of what is happening at the economic level. This conception is called "economism". It leads one easily to suppose that the principal, if not the only problem in building socialism is to ensure the most rapid development possible of the productive forces. On this basis one may be led into accepting that, in certain circumstances, it would be preferable to cut down on the effort of planning in order to give greater scope to the "market mechanisms", on the pretext of making the current functioning of the economy more "efficient".

It is thus essential to determine the *limits* within which the commodity categories help a planned economy to function, and beyond which their action deprives planning of all possibility of really influencing the content of economic development (as regards what is produced and as regards social relations). By working out the theory of social formations in transition between capitalism and socialism, and in particular by working out a theory of prices and economic calculation in these social formations, we shall work out at the same time *a theory of the limits that the working of the commodity categories must not overstep,* if it is desired to prevent the beginning of a process of self-development of these categories. The problems met with here obviously relate also to determining the sphere of operation of the law of value and the conditions under which the latter can be subordinated to the law of social regulation of the development of the productive forces and the requirements for transforming the production-relations.

X Conclusion

The study we have made of the problem of prices in the social formations in transition between capitalism and socialism, and the balance sheet of the discussion of this question that has taken place in the socialist countries of Europe enables me to formulate a few remarks that can be offered by way of conclusion.

First, the problem of prices in these social formations cannot be solved if one starts from ready-made formulae, especially from those constructed on the basis of theoretical concepts specific to another mode of production, the capitalist mode. This has often been forgotten during the discussion I have summarised.

Secondly, in any case, when it is a matter of working out a price policy and concretely fixing the prices of different goods, the problem to be solved is not reducible to laying down "rules" for price-fixing. It consists, in reality, of drawing out the objective laws to which the price-system must conform in order to produce the effects required by the way the economy functions. These laws are not merely those which determine the "regulating magnitudes" of prices but also, and just as much, those which determine both the deviations of prices from these "regulating magnitudes", and also, even, "imaginary prices". There is a certain price-structure which corresponds to the requirements of a socialist planned economy, in the sense that there must be conformity between the objective conditions of production, the targets of the plans, and the price-structure. It is obvious that this means that the price-structure must be subordinated to the targets of the economic plans, something that has often been overlooked by some participants in the discussion on prices.

This leads to a third observation, namely, that the problem of prices cannot be solved if it is regarded as a more or less self-contained one. The search for a satisfactory solution necessarily, and primarily, proceeds by way of analysis of the social relations, and, more particularly, of the production-relations characteristic of the social formation in which the price-system has to operate—both those that exist at a given moment and those that the economic plan aims to develop.[45] These production-relations constitute a structure. The price-system is itself an effect of this structure, and of the changes taking place in it, especially those for which the impetus comes from the political level.

The price-system cannot, for all that, be "deduced" from the present and future production-relations. It has to be built up, and this process demands that *theoretical concepts* be worked out to express the objective *requirements* to which the price-system is subjected, the *functions* it fulfils, and their *limits*. Only when the theoretical concepts have been worked out can one work out the *technical concepts* enabling one concretely to construct a price-system. Too often consideration has been given only to the technical concepts.

The principal aspect of the production-relations of the social formations in transition is the existence of social ownership of the chief means of production. It is because of this social ownership that it is possible to work out a production plan that takes account directly of use-values, and not of exchange-values.

However, the totality of the production-relations of the social formations in transition is dominated by the existence of a fundamental contradiction, resulting from the lack of conformity between the property-relations and the real relations of appropriation. This is the structure determined by the transitional character of these social formations, which is responsible for the appearance of the value-form, and the need for a price-system to operate. This price-system serves to orientate the decisions of the economic subjects in fields where direct intervention, in the form of detailed orders, by the political authorities, would be *ineffective*, or even harmful, because bringing about results other than those explicitly aimed at.

The role played by the price-system in the social formations in transition between capitalism and socialism is thus not to ensure the "autonomy" of the economic subjects, which would presuppose the development of market prices. Its role is—within a structure objectively characterised by *relative autonomy* of the economic subjects—*to serve as a relay-station* for political intervention in the economic field, wherever this intervention cannot usefully take place in any other way.

This form of intervention by the political authority is itself efficient only if the price-system is *coherent* with the political aims pursued and if it answers the demands of expanded reproduction and the transformation of social relations. This implies a certain kind of correspondence between prices and "social costs", the latter term here assuming a *specific* meaning, for "costs" cannot be evaluated in the same way regardless of whether the aim of production is to maximise profit or to satisfy social needs and build a new society.

In order to give greater precision to what has been said, the following observations may be added:

a) The essential role of the price-system in the social formations in transition is to enable the economic subjects to carry out calculations under conditions such that the day-to-day economic decisions taken on the basis of these calculations may, so far as possible,[46] conform to what is most advantageous for the development and changing of the production-relations in the direction of socialism.

b) What is "most advantageous" for the development and changing of the production-relations in the direction of socialism can obviously not be determined either by mere economic calculation or, *a fortiori*, by the economic subjects operating through a market (or a pseudo-market) on which prices are formed spontaneously. Therefore, re-establishment, on a substantial scale, of a system of market prices cannot but hold back evolution towards socialism. This last observation does not mean that, within limited fields, certain prices may not be formed by taking account of demand expressed in money terms, or the indications of a "market" largely controlled by social authorities.

c) The fundamental problems of the development of the social formations in transition *thus do not depend directly on "economic calculation" but on "strategic calculation"* carried out at the level of the central political and economic authorities. The content of this strategic calculation is both economic (in the sense that it concerns the production-relations and the productive forces) and political (in the sense that it concerns relations between classes and between social strata). What corresponds to the economic content of the strategic calculation takes the form of "social economic calculation".

d) Those of the fundamental problems of the development of the social formations in transition which depend on such social economic calculation cannot be solved *by means of economic calculation in money terms* (or, to use other expressions for the same thing, "calculation in prices", or "indirect economic calculation") but only by means of direct economic calculation in the sense indicated in Engels's formulation, quoted earlier

(Engels, No. 21 : see note 2 to this chapter). This kind of calculation operates only with physical quantities (including stocks of means of production, land and labour-power considered concretely, that is, taking account of the workers' degree of skill, where they are, and so on). The aim of this calculation is to bring about that combination of means of production which, under the conditions considered best politically and socially, will ensure maximum satisfaction of social needs, themselves evaluated socially. The end-result of this calculation is the formulating of plans for investment and production.

Thus, it is the working-out of such plans for investment and production that takes priority over the calculation of prices and their fixing, since, *in principle*,[47] these plans are drawn up, independently of any price-system. But a system of "significant" prices will be worked out, at a certain moment or for a certain period, as something *derived* from the investment and production plan (which itself takes account of present and future conditions, and therefore gives expression, in real terms, to real social costs). A system of derived prices like this is consequently only a transla-tion into the language of the price-form of social costs as they result from the present and future conditions of production, themselves inscribed in an economic plan.

This is not just a matter of providing a picture to represent mechanisms that cannot be grasped, but of a proposition referring to definite techniques and procedures. These have already been worked out in principle, even if their practical application on the social scale still gives rise to difficulties. Some of the latter are connected with the need to provide a better definition of the group of *theoretical* concepts which can alone furnish the foundation for calculating a price-system like this. Others are connected with the limitations that the technical means available put in the way of the large-scale calculations that are needed here.[48]

The category of *"dual prices"* refers to one of the forms of such prices, *derived* from a plan regarded as offering the maximum benefits. The works of Kantorovich (No. 28), Novozhilov (Nos. 54 and 55), Nemchinov (Nos. 51, 52 and 53), Fedorenko and Glushkov (No. 22), Kornai (Nos 33 and 34), Frisch (No. 23) and many other economists and mathematicians have opened wide the road in this direction, at least from the technical standpoint.

Such prices derived from plans make it possible to allow the economic subjects to take, *in a certain number of fields*, decisions which, appearing to be the most advantageous from the calculations which these economic subjects can carry out at their own level, that is, with the information available to them, are also the most advantageous for the national economy, and this not in a narrowly economic sense but also in a "political" sense. These are therefore "political" prices,[49] which does not mean prices fixed subjectively or determined in an arbitrary way, but, on the contrary, prices determined objectively on the basis of political and economic needs, that is, taking account of the *principle of maximum saving of social labour*, so far as this can be applied, allowing for social requirements as a whole (especially for the greater or less degree of mobility of the various elements of production, in particular of labour-power).

In order to be prices of this sort, prices must express not only the actual direct expenditure of labour devoted at a given moment to the various kinds of production, but also the potential indirect expenditure, what Novozhilov (Nos. 54 and 55) calls "costs of reverse linkage". They must therefore fulfil very strictly one of the functions that Marx so strikingly pointed out in the passage previously quoted (see *supra*, p. 220: Marx, No. 45, p. 112).

In the construction of a price-system for the social formations in transition between capitalism and socialism, the concepts of *Capital* play a fundamental role: that of matrix of the concepts which are specific to these social formations. On the theoretical plane, that is on the plane they claim to be on, the contribution made by the so-called "modern economic *theories*" is thus absolutely nil, for if anything can be learnt from them, it is not in the *theoretical* but the *technical* field. What these "theories" can, and all that they can, provide are empirical methods and procedures for working-out relations between economic activities. These methods and procedures, so long as one does not take them for what they are not, can be used as helpful tools in certain calculations.

If this can happen, it is, on the one hand, because today, in the most advanced capitalist countries, it has been necessary to try to solve, within the limits imposed by existing production-relations, a set of problems which demand that account be taken of inter-sectoral relations and that attempts be made to forecast the impact of any group of economic and political decisions on future economic development. The economists of the capitalist countries have thus had to solve in advance a certain number of expected problems, within the framework of overall economic calculations. If this can happen, it is, on the other hand, because the development of monopolistic formations has created complex problems of maximising profits (sometimes on the scale of entire branches of production), and, *formally*, these problems are of the same nature as those presented by maximum satisfaction of social needs. The techniques of calculation, and the technical concepts that calculation presupposes, are therefore "tools" which can be used, provided they are correctly modified.

While, however, some of the economic techniques worked out in the capitalist countries can be used in the socialist ones, this is so only provided we not merely refrain from confusing them with the way they are presented ideologically, but also provided they are cleansed of the ideological premises from which they proceed. Moreover, because of the functions they have to fulfil, they do not provide solutions to the *specific problems* of socialism, in particular to those which arise from the need to carry out on the social scale a large number of calculations in physical quantities. One of the characteristics of the calculations carried out in the capitalist countries is that they almost always make use, explicitly or implicitly, of a price-system.

In the conditions of the social formations in transition, however, there are, as we have seen, two levels of calculation which are quite distinct (even if in practice they are far from always kept distinct): calculation on the social scale, which deals, in principle, as has been said, only with physical quantities (including expenditure in labour), and calculation performed at the level of the economic subjects, which is carried out in terms of prices.

This duality of calculation (in so far as it implies the fixing of real prices, that is, prices that are actually to be paid) is the counterpart of the non-correspondence between property-relations and relations of appropriation. In the conditions of the transitional economies, this non-correspondence, when the contradiction it bears is not properly handled, gives rise to a secondary contradiction between "profitability" from the standpoint of society[50] and "profitability" from the standpoint of the economic subjects. A secondary contradiction like this can only be an expression of inadequate handling of the fundamental contradiction.

The duality of economic calculation corresponds to the existence of two levels of decision-making. These two levels are situated differently in relation to time: direct economic calculation (without recourse to money categories) concerns decisions relating to the future, that is, central economic planning; indirect economic calculation (performed by means of a price-system) concerns day-to-day economic decisions, relating to the present and corresponding essentially to the *management* of economic subjects endowed with means of production which have been assigned to them for a more or less lengthy period of time.

The disappearance of this duality requires a long process of transformation of the production-relations and a considerable advancement of the productive forces, which must lead either to social integration of the labour-processes or to a socially controllable degree of interconnexion of these labour-processes. The premises of such a change can already be seen with the formation of increasingly huge economic subjects, sometimes embracing entire branches of the economy (production of electricity, oil, natural gas, railways, etc.) and also with the interconnexion of an increasing number of economic subjects, through the setting-up of calculation centres directly linked with the production-units and capable of grasping their operations in "real time" (Fedorenko and Glushkov, No. 22).

Until this transformation has been fully accomplished, there can be no doubt that the *unification* of *management* and *planning* is still only something for the future.

The present situation therefore demands that the two types of activity (management and planning), while closely connected, with the former strictly subordinate to the latter, should each develop under specific conditions.

At the level of planning, though the actual use of methods of drawing up plans which would involve only calculations dealing with physical quantities is still only beginning, the *structure* of these calculations can already be clearly perceived. It is given us by *matrix calculation* and linear and non-linear *programming* calculations. Here, too, we must mention the contributions of Kantorovich (No. 28), Novozhilov (Nos. 54 and 55), Fedorenko (No. 22), Simon (No. 26), Kornai (Nos. 33, 34 and 35), Frisch (No. 23) and many others,[51] including also the works of engineers and mathematicians who have enabled us to go more deeply into the problems of programming, especially the writings of G. B. Dantzig and Ph. Wolfe (No. 18). Even if some of these works call for critical examination, so as to bring out those of their premises which are not in conformity with the conditions of development of the social formations in transition, they none the less form one of the foundations on which a whole edifice will have to be built.

Even though, however, we have already mastered essential principles regarding the calculations to be made on the social scale, very great problems remain to be solved, both on the plane of operative techniques and on that of their conformity with real economic processes. Furthermore, as regards electronic calculating machines, we are still far from possessing the park of fast and powerful machines that would be needed to handle adequately the enormous amount of data that would have to be handled.

For the moment, therefore, the calculations performed on the social scale deal with aggregated magnitudes, and this deprives the results of these operations of much of their realism. For this reason and some others (which relate particularly to the actual collection of data), one is still obliged to use, even for overall economic calculations, a large number of data expressed in price terms. These prices are later on, in some cases, modified in the light of the results of these calculations. This leads to proceeding by way of successive approximations and the taking of a path which one is not at all sure can lead to satisfactory results (at the purely technical level, because the convergence of the calculations is not guaranteed). However, this state of practice should not cause us to lose sight of the next steps in a genuine process of social direction of the economy.

While waiting, therefore, for direct economic calculation to become capable of developing in complete independence of any price-system, it is necessary to try and make the most of the procedures that enable us gradually to work out a price-system which can be used for certain planning calculations, and later for management purposes (Kornai and Liptak, No. 35; Kornai, Nos. 33 and 34; Malinvaud, No. 41). At the present stage it seems impossible to do without procedures which employ prices even at the level of planning calculations, but this must not make us lose sight of the fact that the aim (dictated by the structure of the problems to be solved) is to "bring down" calculation in prices to the level of the economic subjects alone, and then, later on, to banish it altogether (unless it should seem convenient, even at that stage, to use "imaginary prices" which would therefore not correspond to any "value" in the strict sense of the word).

As regards indirect economic calculation, while waiting for the time when this can be done on the basis of prices worked out in relation to an investment and production plan, that is, on the basis of prices strictly subordinated to this plan, because derived from it, it is clearly essential to establish a price-system which comes as close as possible, so far as this can be judged, to what such a price-system would be. It seems that prices of the "two-channel" type meet this demand most closely, provided that this system takes full account of reverse-linkage costs, which are, in fact, one of the ways in which the priorities of the economic plan, that is, political choices, express themselves.

A price-system constructed in accordance with this conception would already be more suitable than present prices to the needs of the transitional economies. It would make it possible to subordinate the activity of the economic subjects effectively to the requirements of overall development in the direction of socialism, while restricting useless or ineffective interference in day-to-day management. It would make it possible, therefore, for the economic subjects to play the role that corresponds to their real capacities, and this role alone. Consequently, it would make it possible to simplify the plan indices and to develop those direct links between enterprises which are necessary for their successful working, the aim of this being always the fulfilment of the plan and of its indices (and not the satisfaction of a demand taking shape on a market where prices could fluctuate freely).

Finally, what the discussion on prices has shown is, first, the absolute inadequacy of "formulae" aimed at building price-systems according to simplified "models" (for none of these "models" can correspond to the nature of the production-relations of the social formations in transition); secondly, the very serious weaknesses of the existing systems, weaknesses so great that they have made some economists turn towards the reconstitution of market prices; and, finally, the need to formulate a theoretical problematic that will put the price problem back into the only framework in which it can really be thought out and solved, that of the specific structures of the social formations in transition, and so, also, of the requirements for building socialism.

(Study published in *La Pensée*, No. 133, June 1967, pp. 25–56, and No. 134, August 1967, pp. 35–65.)

NOTES TO CHAPTER 6

1   This paper was written in connexion with the preparation of a work on the structures of the transitional economies and economic calculation. The numbered bibliographical references relate to the bibliography given at the end.

2   What Engels said on this point should be recalled here:

"Direct social production and direct distribution exclude all exchange of commodities, therefore also the transformation of the products into commodities (at any rate within the community) and consequently also their transformation into *values*. . . .

"It is true that even then it will still be necessary for society to know how much labour each article of consumption requires for its production. It will have to arrange its plan of production in accordance with its means of production, which include, in particular, its labour forces. The useful effects of the various articles of consumption, compared with each other and with the quantity of labour required for their production, will in the last analysis determine the plan. People will be able to manage everything very simply, without the intervention of the famous 'value'." (Engels, No. 21, pp. 348–9: Eng. edn. *Anti-Dühring*, pp. 339–40.)

3   Even the few large-scale "price-revisions" that have been undertaken in the Soviet Union since the Five-Year Plans began have not been based on theoretically worked-out conceptions, but were in each case responses to a certain number of practical pressures, mainly connected with increasing gaps between costs of production and selling prices.

4   A description of these measures will be found in an article by O. Tarnovsky (No. 60).

5   The last revision of Soviet wholesale prices was undertaken as far back as 1955; in certain branches of industrial production, notably in machine-building, more than 50 per cent of production is now (in 1966) sold at "provisional prices", because no definitive price has been laid down since 1962 for new products (cf. A. Komin, No. 31, p. 10).

6   The following analysis, like the discussion on prices, is mainly concerned with the problem of prices in the state industrial sector. Questions relating to prices on the collective-farm or peasant markets, and the very important questions relating to prices of purchases from and sales to the collective farms and the peasants, or the co-operatives, are thus not dealt with, as such. These questions belong, in part, to a different set of problems from those of industrial prices, because the relations between the working class and the peasantry are very directly involved. A description and a history of the price-system of the USSR as a whole will be found in the book by H. Denis and M. Lavigne (No. 19).

7   They were, indeed, "administered" or "regulated" prices, rather than *"planned" prices*, that is, prices determined as part of a plan. Real planning of prices demands the solving of a number of theoretical problems which are only now being tackled.

8   These organs have varied from period to period, and are different from product to product. It would be pointless to spend time here on these organisational aspects.

9   The only "price reform" carried out on a fairly large scale was that of 1949, but, on the one hand, this affected, in the main, industrial products only, and, on the other, it was largely inspired (like a less substantial "reform" carried out before the war) by budgetary considerations. What

was aimed at was re-establishing so far as possible the financial profitability of heavy industry, on the basis of a profit-norm of 3–4 per cent on
the cost of production. Thereby, industrial wholesale prices were increased by about 80 per cent, but the price-structure continued to lack
much coherence.

10   In the Soviet Union these researches are being carried out mainly
in the Institute of Mathematics Applied to the Economy. This Institute,
which is attached to the USSR Academy of Sciences, was founded through
the initiative of the late Academician Nemchinov. It is now directed by
Academician Fedorenko.

11   It will be observed that he speaks of "the most important principle",
which obviously implies that it is not seen as the *only* principle, and
therefore that prices may "deviate" from value.

12   It should be noted that, even at the time when there was a rather
close similarity between the procedures followed by the different socialist
countries of Europe, there were nevertheless a certain number of differences
as regards the conditions of price-fixing. These differences related not
only to "standards of profitability" but also to the *calculation of costs of
production*. Costs of production are, indeed, *not ready-made absolutes*:
they are worked out in accordance with definite rules (concerning the
evaluation of production funds, depreciation norms, allocation of expenditure common to complex forms of production, etc.), and these rules vary
not only from one country to another but, even within a single country, from
one period to another and even sometimes from one industry to another.

Though these rules determine the price level, whenever a connexion
is established between selling price and costs of production (which makes
the conditions for calculating costs of production extremely important),
the discussion dealt little with the rules for working out costs of production. This is, however, a problem that is beginning to be given more
attention (e.g., Sitnin, No. 57, pp. 45–6).

13   I have already pointed out that the problem of the "rules" for evaluating these investments and the problem of "rules" for depreciation are both
far from having been solved, and are giving rise to a certain amount of
discussion.

14   In a passage in Book III of *Capital* Marx brings up the problem of
changes in value or price of production as a result of general laws. He
does this by emphasising that the sale of products at certain prices is
bound up with a distribution of social labour among the various activities
which is proportional to social needs. Thus, he writes:

"If this division is proportional, then the products of various groups
are sold at their values (at a later stage [*bei weiterer Entwicklung*] they
are sold at their prices of production), or at prices which are certain
modifications of these values or prices of production determined by
general laws." (Cf. Marx, No. 46, p. 685, corresponding to p. 648 of
Vol. 25 of the Dietz Verlag edn.: Eng. version from F.L.P.H. edn.,
Vol. III, p. 620.)

As will be seen, this idea is especially important in that it stresses that prices which are *modifications of value "determined by general laws" also express the socially necessary expenditure of labour*; since production is commodity production, *a distribution of labour proportional to society's needs* is possible only when equivalent quantities of social labour are exchanged.

15 The problems presented by calculating costs of production, and "choosing" significant costs of production, are the same here as in the system of "own costs" (see above, note 12). Among the economists who support a price-system of the "price-of-production" type there reigns a great variety of attitudes to the solving of these problems.

16 The latter writes, for example:

"It is easy to increase the rights of the enterprises. But it is more difficult to ensure that the interests of those who work in these enterprises shall coincide with those of the national economy, and, in a rational planned economy, independence can be given to enterprises only in those fields where the interests of the production-unit have been brought into line with the plan. To achieve this, a complex system of measures is needed . . . which demands that centralised economic direction be increased and improved." (Novozhilov, No. 55.)

In the same article Novozhilov points out the meagre amount of information contained in any price-system and the need, in consequence, to carry out calculations that explicitly take into account use values and social needs.

17 This rate of about 10 per cent did not save a number of branches of heavy industry from working at a loss. Komin, who quotes the figure of 10 per cent, also shows that, in order to increase the profitability of heavy industry by 1 per cent, it is necessary to agree to an average increase of 2.2 per cent in the wholesale prices of heavy industrial products. Thus, an increase of profitability by 5 per cent, equalised throughout all branches, would entail an increase of 20 per cent in the general price-level. This explains why there is no question, for the moment at any rate, of equalising the rates of profitability of the different branches. It is clear that as soon as one applies rates that differ between branches, a "price-of-production" system in the exact sense of the word is no longer being applied.

18 In relations with the capitalist countries the socialist countries use the same prices as the former, except when they wish to accord to some of them (e.g., certain "developing" countries) conditions which are more advantageous than would follow from application of the prices current on the capitalist market.

19 Incredible as it may seem, this sort of question often comes up in the discussion on prices, and is given a wide variety of answers, sometimes "supported" by quotations from *Capital*.

20 As illustrations of how these questions arise concretely, here are some examples. In the G.D.R. down to 1 April 1964, when a new price-system

was introduced for fuel and power products, the price per ton of lignite was the same, regardless of quality: 3·51 DM, in the crude state, and 16·56 DM, in the form of bricks. This was because the cost of production of the different qualities was the same. After April 1964 the existence of different qualities of lignite was recognised, with a price-range of 6–9·2 DM for a ton of crude lignite and 30–42 DM for a ton of lignite bricks (Tarnovsky, No. 60). Quality was defined by caloric power. Following the introduction of the new prices—which, it will be observed, are higher than the old ones—industry's consumption of units of fuel and power has fallen (Lefranc, No. 37, p. 88).

21   As I have already mentioned, in the USSR the basis of the price-system was, until recent years, the prices of 1926–7; whatever the changes made since then in different individual prices, the weight of this basis continues to be felt in the system as a whole. In the G.D.R., down to the recent reform, the "basis" of prices was 1937 in the engineering industry and 1944 for fuel and power prices (Lefranc, No. 37, p. 80).

22   Thus, in the G.D.R., building the Schwedt petrochemical complex involved the participation of over 3,000 enterprises (Lefranc, No. 37, p. 89).

23   On the grounds that only living labour produces value, some thought it right to conclude that only living labour need be economised to the maximum.

24   One of the positive results of the discussion has certainly been to draw attention to the inadequacy of past practices. Thus, P. Bunich wrote in 1965:

"It is inadmissable that a large number of office workers should be occupied in checking on the presence or absence of the workers in a factory while no account is taken of the periods during which the machinery is at a standstill; that every kopeck paid in wages should be counted meticulously while investment funds a hundred times as big as the wages bill are spent without the necessary analysis; that entire offices should be engaged on working out norms of living labour, while revision of the norms for return on production funds and volume of production-capacity is carried out in random and occasional fashion." (Bunich, No. 16, p. 22.)

25   As a whole, though the annual rates of growth of their national incomes have noticeably fallen, these countries still enjoy growth-rates a little higher than the industrialised capitalist countries. However, in recent years the growth-rates of these two groups of countries have come noticeably closer. In the most highly industrialised socialist countries, rates of growth have been as follows, since 1958: (see table on p. 239)

Before 1958, the rates were of the order of 10–12 per cent; they are still at this level in Romania, Albania and Bulgaria. They are 6–7 per cent (average for 1961–5) in Poland and Hungary, with a downward tendency in the latter country in 1964 (4·7 per cent) and 1965 (2 per cent). (Source: United Nations, No. 50, and Babaikov, No. 7).

Annual growth-rate of the national income

	USSR	Czechoslovakia	G.D.R.
1958	12·5	8·0	11·0
1959	8·0	6·0	8·5
1960	8·0	8·3	4·6
1961	6·8	6·8	3·5
1962	5·7	1·4	2·2
1963	4·1	2·2	2·9
1964	9·0	0·9	4·5
1965	6·0	2·5	4·7
1966	7·4	—	—

26   Among which must be mentioned a reduction in rates of accumulation. In some years this reduction has lowered the absolute value of current accumulation.

27   On the notion of an "empirical concept", see L. Althusser's article, No. 2.

28   In France, for instance, Maurice Godelier, in his book on economic rationality (No. 25), has accepted a series of propositions borrowed from Pareto and developed by the chief theoreticians of "welfare economics", without subjecting them to the rigorous criticism which is essential.

29   The article by A. N. D. McAuley (No. 40) gives an interesting critique, from a non-Marxist point of view, of the premises of the theory of "welfare economics". He shows how very narrow are the limits within which the "theorems" of welfare economics are valid, bringing out, in particular, the point that among these premises are conditions that contradict present-day conditions of production, since "welfare economics" theory assumes continuity of functions of production, absence of decreasing marginal costs in all industries, no external costs, and so on.

30   To do this would be to respond to the demand formulated by Engels when he wrote: "With these discoveries [by Marx] socialism became a science, which had in the first place to be developed in all its details and relations" (No. 21, p. 58) (Eng. version from *Anti-Dühring*, p. 33).

31   Thus, Marx writes:
"As the co-operative character of the labour-process becomes more marked, so, as a necessary consequence, does our notion of productive labour, and of its agent the productive labourer, become extended. In order to labour productively, it is no longer necessary for you to do manual work yourself; enough, if you are an organ of the collective labourer, and perform one of its subordinate functions." (Marx, No. 44, pp. 183-4: Eng. version, *Capital*, Vol. II, p. 517.)

32   In the *Critique of the Gotha Programme* (No. 47), Marx replies to this stuff when he writes:
"Labour is not the source of all wealth. Nature is just as much the source of use-values (and it is surely of such that material wealth consists!) as labour, which itself is only the manifestation of a force of

nature, human labour power. . . . The bourgeois have very good grounds for falsely ascribing *supernatural creative power* to labour. . . ." (*Op. cit.*, pp. 17–18: Eng. edn., pp. 14–15.)

33 Attempts at measuring, within capitalist economy, certain empirical magnitudes corresponding approximately to the theoretical concepts of *Capital*, like "price of production" or "average rate of profit" are, of course, quite a different matter. Here it is a question of *measurement carried out on, the basis of prices which are already given, and not of measurement of empirical magnitudes other than prices in order to construct a price-system*. This is why there is point in observing the historical evolution of prices under capitalism: it enables us to observe the objective tendencies of a certain number of magnitudes within a social formation in which these magnitudes express themselves spontaneously through determined concrete categories.

34 If one is not in a position to solve theoretically the questions that are raised by the establishment of a price-system, one is easily led to leave these problems to settle themselves in practice, through market mechanisms. But the prices that the market can set up are no longer those that correspond to the needs of planned economic development; they therefore come into contradiction with planning, and so with the development of the socialist mode of production.

35 Including the re-establishment of free convertibility of currency; and of bankruptcy, as a way of eliminating "unprofitable" enterprises.

36 It should be observed at this point that a distinction must be drawn between re-establishing "market prices" (which implies a possible reaction by prices on quantities produced) and allowing some latitude to some social authority or other to modify certain prices in order to take account of the level of demand (for example, selling-off perishable goods at relatively low prices, or doing the same with stocks of consumer goods which cannot find customers at the prices previously fixed). These are two quite different things.

37 Notably in Book III. On this see note 14, *supra*.

38 To clarify the above remarks, we can illustrate the problems involved by means of some examples. Let us take the question of the price of electric power. It is one thing to determine the average price at which power has to be sold to users, in order to conform to the laws of price-determination which govern expanded reproduction and the development of the productive forces; it is quite another to fix the prices at which power will be sold depending on the hours between which it is to be used, and by whom. In the latter case, indeed (if prices are to be used as one of the ways of directing the economy and subordinating the decisions of the enterprises to the targets of the plan), it is necessary to determine the divergences from these average prices, so that the capacity for producing electric power may be utilised as fully as possible throughout the day and throughout the year, and so as to render it less advantageous for certain users to use power at certain times, and more advantageous for others, and so on.

Similarly, it is one thing, where railway charges are concerned, to fix the average price per ton-kilometre, and quite another to determine the price which the enterprises of a particular locality, producing a particular kind of goods, will pay for transport, and to do this in such a way that the trucks are as full as possible, both coming and going. This sort of problem arises continually. It presented itself on a large scale when the Ural–Kuznetsk combine was set up. The price of transport was then fixed at a "very low" level, which was regarded as "artificial" by some commentators. In reality the price corresponded, at least intuitively, to the requirements of maximum saving of labour, once the two centres of production of coal and iron ore had come into being, having been established during the Soviet Union's First Five-Year Plan.

39 Cf. E. Balibar, No. 9, especially pp. 212 et seq.

40 I have developed this point earlier in various articles (Nos. 12, 13 and 14).

41 Saying that one can think out the conditions for a certain calculation clearly does not mean that one can actually perform the calculation; to do that the necessary conditions have to be objectively realised. At the present time, these conditions are as yet only partially available; this is precisely why the calculations that serve as the basis for planning have to be completed by calculations carried on in prices, at the management level.

42 It will be recalled that, in the *Grundrisse*, Marx (No. 48) emphasises that the very development of large-scale industry tends to deprive the value form of its content, by weakening further and further the link between value and labour-time. He writes in this connexion: "From the moment when labour in its immediate form ceases to be the great source of wealth, labour-time ceases to be its measure, and must cease to be the measure of use-value. . . . Thereby, production based on exchange-value breaks down." (No. 48, p. 593.)

When Marx speaks here of "labour in its immediate form" he means labour *directly* devoted to producing an object, or to producing the means of production used to obtain this object. In large-scale industry, he says, the wealth created depends less and less on this immediate labour and more and more "on the general level of science and the progress of technology, the application of science to production" (No. 48, p. 592).

The socialist economies of today have not yet reached this level in the development of their productive forces, but their production-relations are already prepared for it. This is why, when plans are drawn up, it is necessary to work essentially in terms of use-values and concrete labour and not in terms of exchange-value; at the level of planning and social calculation, exchange-value is already stripped of meaning.

43 In practice, by pointless considerations of financial "profitability".

44 J. V. Stalin (No. 58).

45 This observation entails especially important consequences as regards the prices at which exchange takes place between the different "sectors"

of the economy: the state sector, the co-operative sector, the private sector, the capitalist sector, and so on. This is a problem which has not been specially examined in this article.

46   The reservation expressed here is important, because it seems clear that it is not possible to build a price-system such that all the day-to-day economic decisions that the economic subjects may take as a result of calculations made in price terms will coincide with the politically decided aims for the development of the social formation. Hence the need to combine a variety of forms of intervention at the economic level from the political level.

In any case, calculations in price-terms carried out by the economic subjects can have point only in relation to day-to-day economic decisions. This excludes, in principle, decisions regarding investments. Where the latter are concerned, the taking of decisions that are coherent and ensure the best use of accumulation funds demands knowledge of "future economic conditions", that is, of all the decisions about investment that are being put into effect, or which are to be implemented in the forthcoming period. This is beyond the horizon of the economic subjects and cannot be expressed by the price-system.

47   This is clearly only a principle. In reality, given the present state of the techniques and means of calculation, it is inevitable that some of the planning calculations have to be made using a price-system. However, calculations made in this way must always be seen for what they are— substitutes for more fundamental calculations, the results of which require to be evaluated socially and politically.

48   These calculations require, indeed, the solving within a limited period of time of tens of thousands of simultaneous equations. Some years ago this task would have been impracticable. In 1956 for instance, given the solution codes available, it was only possible to solve, as a practical proposition, in the form of linear programmes, problems of some 60 equations and 100 variables, and the solution took about ten hours to obtain. In 1958 it became possible to deal easily with problems of 300 equations, and it began to be possible to ensure the management and self-checking of the matrices by the computers themselves. In 1960 problems involving 500 equations were being handled with ease, and they were beginning to go over to linked calculations which made it possible to deal, in acceptable conditions, with several neighbouring fields of possibility, and to test the sensitivity of the results to slight variations in the data (which is necessary when the data relating to the future are more or less uncertain). By 1962 they were dealing fairly easily with systems with 2,000 equations and 35,000 non-zero coefficients. In 1967 it is expected that it will be possible to handle problems involving up to 8,000 equations; moreover, studies which have been undertaken in a number of countries on decomposition algorithms give the prospect of soon solving problems involving 20,000 equations. Thanks to this progress we are nearing the stage when computers will actually be able to deal in a really

useful, that is, a sufficiently concrete, way (bringing in only so many averages and aggregates as are acceptable because they do not distort the nature of the problems too much) with problems covering the whole of a national economy. In addition to the improvement in codes and languages and the increase in the power and speed of computers, two developments should help to achieve this result: the techniques of automatic generation of matrices on the basis of prototypes, and above all, the perfecting of an effective algorithm for solving problems involving non-continuous values.

49 It is obvious that today, in most of the capitalist countries, the most important prices *are no longer market prices but political prices,* that is, they result from the "strategy" of certain capitalist groups and of the state. Here, too, this does not mean that these prices are not determined objectively: they are based on the objective economic and political requirements of state monopoly capitalism, including those that result from the class struggle.

50 The expression "profitability from the standpoint of society" is obviously only a metaphor the use of which can be justified not only by its convenience but also by the contrast it enables one to stress, between two levels of calculation. This metaphor should not, however, lead us astray for "profitability from the standpoint of society" is not measured in terms of surplus of receipts over expenses but in terms of development of the productive forces and changing of social relations.

51 Some of these writers have on occasion taken up positions favourable to a very extensive decentralisation of economic management, but these positions are not logically bound up with their analysis of the conditions for significant economic calculation; quite the contrary. It is therefore mistaken to proceed from criticism of these positions to refusal to recognise the importance of the contribution made by these writers to the solution of serious problems in the field of economic calculation.

Appendix to Chapter 6

Bibliography on the problem of prices in the socialist countries of Europe

1　USSR Academy of Sciences, *Manuel d'Economie Politique*, Institut *d'Economie*, Paris, Editions Sociales, 1956 (2nd edn., 1958). (Eng. version: *Political Economy: A textbook issued by the Institute of Economics of the Academy of Sciences of the USSR*, London, 1957.)

2　L. Althusser, "Sur le travail théorique" (On theoretical work), *La Pensée*, No. 132, April 1967.

3　G. C. Archibald, "Welfare Economics, Ethics and Essentialism", *Economica*, November 1959.

4　Z. Atlas, "On the profitability of socialist enterprises" (in Russian), *Voprosy Ekonomiki*, 1958, No. 7, pp. 115–28.

5　Z. Atlas, "Profitability and value in a socialist economy" (in Russian), *Voprosy Ekonomiki*, 1960, No. 10, pp. 71–82.

6　Z. Atlas, "The basic principle of socialist economic management and its realisation in practice" (in Russian), *Voprosy Ekonomiki*, 1965, No. 8, pp. 66–79.

7　G. V. Babaikov, Report to the USSR Supreme Soviet, December 1966.

8　A. Bachurin, "The economic reform: problems and first results" (in Russian), *Ekonomicheskaya Gazeta*, No. 45, XI, 1966, pp. 7–8.

9　E. Balibar, "Sur les concepts fondamentaux du matérialisme historique" (On the fundamental concepts of historical materialism), *Lire le Capital*, by Althusser, Balibar, Establet and others, Vol. 2, Paris, Maspero, 1966. (Eng. edn., *Reading Capital*, New Left Books, 1970.)

10　W. J. Baumol, *Welfare Economics and the Theory of the State*, 2nd edn., London, 1965.

11　V. D. Belkin, *Tseny edinogo urovnya i ekonomicheskie izmereniya na ikh osnove* ("Uniform-level prices and economic measurements based on them") (in Russian), Moscow, 1963.

12   Ch. Bettelheim, "Formes et méthodes de planification socialiste et niveau de développement des forces productives" (Forms and methods of socialist planning and level of development of the productive forces), *La Pensée*, No. 113, 1964. (See Chapter 3 of this book.)

13   Ch. Bettelheim, "Les cadres socio-économiques et l'organisation de la planification sociale" (The social and economic framework and the organisation of social planning), *Problèmes de Planification*, No. 5, École Pratique des Hautes Études, C.E.P.S., 1965. (See Chapter 2 of this book.)

14   Ch. Bettelheim, "La Construction du socialisme problème de l'économie de transition" (Building socialism: the problem of the transitional economy), two articles, *La Pensée*, Nos. 125 and 126, February and April 1966. (See Chapters 4 and 5 of this book.)

15   A. Brody, "Three Types of Price Systems", *Economics of Planning*, No. 3, Vol. V, 1965, pp. 58–66.

16   P. Bunich, "Economic stimulation of higher efficiency and profitability of investments" (in Russian), *Voprosy Ekonomiki*, 1965, No. 12.

17   B. Csikos-Nagy, "Two Stages of the Hungarian Debate on Prices", *Acta Oeconomica*, Academy of Sciences, Budapest, Vol. I, fascicle 3–4, 1966, pp. 255–66.

18   G. B. Dantzig and P. Wolfe, "The Decomposition Algorithm for Linear Programs", *Econometrica*, 1961, No. 29, pp. 767 et seq.

19   H. Denis and D. Lavigne, *Le problème des prix en Union Soviétique*, Paris, Ed. Cujas, 1965.

20   A. Emmanuel, "La Division internationale du travail et le marché socialiste" (The international division of labour and the socialist market), *Problèmes de Planification*, No. 7, École Pratique des Hautes Études, C.E.P.S., Paris, 1966.

21   F. Engels, *Anti-Dühring*, trans. Bottigelli, Paris, Editions Sociales, 1950.

22   Fedorenko and Glouchkov (Glushkov), "Pour appliquer largement les techniques de calcul à l'économie nationale" (For large-scale application of calculation techniques to the national economy), *Problèmes de Planification*, No. 6, École Pratique des Hautes Études, C.E.P.S., Paris, 1966.

23   R. Frisch, "Rational Price-Fixing in a Socialistic Society", *Economics of Planning*, No. 2, Vol. VI, 1966, pp. 97 et seq.

24   S. Ganczer, "Price Calculations in Hungary on the Basis of Mathematical Methods", *Economics of Planning*, No. 3, Vol. V, 1965, pp. 67–79.

25 M. Godelier, *Rationalité et irrationalité en économie*, Paris, Maspero, 1966. (Eng. edn., *Rationality and Irrationality in Economics*, New Left Books, 1972.)

26 G. Simon, "Ex-post Examination of Macro-economic Shadow Prices", *Economics of Planning*, No. 3, Vol. V, 1965, pp. 80 et seq.

27 J. Kosta, "Czechoslovak Economists Discuss Ways of Improving the System of Planned Management", *Czechoslovak Economic Papers*, No. 4, Academy of Sciences, Prague, 1964, pp. 139 et seq.

28 L. V. Kantorovitch, *Calcul économique et utilisation des ressources*, trans. C. Sardou, Paris, Dunod, 1963.

29 E. Kats and A. Rozhansky, "Price-formation taking account of the capital-intensity of goods" (in Russian), *Voprosy Ekonomiki*, 1966, No. 10, pp. 33–8.

30 T. Khachaturov and D. Lvov, "Hastening scientific and technical progress and increasing the efficiency of social production" (in Russian), *Voprosy Ekonomiki*, 1966, No. 8, pp. 3 et seq.

31 A. Komin, "Problems of bringing wholesale prices up to date" (in Russian), *Planovoye Khozyaistvo*, 1966, No. 10, pp. 10–16.

32 T. C. Koopmans, *Three Essays on the State of Economic Science*, New York, 1957.

33 J. Kornai, "Mathematical Programming as a Tool in Drawing up the Five-Year Economic Plan", *Economics of Planning*, No. 3, Vol. V, 1965, pp. 3 et seq.

34 J. Kornai, *Mathematical Planning of Structural Decisions*, Amsterdam, 1967.

35 J. Kornai and Th. Liptak, "Two-level Planning", *Econometrica*, 1965, Vol. 33, No. 1, pp. 141 et seq.

36 Ya. Kronrod, "The economic reform and some problems of the political economy of socialism" (in Russian), *Voprosy Ekonomiki*, 1966, No. 10, pp. 19–32.

37 P. Lefranc, "La situation économique et le nouveau système de planification de la R.D.A." (The economic situation and the new planning system in the G.D.R.), *Economie et Politique*, June 1965, pp. 77–91.

38 E. Liberman, "On the planning of industrial production and material stimulants to its development" (in Russian), *Kommunist*, 1956, No. 10, pp. 75–92.

39 [E. Liberman], "Discussion on [Liberman's views on] economic stimulation of enterprises" (in Russian), *Voprosy Ekonomiki*, 1962, No. 11, pp. 87–142.

40 A. N. D. McAuley, "Rationality and Central Planning", *Soviet Studies*, Vol. XVIII, No. 3, January 1967, pp. 340 et seq.

41 E. Malinvaud, *Decentralised procedure for planning*, Cambridge, International Economic Association, 1963.

42 I. Malyshev and V. Sobol, "The scientific basis for studying the socialist economy" (in Russian), *Kommunist*, 1961, No. 8, pp. 82–8.

43 K. Marx, *Le Capital*, Paris, Editions Sociales, Vol. I.

44 K. Marx, *Le Capital*, Paris, Editions Sociales, Vol. II.

45 K. Marx, *Das Kapital*, Book I, Moscow and Leningrad, Marx-Engels-Lenin Institute, 1933.

46 K. Marx, *Das Kapital*, Book III, Moscow and Leningrad, Marx-Engels-Lenin Institute, 1934.

47 K. Marx, *Critique du Programme de Gotha*, Paris, Editions Sociales, 1950.

48 K. Marx, *Grundrisse der Kritik der Politischen Oekonomie*, Berlin, Dietz-Verlag, 1953.

49 E. J. Mishan, "A Survey of Welfare Economics, 1939–59", *Economic Journal*, June 1960.

50 United Nations, *Statistics of the Economic Commission for Europe*, Geneva, 1966.

51 V. Nemchinov, "Some quantitative relations in the reproduction formula" (in Russian), *Voprosy Ekonomiki*, 1962, No. 2.

52 V. Nemchinov, "Value and price under socialism" (in Russian), *Voprosy Ekonomiki*, 1960, No. 12, pp. 94 et seq.

53 V. Nemchinov, "Socialist economic management and the planning of production" (in Russian), *Kommunist*, 1964, No. 5, pp. 74–87.

54 V. V. Novozhilov, "Mesures de dépenses (de production) et de leurs résultats en économie socialiste" (Measurement of costs of production and their results in a socialist economy), trans. from Russian in *Cahiers de l'I.S.E.A.*, No. 146, February 1964, pp. 43–291.

55 V. V. Novozhilov, "Problems of planned price-formation and the reform of industrial management" (in Russian), *Ekonomika i Matematicheskie Metody*, 1966, Vol. II, No. 3, pp. 327–39.

56 B. Rakitsky, "The lessons of *khozraschet* (business accounting)" (in Russian), *Komsomolskaya Pravda*, 19 October 1966.

57 V. Sitnin, "The economic reform and the revision of wholesale prices of industrial goods (in Russian). *Kommunist*, 1966, No. 14, pp. 37 et seq.

58   J. V. Stalin, *Les problèmes économiques du socialisme en URSS* (Economic Problems of Socialism in the USSR), Paris, Editions du P.C.F., 1952.

59   S. G. Strumilin, "Processes of price-formation in the USSR" (in Russian), *Planovoye Khozyaistvo*, 1928, Nos. 5, 6 and 7, article reprinted in the symposium *Na planovom fronte* ("On the planning front") (in Russian, articles of 1920–30), Moscow, Gospolitizdat, 1958, pp. 503–80.

60   O. Tarnovsky, "Price-formation in the industries of the Comecon countries" (in Russian), *Voprosy Ekonomiki*, 1966, No. 7.

61   N. A. Tsagolov, ed., *Kurs politicheskoi ekonomii* ("A course in political economy") (in Russian), Vol. II, Moscow, 1963.

Index

Accumulation funds, 52, 87–8, 179, 180
Administrative centralisation, 23, 26, 85, 92; in planned economies, 31, 176–7; quality and quantity control in, 93
Administrative management, bureaucratisation of, 83, 86, 90–2; and economic subjects, 74, 83, 85; role of, 86
Administrative share-out, 56–7, 60
Administrative subordination, 82, 85, 90–3
Agricultural cadres, 78
Agriculture, and economic subject, 73–4, 75; industrial products consumed by, 48–9; and nationalisation of land, 46; new techniques in, 51; planning in communes, 78–9; transition period in, 123–4; vertical integration in, 66–7; working groups in, 76–8; *see also* Collective-farm sector
Alienation, 155, 156
Althusser, Louis, 13, 14–15, 144, 155, 156
Anti-Dühring (Engels), 33, 34, 43, 48, 166
Appropriation, formal and real mode of, 24, 25–6, 29, 127–8, 134, 225–6; homology of forms of, 25–6; and level of productive forces, 152–3
Authority, and effective capacity, 45
Automation, 54, 70, 174, 176

Bachurin, A., 210
Balibar, Etienne, 15, 24, 25, 28, 226
Banking system, and centralised allotments, 58–9; funds for investments of, 102; of state, 32, 88
Berri, L., 49–50
Bettelheim, C., 180
Böhm-Bawerk, 151
Bolshevik Party, Ninth Congress 1920, 181
Bonuses, 97, 101
Bottigelli, E., 155, 163
Brody, Andras, 202, 212–13
Bukharin, Nikolai, 31, 111, 125–6, 132, 150, 172

Bulgaria, 201
Bunich, P., 238
Bureaucratic domination, bureaucratisation, 62–3, 64, 82; in administrative hierarchy, 90–1; and economic subjects, 74, 83, 117
Business accounting, 100, 115–16, 137, 174, 186; *see also* Calculation, economic
Buying and selling, 110; central office for, 57–8, 64; contracts for, 86–7; joint services for, 69; of means of production, 174; planned obligations in, 56–60; in state sector, 133

Calculation, economic, 77, 80, 186–9 *passim*, 212, 225, 229–30, 232–4; electronic, 64, *see also* Electronic tools; internal, 79; requirements of, 38, 57, 62; strategic, 229, 243
Capacity, effective, to account and allot, 127–8, 129–30, 168–9; and authority, 45; to dispose of means of production, 45, 130, 140; of economic subject, 75
Capital (Marx), 14, 151, 160, 163–4, 224; on price-systems, 195, 208, 211–12, 214–15, 218, 220, 223, 231, 236
Capitalism, capitalist modes of production, 14–15; British, 15; calculation techniques in, 231; contradictions of, 164–5; dissolution of, 20–1; fragmentation under, 135; horizontal concentration in, 65; labour-process in, 217–18; price system of, 195–6, 201, 211, 213, 240, 243; social forms of ownership in, 43, 52, 164; in socialist structures, 17; theoretical foundations of, 151, 212; transition to, 15, 24–5; vertical integration in, 66–70
Capitalist property, 163–4
Centralisation, functional and bureaucratic, 64–5
Centralised allotments, 56–60, 62, 106, 110